HOW TO BUY AND SELL REAL ESTATE FOR FINANCIAL FREEDOM

D1132816

James Dicks

JW Dicks

McGraw-Hill

New York   Chicago   San Francisco
Lisbon   London   Madrid   Mexico City   Milan
New Delhi   San Juan   Seoul   Singapore
Sydney   Toronto

The *McGraw·Hill* Companies

1 2 3 4 5 6 7 8 9 0   DOC/DOC   0 9 8 7 6

ISBN: 0-07-146867-6

First Edition

This publication is designed to provide accurate and authoritative information in regard to the subject matter covered. It is sold with the understanding that neither the author nor the publisher is engaged in rendering legal, accounting, or other professional service. If legal advice or other expert assistance is required, the services of a competent professional person should be sought.

> —*From a Declaration of Principles jointly adopted*
> *by a Committee of the American Bar*
> *Association and a Committee of Publishers*

McGraw-Hill books are available at special quantity discounts to use as premiums and sales promotions, or for use in corporate training programs. For more information, please write to the Director of Special Sales, Professional Publishing, McGraw-Hill, Two Penn Plaza, New York, NY 10121-2298. Or contact your local bookstore.

Library of Congress Cataloging-in-Publication Data

Dicks, James.
  How to buy and sell real estate for financial freedom / by James Dicks and J.W. Dicks.
      p. cm.
  ISBN 0-07-146867-6 (pbk. : alk. paper) 1. Real estate investment—United States. 2. Real property—Purchasing—United States. 3. House buying—United States. 4. House selling—United States. I. Dicks, J. W. (Jack William), 1949– II. Title.
  HD255.D53 2006
  332.63'24—dc22

                                                                2005037481

 This book is printed on recycled, acid-free paper containing a minimum of 50% recycled de-inked fiber.

This book is dedicated to David Edmunds, Jim Dicks, and Bert Rodgers, three real estate mentors

ACKNOWLEDGMENTS

Real estate is a relationship business. The people you meet and the contacts you make are invaluable in building a successful business. We want to take the opportunity to thank some of the people who are part of our current real estate world:

- Roger Soderstrom and Chocky Burks of Stirling International Real Estate, two of the best Realtors we have had the pleasure of working with.
- Mike Morgan who heads up our real estate development division and deals with all the hard stuff.
- Bob Reynolds, a model for the ultimate Buyer's Broker, who bird-dogs and negotiates properties as well as the best in the business.
- Lindsay Dicks, Director of Sales and Acquisitions for PremiereTrade™ Realty, LLC.
- Scott Thompson, one of the brightest and most talented real estate attorneys we have had the opportunity to work with.
- The entire staff and associates at PremiereTrade™, LLC, whose dedication and hard work help us spread the message and ideas contained in this book and our company products.

Contents

PART 1

How to Get Started in Real Estate

CHAPTER 1

Real Estate and the Law of Success Duplication

R eal estate has been in our family's blood for generations. Not necessarily big-time development (although we have done that, too), but the core of real estate investing, which makes real estate so appealing to so many people: buying a little property, fixing it up, and selling it for a profit. It's the American dream in action. "Real estate is something everybody should own a little of," as our mother/grandmother used to say. We agree!

Just this year, for example, we bought two single-family lots with a small option and flipped them for a 290 percent profit in one year. We bought an 800-acre ranch that has already zoomed in value by 100 percent in a single year. We bought a 26-acre parcel on a lake and began its transformation into an exclusive multimillion-dollar residential development. We put 5 percent down on a $12 million commercial condo space that has jumped 25 percent in price on the total value (not just our down payment)—and we haven't even closed yet! And we did all of this part-time, while we spent our "full time" growing our financial software and service business.

We aren't giving you this brief bit of recent history to pat ourselves on the back. Later on, we'll tell you about some of our real estate deals that *haven't* worked out so well—and there have been plenty of those. No, the reason we recite the good news from our recent past is to make the point—*from the very beginning of this book*—that the real estate game is far from over. Don't listen to the gloom-and-doomers. Real estate is still one of the best investments you can make. In fact, real estate is the most promising way for someone who starts with nothing to end up with a fortune. Not everyone *will*, of course. But the exciting thing is that anyone *can.*

There are good markets, great markets, and, yes, the occasional bad market in real estate. There are seller's markets, where you have to compete for the properties you want. There are buyer's markets, in which you'd better hope you don't own any property with negative cash flow, because you are going to need deep pockets to "feed the alligator." (In real estate, "alligators" are properties that you have to pour money into constantly. They are *hungry* properties.)

What you have to do to be successful in real estate, over the long term, is learn how to invest in each of these markets—and, in particular, know *how* you are going to make money. We have bought and sold property in the days of 16 and 17 percent interest rates, and we have bought and sold with interest rates of less than 6 percent. You can make money in both markets, but you have to learn to adjust—or you can lose your shirt.

As we write this book (in the fall of 2005), we are in a powerful seller's market. People are making big money flipping condos, even before the ink on the first deal is dry. Residential development is hot. Everyone is jumping on the real estate train, and praying they aren't too late. Even Alan Greenspan, as chairman of the Federal Reserve, took note of the success that people are experiencing—and warned that the same conditions that ended the tech bubble of the late 1990s could put an abrupt end to the real estate party.

Will this market slow down? You bet. It has to happen, and very likely will by the time this book is published. But that's why you need to read this book. The great advantage of real estate is that *you can make money in both types of markets*; you just have to change your strategy. You have to go from making money in a seller's market to doing so in a buyer's market. No, it isn't always easy, but the rewards can make the learning process worthwhile. In fact, we are actually excited about the prospect of opportunities resulting from a slight slowdown, because it decreases the competition for the best properties.

Getting Started Strategy No. 1: Buy Real Estate

Should *you* own real estate? Yes. As our mother/grandmother said, everyone should own (at least) a little. The best way to start, of course, is to buy a home to live in, and then build on that learning experience. To advance beyond that, you will have to learn the *art* of investing in real estate—the art of buying and selling in your own style and developing your own niche. Some of you will never leave the world of residential real estate, and that's a perfectly good strategy for many people. We know and admire many people who make "big money on little deals," as one of them phrased it. These real estate entrepreneurs use single-family homes like pieces on a chessboard. Some of them build portfolios of hundreds of houses, and then sit back and collect rents. Others buy houses, fix them up a little, and flip them for a quick profit. Again, very different strategies are appropriate for people with different resources, skills, goals, and time frames.

Some of you will read this book, catch the real estate bug (if you don't have it already!), and go on to develop big parcels of real estate. Some of you will never buy real estate directly, choosing instead to finance other people's transactions. Either way, you can still be a winner, no matter which direction the market goes. There is a *big world* out there in real estate. We are going to open the doors for you, show you how it works, and help you figure out the best opportunity for *you* to get involved in.

What Will *You* Do?

We have written this book to help you figure out what type of real estate is right for you, and where you can make the most money. We take you through the relevant processes step by step: everything from finding your real estate niche to protecting your assets once you have made your fortune. We've tried to make the book easy to read, but make no mistake: this is not "real estate for dummies." We take real estate very seriously, and we *don't* think it's a good field for dummies. The stakes are too high, even if you're buying only a single property. We take a no-nonsense approach to buying and selling real estate—and that's what's described in the following pages.

Getting Started Strategy No. 2: Use the Law of Success Duplication

First, though, let's look at the issue of *habits* and *patterns* in our lives. We can't take a new path unless we understand the one we're already on.

Making money really isn't very hard. Most of us do it every day. Sometimes we even make a little extra, and we set that surplus aside for a rainy day—an important part of anybody's personal financial strategy, and one that we advocated in our best-selling book, *Operation Financial Freedom*. The truth is, almost anyone who has even a little bit of drive can succeed at this level.

What is far more difficult, for most people, is figuring out how to get out of our present financial circumstances and vault to the next level. How do you get from where you are right now to where you want to be?

When you *can't* answer that question, it is like being caught in a giant rut in the road. You can see opportunities all around you—left turns that look promising, right turns that seem intriguing—but you're stuck in a groove. You can't get your wheels out of the rut and pointed in a new direction.

The problem with the "I'm in a rut" mode is that it is very likely to continue indefinitely—you'll *stay* in that rut unless some sort of life-changing event forces you out of it, or you make a conscious, deliberate effort to *change your circumstances.*

Let's be clear about this point. If you're in a rut, you're not all that unusual. For the most part, we humans are creatures of habit. We land in a certain place, and, unless we make an extraordinary effort, we tend to stay in that place. We do what we do pretty much because that is the way we have always done it. We tend to reinforce the status quo, and we tend to do it automatically. We *duplicate* ourselves and our circumstances, as if we were running them off on a photocopier: one day looks a whole lot like the other days. It's *efficient*, yes, but it doesn't allow for easy changes.

Examine your own life in this light. Isn't it true that your life is a series of duplicated events, many of which are simply repeated automatically? Here's another measure: Is your financial life very similar to that of your parents? (This is certainly true for many people. After all, whom do we learn our financial habits from?) And unless you break this paradigm, your children's financial life will be similar to yours.

Should you break that paradigm? If one generation copies the previous one, or if you copy yourself, is that good news or bad news?

The answer, as you might suspect, is that it can be either good news *or* bad news, or sometimes even both. If you continue doing what you are doing, you will remain in your present circumstances (your rut) with only minor changes. Another way we like to phrase this idea is, "If you always do what you've always done, you'll always get what you have always gotten." Well, if you are happy with what you have, fine. (Ruts aren't necessarily negative.) But if you aren't happy with what you have, then you have no choice but to change it.

Some people take this as bad news. We see it as *exciting* news. Why? Because we all possess the *ability* to change. If you want to change, all you need to do is change your behaviors to routines that are more successful, and then repeat them over and over until they become habits. Once they are habits—once they are automatic—your life will continue in its new state, including its new financial state.

Now let's apply this way of thinking to real estate. Buying and selling real estate is a process that anyone can learn. Additionally, the field is so broad that you can definitely find an area or subspecialty that you can become good at. Once you do that, you can develop a set of routines that are repeatable over and over again until they become a habit. Let's assume that you've undertaken this process wisely, and you've selected a process that will deliver the kind of money you need to achieve financial freedom. Once that process becomes a habit, your rewards and financial success will follow automatically.

What does this mean specifically? Of all the people we know who are actively involved in making money in real estate, almost *none* of them do more than one specific type of real estate investing. They flip, or they do options, or they invest in groups that develop real estate, or they build, or they pursue any one of the other dozen ways to make money in real estate to be discussed in subsequent pages. A few do more than one, but it is extremely rare for someòne to do more than two.

The reason for this is the law of success duplication. When you are successful, you tend to repeat over and over the habits that made you successful. Why would you branch out in an entirely new direction, unless the old formula suddenly stopped working?

There is another point about the law of success duplication, and it has to do with mentors. Mentors can be extremely important to the success of the "apprentice." The apprentice copies what the mentor does to be successful, and the law of success duplication kicks in almost automatically. Keep in mind, though, that your mentor—the person you choose to copy—doesn't have to be someone you know. It can be almost anyone whom you can study, figure out, and emulate, even from afar. Not having a mentor in your building, or on your block, is no reason not to have a mentor at all!

When it comes to the concepts and strategies contained in this book, your job is to find the one or two nuggets that appeal to you most. Study them. Learn them. Specialize in them, and repeat them as often as you can. Make the practice of successful real estate investing an automatic in your life.

Real Estate Action Plan

Here's a two-step real estate action plan to get you on the road to financial freedom through real estate:

1. Complete the Financial Freedom Planner below. Based on your answers, you can quickly develop a goal that you can concentrate on throughout this book.
2. Review the 10-Year Retirement Plan that follows the Financial Freedom Planner. Note, for example, that by developing a systematic plan to acquire just one house a year for 10 years, you can create a continuous income stream for life.

FINANCIAL FREEDOM PLANNER

To develop your own real estate Financial Freedom Plan, complete the following form to see how many houses you need in order to reach your goal.

1. How much annual income will you need to live the way you want to at retirement? $_____

2. Multiply line 1 by 10 to get the value of the portfolio that is needed to generate your income. This is an old rule of thumb for income-producing real estate.
                                                               $_____

3. What is the value of your investment portfolio today?
                                                               $_____

4. Subtract line 3 from line 2 to find out how much of an increase in portfolio value you need in order to meet your goals. $_____

5. How many more years do you want to work for your financial freedom? $_____

6. Divide line 4 by line 5 to arrive at the annual increase needed in your portfolio values. $_____

7. What is the value of the average house in your town today? $_____

8. Divide line 4 by line 7 to arrive at an estimated number of houses needed to fulfill your goals. $_____

Getting Started Strategy No. 3: Develop Your 10-Year Retirement Plan

As a broad rule of thumb, a good house will approximately double in price every 10 years. [This is more likely when (1) the house is purchased wholesale, or (2) you use the ideas contained in this book.] The following example shows you how this appreciation can be harvested annually to provide a retirement income into perpetuity after the tenth year.

Let's assume that you buy a house today with a fair market value of $160,000 for 10 percent below market with 10 percent down.

$160,000	Today's fair market value
– 16,000	10 percent discount through negotiation
$144,000	Your purchase price
– 14,400	Down payment
$129,600	Loan balance (may be a combination of first and second mortgages)

Ten years from today, you refinance the same house, which has now reached a fair market value of $320,000. You get an 80 percent investor loan.

$320,000	Fair market value
x 80%	Non-owner-occupied loan
$256,000	
– 111,000	Pay off old loans
$145,000	Equity
– 6,000	Loan and closing costs
$139,000	Net loan proceeds (tax deferred from refinance)

If you purchase one house each year for 10 years, by the eleventh year, you can harvest the first one as shown here. In each succeeding year, you harvest another house until all have been refinanced, at which time you start the refinancing cycle again. And while there can certainly be variations on this basic theme, it at least gives you an idea of what a simple and systematic plan can do.

THE SUCCESS-DUPLICATION CHECKLIST

☑ **BUY REAL ESTATE—OF ONE KIND OR ANOTHER—TO TAKE ADVANTAGE OF THE MULTIPLE ADVANTAGES IT OFFERS OVER OTHER INVESTMENTS.** No, real estate shouldn't be your only kind of investment. But even the most conservative institutional investors, like corporate pension plans, allocate up to a fifth of their assets to real estate. You can probably allocate far more. (You probably already do, in terms of your net worth.) But even if you don't, everybody should own (at least) a little real estate.

☑ **USE THE LAW OF SUCCESS DUPLICATION FOR MAXIMUM ADVANTAGE.** This is a dressed-up way of saying that you should copy what's profitable and promising in your life and not duplicate the dead ends. If nothing seems particularly profitable or promising, you need to get out of your rut. Once you're out, *stay* out by duplicating your new good habits.

☑ **DEVELOP YOUR 10-YEAR RETIREMENT PLAN USING REAL ESTATE.** Study the example provided: through the purchase of one house a year for 10 years, you can position yourself to harvest appreciation, giving you substantial retirement income in perpetuity after the tenth year. Of course, this is only one of an infinite number of strategies, but it shows you the power of investing in real estate and the appeal of "success duplication."

CHAPTER 2

Ways to Make Money in Real Estate: A Baker's Dozen

The traditional approach to making money in real estate has been to buy a property, rent it out, and then, at some time in the future, sell it for a profit.

This approach certainly is tried and true, and it works well enough for some people. But at the same time, it has kept many other people out of the real estate investing arena, either because it entailed working in areas of real estate that they weren't interested in, like property management, or because it was simply too *boring*.

There are investors who never learn to trade in the stock market because they don't want to be "tied to a computer screen all day." But this is simply a mistaken view of what it takes to buy and sell stocks successfully. In fact, stock traders *don't* have to sit in front of their computers all day long. And similarly, real estate investors don't *have* to deal with the day-to-day routines of things like property management if they don't want to.

The truth is that there are many different ways to make investments in real estate and harvest profits. The trick is to find out which area of real estate you are most interested in (and probably best at), and apply your skills, time, and talents there. Don't let anyone tell you what you should do, or what is best for you. You have to decide that for yourself. If you do, you will be happier, and you will make more money.

This is one of life's few certainties. As we always tell our children, "First find out what you like to do in life, and then figure out how to make money at it."

Getting Started Strategy No. 4: Discover the Many Ways to Make Money in Real Estate

In this chapter, we explore 13 ways to make money in real estate, in terms of both strategies and specific subprofessions within the industry. Don't be daunted by this large menu of choices. You need to find only one that works for you in order to be successful. (Remember, "working for you" means not only financial success but happiness.) And you can always refine your course, or even change it, in later years as you grow in both experience and expertise.

1. *Buy, hold, and sell.* This is the strategy introduced at the beginning of this chapter. Over the years, buying, holding, and ultimately selling has been the most common way that people made money in real estate. They bought a house, lived in it, and at some point sold it. Or—going a big step further into the real estate investing game—they bought a rental property, fixed it up, managed it, and sold it. In recent decades (and, in fact, for much of American history), if you adopted this strategy, you were likely to make money. In fact, you probably wound up

wishing you had pursued this strategy more aggressively and bought more real estate earlier in your life.

We hear this very often from retirees who have dabbled in real estate. "If only I had bought a little more real estate," they tell us. Almost without exception, we tell them that *it's never too late!* Even at a relatively advanced age, if you have the necessary funds to buy and maintain more property, a second home or a rental property in a good area is almost always worth looking into. Some of our relatives who are in their eighties are not only managing their existing real estate assets (and earning a good income today), but also building for their future, and for their family's future.

2. *Buy, renovate, and hold (or sell).* For the slightly more aggressive investor, learning to buy and renovate property has traditionally offered two key advantages. First, it opens up a whole new category of potential purchases: properties that are undervalued because they need work and therefore scare off buyers who don't want to get in over their heads. Second, when you do the work yourself, you create "sweat equity," thereby adding a second element of profit—that is, in addition to the normal appreciation that your investment property would otherwise experience.

If you are handy (if improving a property comes naturally to you), then using your talents in this way is one of the best ways to take control of your financial future.

Obviously, you can keep building sweat equity for as long as you own the property. Our parents and grandparents supplemented their income throughout their lifetimes with rental income. We can still remember family "outings" in which we all trooped over to the rental properties to do some work. Everyone was involved—including the little kids as soon as they could pull a rake or wield a paint roller. In fact, this was one of the ways in which our parents and grandparents taught us the importance of investing in the future—as well as the fun of doing things as a family.

There are two more things to consider when it comes to sweat equity. First, like everybody else, you're most likely good at some things and not so good at others. (Maybe you're a great painter but not such a hot finish carpenter.) Sometimes it makes more sense to buy or barter for a certain skill than to try to master it yourself—especially if the skill in question involves specialized and expensive tools, or if mistakes in this area can be costly. And this leads to the second and related point: you need to keep an eye on *how much your time is worth*. If there's something else you could be doing that would earn you more money overall, you might be better off spending more time doing that and less time doing renovations.

Of course, some people really *enjoy* redoing a fixer-upper. If that's the case, you have to figure the "fun factor" into your calculations, as well.

3. *Flipping properties.* The art of buying properties to flip has gotten a great deal of press recently, and not all of it has been good. (We'll return to this subject in a minute.) To "flip" a property simply means to buy it at a low price and then sell it to someone else for a quick profit. Flipping goes on constantly, for a variety of reasons. First, some sellers simply get it wrong. They sell their property at below market value, thereby creating a flipping opportunity for a shrewd purchaser.

Another reason is differing views of investing or differing levels of risk tolerance. Many investors don't like to spend the time needed to find a property that is undervalued. (Their time may be too valuable.) They would much rather let someone else do it for them, and then bring them the property to buy and hold for the longer term. In other words, they choose to have properties flipped to them, and they are willing to pay the flipper's premium. In this scenario, both parties get a good deal, and both bring a different kind of value to the marketplace.

At different points over the years, we have been on both sides of flip transactions, usually depending on how we were trying to make money at that juncture. If our goal at the time was to make money to feed the family, we naturally tended to focus on the quick profit. Having achieved a certain level of financial security, we're now more inclined to take a longer-term approach, and we're happy to let people make some money finding good deals that they flip to us.

These flippers are often called "bird dogs" in the trade, because they sniff out the best deals. Sometimes, they are real estate agents. Other times, they are individual investors who have decided to specialize in this area of the market—and some of them are *very good* at it. When you're an investor in the long-term mold, as we are today, good bird dogs can be worth their weight in gold. You don't negotiate too hard with them, because you want them to keep bringing you the best deals first. They are happy doing what they do best, and you are happy building long-term value. To us, a real estate transaction is most satisfying when it's a win/win proposition for all parties.

Back to that issue of bad publicity: when you hear the argument that flipping properties is somehow "wrong," it's usually because a bank has been burned as a result of the flip. Here's how it typically happens: someone buys a property and pays off an appraiser to generate an inflated appraisal of the property. The buyer then refinances to that appraised amount, which means that the property is overfinanced. (In other words, there's no built-up equity in the property, and there's more money loaned against the property than it is currently worth.) If for some reason the buyer then can't hold onto the property, the bank has to take it over through foreclosure, sell it at a discount, and lose money.

Obviously, banks aren't in the business of losing money, and they complain loudly when they feel they've been conned. But as we see it, the problem isn't in the flip itself; it is in the bogus appraisal. Never mind that the bank could have (and should have) looked after its own interests more effectively. Buying an inflated appraisal is simply dishonest, and dishonesty is *never* the right way to do business. And it's unnecessary: if you're any good at flipping, there are always legitimate opportunities out there, and you don't have to resort to crookedness to make money.

Flipping also gets bad marks when it is seen as contributing to the overheating of a real estate market. A rising tide of condo flips, in particular, tends to signal a hot real estate market—in many cases, an *overly* hot market. Investors rush to buy preconstruction condos and flip them prior to closing. In Miami, as of this writing, things are so hot in the condo market that there is talk of creating a Web site exchange just for flipping condos before they close.

We agree that this level of froth has negative consequences. It creates an overpriced market, which usually means that people (generally unsophisticated investors) take a financial beating when reality finally sets in. (In the past, banks also took a beating, but after the 1989–1990 real estate crash, they became much more conservative in their lending.) We're *less* sure about the best way to take some of the hot air out of a "flipping bubble." In some cases, lenders refuse to loan money to developers who don't have strict anti-flipping provisions in the contract. Others refuse to loan money based on an appraisal that is higher than the original construction appraisal.

These are reasonable steps. But the truth is that when investors get caught up in a bubble mentality, it's very hard to protect them from themselves.

4. *Lease options.* The lease option has become one of the featured strategies for real estate wealth builders because it has legitimate win/win features for both the buyer and the seller. We will talk about lease options extensively in Chapter 16. For now, though, you should recognize that the lease option is an excellent way to buy property if you don't have much money to put up for a real estate purchase.

Using the lease-option strategy, you find a property that you are interested in, and you offer to lease it for a certain number of years with the right to buy it at any time during the period of the lease for a set price (normally more than the property is worth at the time of the agreement). You lease the property and hope that it will appreciate faster than your set purchase price. If it does, you exercise your option and sell the property, making the profit. If it doesn't, you let your lease expire and try again somewhere else.

This can be a very successful technique for getting ownership of a property at a good price. You might think it would be difficult to get people to offer a lease option on their property, but in fact, there are many circumstances under which people will do so happily, even in hot markets. In Orlando, Florida (one of the hottest real estate markets in the country), for instance, we recently structured a type of option transaction on a commercial building worth more than $12 million, and the property has already appreciated (at least on paper) by 25 percent or more. Will we make 25 percent on our money? Who knows? If we time it right, we'll do fine. If we *don't* time it right and things get overbuilt and commercial rents and prices decline, then we won't make any money. Ah, but that is the joy of real estate investing!

5. *Equity-sharing partner.* Maybe you're reading this book because you have dreams of building wealth and achieving financial freedom, but you don't have the cash to realize those dreams. We have all been there. Not having cash is neither a cause for embarrassment nor a reason not to make money. You just have to *think harder* and work harder. You have to be willing to do what other people won't or can't do—and that is where you will make your money. In real estate, the opportunities are endless.

If you take the time to learn what we teach you in this book, you will know things that most people don't. Furthermore, if you are willing to work hard, and especially if you have skills at fixing up property yourself, you bring a lot to the party. All you lack is the cash. One way to get the money for your enterprise is to get a partner to put up all the money, and possibly even to "use your partner's financial statement" by getting that person to be the co-borrower with you. We call this equity sharing, and it is a type of partnership arrangement that is good for both parties. Investors who have made a lot of money generally want to keep doing whatever it is that has made them the money. (You don't change a formula that's working well.) They would rather give up some of the return and let *you* do the work, which, of course, frees them up to keep making money elsewhere.

Where do you find those kinds of investors? Amazingly, they are all over. We will tell you where and how to find them in Chapter 4, "Creating Your Real Estate Master Mind Group."

6. *Real estate agent.* Maybe you've never thought about becoming a real estate agent. Or maybe you have—and you've already decided that it's the last thing in the world you want to do. As we have already said in other examples, it all depends on your perspective. You have to do what works for you. But becoming a real estate agent may be the right move for a number of reasons.

First, you may find that you *like* this aspect of the real estate field—in fact, you like it so much that you want to get a Realtor's license and make a full-time job of it. This is a career that in effect pays you to search for properties (which you are probably doing anyway, as an investor), and also pays a very nice commission when you close a sale for someone else. Since you can't buy everything yourself, you might as well make money on the properties you can't or don't want to buy.

Even if you don't like representing other people, you may still find that having a license is worth your while. The money can be good, especially in a hot market, and it can come not only from commissions, but also from referral fees when you put investors together with sellers. You can also make invaluable contacts in the real estate community and position yourself to hear about good investment opportunities.

If you don't want to work full time as a agent, consider getting a license for use on a part-time basis. Real estate offers great opportunities for people who need flexible hours, whether because of family commitments or because of other employment.

7. Property manager. Most rental properties have someone, on- or offsite, who manages them. The property manager collects the rents, fields questions from current and prospective tenants, arranges for maintenance and repairs, and otherwise acts as the owner's representative. Again, this may be something you've already thought about doing. If not, it's worth considering. After all, *somebody* has to manage all of this property that people are buying, and you may find that this is exactly what you like doing. Even after you get your own properties to manage, you may find it is worth your while to manage properties for other owners as well.

Property management pays well, in part because not everyone likes to do it. You also have the advantage of having a *residual* form of income, which simply means that you have year-long contracts that pay you a percentage of the income you collect each and every month. Unlike the commissions paid to a real estate agent, residual compensation provides a steady income stream that you collect each month. Additionally, when you manage a property, you are generally the first to know when it comes up for sale. Because you manage it, moreover, you have a good sense of whether or not it's a good buy.

If it is a good buy, you can acquire it for your own portfolio. If you don't like it for yourself, you can list it and make a good commission when it is sold to someone else. Sales commissions on properties you manage in effect increase your compensation for the time you spend managing them.

Once you gain experience in the property management field, you can expand to bigger properties, such as strip centers, office buildings, and other commercial properties. The management compensation on residential properties is generally 10 to 15 percent of gross rents and on commercial properties, 5 to 7 percent. The more expensive the properties you manage, the more your income goes up—even though your workload remains about the same. In fact, larger and more expensive properties sometimes require *less* work, because the tenants you deal with in these settings tend both to be more professional and to have more realistic expectations of you and the property. They tend to be less emotional and more businesslike.

8. *Mortgage broker.* Being a mortgage broker, which involves arranging the financing for real estate that is being bought or refinanced, can be another profitable side of the real estate industry. Mortgage brokers make their money through commissions. Fees range from 1 percent on conventional loans to 5 percent or higher on hard-to-place financing. With the average home today

selling (or being refinanced) for well over $200,000, you can do very well for yourself by putting together buyers and lenders.

The key to success as a mortgage broker is having great contacts in the real estate field. The more agents you know, the more buyers you'll have referred to you, and the more successful you will be. This field has gotten very active in recent years, in part because of increased levels of home buying, but especially because of all the refinancing activity prompted by lower interest rates. Lower rates, of course, encourage homeowners to refinance their homes to lower their monthly payments.

Refinancings are likely to slow over the next few years, since interest rates have apparently bottomed out for this economic cycle and will probably to begin rising. That doesn't mean, however, that you should exclude this area of real estate from serious consideration. Again, there will always be money to be made in the mortgage-brokering business.

9. *Appraiser.* Appraisal is a specialized corner of the real estate business. Before a financial institution will make a loan on a property, that property must be inspected and assigned a realistic market value to ensure that the lender isn't lending too much. This valuation process is the appraisal. Since most properties are purchased with financing, that translates into a lot of appraisals—and a lot of business.

Appraisers learn the business through an apprentice system, very similar to the guilds of yesteryear. Although anyone with a real estate license can do an appraisal (and can charge a fee for that service), banks require the appraisers they use to have a special designation as either as a residential or a commercial appraiser. Getting such a designation requires years of apprenticeship to someone who already has the designation, meaning that during your apprenticeship, you are more or less in a situation of indentured servitude. The designated appraiser to whom you are apprenticed is likely to think of you as future competition for business and therefore is unlikely to pay you much money during your apprenticeship.

So the challenge is to "float" your apprenticeship, just as you'd have to find ways to pay for any other kind of education. And although being a designated appraiser is not an automatic road to riches (and again, the state of the real estate market either hurts or helps appraisers), getting that designation is usually worthwhile in the end.

Why? In part because being an appraiser puts you squarely in the middle of the real estate marketplace. As an appraiser, you will be in a key position to see and spot properties that are coming on line, whether they are established properties or new construction. Meanwhile, assuming that you're good at what you do, no one will know the real value of property better than you do. The combination of these two information streams can offer you continuous opportunities in the local marketplace.

10. *Auctioneer.* Until very recently, the profession of real estate auctioneer has been largely invisible. As the name implies, the auctioneer runs the sale of properties in an auction format. Awareness of the auctioneer's job, and the opportunities it presents, has increased in recent years, thanks to the entry into this field of big-name auction houses. When a firm like Sotheby's starts selling big estates at auction, instant attention and credibility are brought to the job.

Selling through an auction is a very specialized type of marketing. Most people assume that mastering the "calling" of the auction (that is, standing in front of the crowd, managing the bidding process, and generally doing your best to drive the selling price upward) is the most difficult aspect of the auctioneer's job. In fact, marketing the auction in a way that attracts strong buyers is the toughest part of the job. In addition, you typically need fairly deep pockets to get you from one end of the auction process to the other.

As in the appraisal field, you get to be an auctioneer through an apprenticeship program. Yes, you can theoretically get there on your own, but we've never run across anyone who got started that way.

11. *Developer.* In the real estate industry, the word *developer* is a broad term. It covers everyone from the people who buy raw land and get it ready for development to the people who spend years putting together big tracts of property and building major planned-unit developments—and lots of people in between. For many people, this is where the action is. It's where most of the money in real estate is made and lost.

In many industries today, the freestanding, lone-wolf entrepreneur is nearly an extinct species. Not so in real estate! The big-time developer is a throwback to a bygone era—an earlier, more buccaneering stage of capitalism. As a developer, you have to have vision, luck, great contacts, lots of money, and nerves of steel. It may take years to put together a big project, and in the meantime you are doing nothing but paying out large sums of money. The regulatory climate has continued to get tougher and tougher, and the red tape surrounding environmental impact statements (to cite just one example) can be a nightmare.

We speak from experience. We have had entire projects held up by nesting whooping cranes. In another case, we had gopher turtles (a grand total of four of them) living on a tract of land we owned. Gopher turtles are neither "endangered" nor "threatened" in the official bureaucratic categorizations; they are a "species of special concern." Nevertheless, those four foot-long turtles held up our project so long that we finally offered to put them up at the Four Seasons Hotel next door to our property if the government would just let us get started with the project. The agency in question didn't take to the idea, and the issue took another six months to resolve—six more months of money flowing out the door.

On the other hand (and yes, in the real estate business, there is almost always another hand), development can be very, very profitable. Yes, you have to learn to roll with the punches that can be served up by a fickle market or an overeager regulator. You have to learn how to behave in all phases of the larger real estate cycle—not just the good times. And, no, this isn't easy. But when you *do* pull it off, it can make you rich.

12. *Syndicators.* These are people who put together deals using other people's money. These passive investors buy shares in the deal in proportion to their share of the total investment. Most people have heard of racehorses being "syndicated" (that is, bankrolled by a group of investors who are betting that the horse will someday make big returns), but fewer people are aware that real estate can be syndicated in basically the same way.

Real estate syndications come in all sizes. There are small syndications (e.g., a single-family home), and there are big syndications (e.g., the Empire State Building), and everything in between.

Syndication can be very lucrative. When you put together deals using other people's money, though, you have to keep in mind that these people are expecting a good return on their money. So there can be a great deal of pressure on you to be successful if you want to stay in the syndication game. If you put together a good track record, you will never lack for investors. Unfortunately, the first time a deal goes south, you may have some very angry partners to deal with—and that's never fun.

Over the years, we have learned that an investment partnership is a lot like a marriage: it's easy to get into, but very ugly and expensive to get out of. Neither of us has gone through a divorce, thank goodness, but we've certainly been through unpleasant business breakups. Even so, we don't shy away from a promising partnership. In many cases, partnerships make things possible that otherwise wouldn't be possible. The first key to success in a partnership is for all parties to *go in with their eyes open,* that is, understanding as much as they can about the relationship and what each person expects to get out of it. The second key to success is *open and effective communication.* If you're not a good communicator, you may not be a good syndicator. You can't be a stranger to your investors.

13. *Trainer/mentor.* After you do something for a while and get a reputation for being good at it, people start trying to figure out your secret formula. Two observations: first, the secret to your success is probably your willingness to put in the long hours and do the hard work that no one else wants to do. Second, almost nobody wants to hear that story. They want to hear about the shortcuts to success—the get-rich-quick strategies.

By the time you achieve this kind of success, you'll be wise enough to know that there really aren't any shortcuts. At the same time, you will have learned a great deal, and there are almost certainly worthwhile elements of your expertise that you can pass along as a trainer or mentor. Depending on your particular skills and interests, this may take the form of teaching, writing, or speaking about your experiences.

Unless you're really good and really lucky, you're unlikely to make a lot of money as a trainer or a mentor. But these activities bring their own special kinds of rewards. It can be extremely gratifying to see young people follow your example—without making some of the same dumb mistakes that you made early on. Being a trainer or a mentor also forces you to be explicit about exactly how you do what you do, and this can be a very valuable exercise as you think about the next phase of your own professional life. What works? What's interesting? What's fun?

For serial entrepreneurs like ourselves (and maybe like you), figuring out the answers to these questions is the *real* challenge of our business lives.

Getting Started Strategy No. 5: Find a Corner of the Industry That Matches Your Skills and Interests

As this chapter suggests, there is an almost infinite number of ways to make money in real estate. We've barely scratched the surface. In addition to the 13 approaches described, you can and should explore multiple other avenues: hard-money lender, home inspector, private investor, discount paper broker, tax lien specialist, nothing-down buyer, and so on. In the chapters ahead, we will explore and explain many of these real estate niches in detail.

Those who tell you that you're not cut out to succeed in real estate are probably demonstrating their own ignorance of this huge and incredibly diverse industry. Don't be dissuaded. If you're reading this book, you're already demonstrating the kind of curiosity and determination that is needed for success. You will need to develop a plan, and start implementing it as soon as possible. You will need to work hard, and you'll need to work smart.

But you *can* succeed.

THE GETTING-STARTED CHECKLIST

☑ **START LEARNING ABOUT THE MANY DIFFERENT WAYS TO MAKE MONEY IN REAL ESTATE.** Real estate, as we've said, is an incredibly diverse field. It's full of people pursuing very different strategies and doing very different things, minute by minute and day by day. In this chapter, we presented only 13 of these strategies and professions. There are many, many more. Based on our brief descriptions, start digging more deeply into one or more particular subspecialties of the industry that sound appealing to you. Talk to people who actually pursue that strategy or do that job. Would they do it again if they were starting over? How does it feel to be an auctioneer (for example) at both the high and low points of the real estate cycle? What are the success factors? But remember, you have to discover these things firsthand, for yourself. Never make career decisions based on guesses, rumors, or hearsay.

☑ **FIGURE OUT WHAT YOU'RE ALL ABOUT, AND FIND A CORNER OF THE REAL ESTATE INDUSTRY THAT SEEMS TO MATCH YOUR SKILLS AND INTERESTS.** Maybe you've noticed how many people around you are eager to tell you what's good and bad for you. Listen hard to them, if you value their opinion, but don't be overly influenced. *You* have to figure out what's good for you. As you're learning about the real estate industry, you'll also be learning about yourself. If something sounds very appealing to you (or very unappealing), try to figure out what that says about you. Do you cherish your independence? Do you perform well under pressure? Are you a good communicator? Bringing together your growing knowledge of a complex industry and your growing knowledge of yourself is the best way to succeed in real estate.

CHAPTER 3

How Real Estate Can Make You Wealthy

Investing involves an unending series of choices: Which investment vehicle should I put my money in? How much should I put there? How long should I leave it there? Before looking at the specifics of investing in real estate, and explaining how it can make you wealthy, we should probably take a quick look at the other alternatives. If you want to get rich, what's the best way to get there?

In our recent best seller *Operation Financial Freedom,* we discussed the importance of a strategy called "pay yourself first." The idea is to set aside 10 percent of your monthly income for long-term growth. We make the case that by following this strategy, anyone can build a satisfactory retirement nest egg over the long term.

So let's assume for a moment that you decide to follow this advice, and you start setting aside 10 percent of all your income so that you can begin to build an investment program for yourself. Maybe you start putting the money in a money market account, or you open up an IRA to build your long-term wealth. In either case, you're *taking action*, and that is a great start.

For the sake of discussion, let's assume that during your first year of saving, you are able to put away $4,000, 10 percent of your $40,000 gross income. If so, you probably feel pretty good about that, especially if this is the first time you've actually succeeded in starting a systematic savings plan. Let's assume, too, that you take another piece of advice from us and give yourself a big pat on the back. We strongly believe in celebrating these kinds of successes!

Now let's assume that with your new savings program in place, you start thinking about making a little extra money *on* your money, so that you don't always have to rely exclusively on your salary to provide for you and your family. After some calculations, you decide that it would be great if you could get to the point where you were making an extra $10,000 per year just from your investments. Seems reasonable, right?

Here's the rub: you continue your calculations, and pretty soon this reasonable target doesn't look so reasonable. You know, for example, that your money market fund is paying 2 percent annual interest, and you calculate that to get an extra $10,000 per year from that in the form of interest, you're going to have to build a nest egg of $500,000. *That's* depressing, you think to yourself.

What about the stock market, you ask yourself. Well, a little research shows that the stock market produces about a 12 percent annualized return, on average. That is a little better. Now you need only an $83,000 nest egg to generate your desired $10,000 per year extra return. And if you "margined" your money (borrowed up to 50 percent) in the stock market, you could get that sum down to $41,500 of your own money. Unfortunately, though, you also realize that it will take you 10 years of saving at your current rate of $4,000 per year to get close to the required

$41,500—and, of course, you'll have to average that 12 percent return each and every year. As anyone knows from the experience of the last few years, the stock market doesn't always turn in a double-digit performance, and a downturn can have severe consequences for someone who's trading on margin.

If your analysis stopped there, you'd have ample reason to be depressed. We're going to argue, though, that you shouldn't stop there. You should continue with your analysis, and look at the returns in real estate. Why? Because real estate has one thing going for it that no other investment vehicle has. We call it the *power of OPM*, or other people's money.

Getting Started Strategy No. 6: Use the Power of OPM

The advantage that real estate offers over all other types of investing is that you don't have to have money to start investing. With real estate, you don't have to have money to make money. In some ways, the less money you have, the more money you can make.

Let's go back to our example. How long do you think it would take to turn your $4,000 nest egg investment into a million dollars, assuming that you could consistently earn a 20 percent return on your money? The answer: 30 years. Well, what if you don't *have* 30 years? Should you just give up (as many people do) and say to yourself, "I'm just too old to make any real money"?

What if you were to say to yourself, "I have only five years"? Could you do it? Well, you would have to make a 200 percent annual return on your money—impossible in a money market account, and nearly impossible in the stock market. So how can you do it?

The answer, of course, is real estate. Here's how. Let's say you are going to buy a $50,000 property paying all cash. (Don't worry about the price; it's just an example.) Let's say the property appreciates 10 percent, or $5,000, in one year. Your return on your $50,000 cash investment, therefore, is 10 percent—a respectable return, but not spectacular.

But let's say you don't *have* $50,000. Instead, you have only $5,000 to invest in the property. So you invest your $5,000 and take out a loan for the balance of the purchase price. The house still goes up 10 percent in value, but your return is now $5,000 on your original $5,000 investment—in other words, a 100 percent return on your money. This is a central concept, so if you didn't follow it, try walking through it again, and look at the next example, as well.

Suppose you could scrape together only half of the down payment, or $2,500, and borrowed the rest. If the same scenario unfolded (a 10 percent appreciation of the property in a year), you would earn a 200 percent return on your money. Keep going in this direction: what if you put *no* money down? Your return would be, well, *amazing*. And that is how you build wealth: through "leverage." You use the power of OPM (other people's money) to tap into returns that normally would go to somebody else.

Let's acknowledge quickly that this is a very simplified example. It doesn't take into account the interest that you'd pay on your loan (nor does it reflect any offsetting rents that you might collect on the property). The example doesn't include capital investments or maintenance expenses, nor does it consider the tax advantages of investing in real estate. But what this simplified illustration *does* do is show you how leverage, and using the power of OPM, can work for you, in the right circumstances.

Do you have to go into debt to get these returns? Yes, you do. But you're doing so to invest in something that traditionally has been an appreciating asset. There *are* risks involved, but most ambitious people decide at some point that to get ahead, they are going to have to take a calculated risk.

Again, if you're just starting out, we suggest starting with the single-family home that you're going to live in. Risky? Well, yes; and writing those big checks at the closing is always a little nerve-wracking. But most likely, your risk *feels* lower (and, in a sense, it *is* lower) because you would have to pay to live someplace, in any case. See how the definition of "risk" shifts, depending on your perspective?

You should also keep in mind that real estate debt is *not* the same as consumer debt. Most of what you buy with your credit cards (and similar kinds of consumer debt) is considered a "wasting asset," because it loses value starting from the moment you buy it. True, some real estate also has gone down in value, but a much greater percentage increases in value year after year. Declines in real estate values usually result from some very unusual and specific circumstances, and one of the main goals of this book is to help you avoid those problems.

How Do You Find OPM?

Most of the time, money for real estate purchases is readily available. The money most often comes from banks, but there is a myriad of other potential lenders out there, including private investors, second mortgage lenders, sellers, Realtors, hard-money lenders, sellers, and even other real estate investors. At various times, and under varying circumstances, each can play a very active role as a lender in the real estate market.

The past decade or so has been a very good period in which to borrow money, whether from conventional or less conventional sources, because interest rates have been very low by historical standards. Low interest rates enable you to buy more expensive properties, because your payments are driven not only by the size of the loan, but also by the rate of interest on that loan.

This is important not for reasons of prestige, but for a very practical reason: being able to buy a larger property means a higher return, in terms of equity buildup, if the property appreciates. In our previous example, our $50,000 property increased 10 percent, yielding you $5,000 in equity on your $5,000 investment. But if interest rates are low enough to enable you to carry the loan on a $100,000 property, and if that property goes up 10 percent, your equity buildup will be $10,000, giving you a 200 percent return on your original $5,000 cash investment.

As of this writing, there are large numbers of private investors who are fed up with the very low returns they can make by putting their money in banks. Most of these investors aren't fools. They know that, in many cases, the bank is investing their money in real estate and earning good returns that way. Many of these investors are willing to cut out the middleman (the bank) and make the loans themselves, as equity partners, members of a real estate syndicate, or some other kind of real estate investor.

One reason why private lenders may be more attractive to you than conventional lenders is that you don't usually pay "points" (an assessed fee) on your loan. In addition, the closing expenses are substantially lower, usually by as much as 1 percent of the total amount of the loan. Borrowing from private lenders is frequently less cumbersome, too, because they aren't subject to government regulation and usually don't require credit checks or financial statements.

We're not trying to oversell the power of OPM. (In fact, we're not trying to oversell *anything* in this book.) At the same time, we hope these simple examples get you excited about the real opportunities that await you in real estate. Leverage—using the power of OPM—is the real secret to success in real estate.

Getting Started Strategy No. 7: Use Nonconventional Financing

Especially when your cash is low, it is wise to use nonconventional financing to get a fast start in real estate.

How to Print Your Own Money

Once you own real estate and have built up some equity in the property or properties, you also open the door to your own mint. You get the power to print money.

How does this work? Simple. You take out a second mortgage on the property to tap into your built-up equity. This is no more complicated than going down to your local office-supply store, picking up a blank mortgage form (or deed-of-trust form, depending on your state), and filling in the blanks to specify a value for the property that you think you can justify. (Obviously, this stated value has to exceed the amount of the existing mortgage on the property and the amount of your proposed second mortgage.)

After creating the mortgage, you run an ad in the newspaper and sell the mortgage on your property to an investor, either at face value, or perhaps at a discount off face value in order to entice the investor to make the loan. (See the discussion of discount mortgages in Chapter 18.) Such a discount may be necessary because your mortgage is new. It isn't a "seasoned loan"—in other words, a loan with a payment history.

Depending on how long you have had your property and how much equity has built up, the lender (your second-mortgage investor) may feel that there is not enough equity in the property in the event that you default and the lender has to foreclose on the property (i.e., take the property in settlement of your debt). If that becomes an issue, you can create additional security for the investor by signing a promissory note with your personal guarantee to repay. As a rule, though, your goal should be to give a "mortgage without recourse," meaning that the lender can look only to the property itself, and not to your other assets, to collect from in the event of a default by you.

Why would a lender agree to a mortgage without recourse? Because the lender believes in you and believes that you will make every effort to avoid a default. He knows that you are trying to either build or protect your reputation as an investor and that a good credit history is almost as important to you as cash. And finally, the investor believes that the money is there to be gotten back out of the property, or he wouldn't have gone in on the deal in the first place.

Many first-time real estate buyers who hear us talk about creating their own mortgages on their property think this scheme sounds too good to be true. It's not. Seasoned real estate investors do this all the time, and there is a big market for discount mortgages, because they offer good returns and are backed by real estate. Your biggest challenge will be to show that there is equity in the property. Maybe this is because you put down a substantial down payment. Maybe it's because properties like this, in this neighborhood, have appreciated. Or maybe it's just because you got a good deal in the first place. The truth is, nonconventional lenders don't care where the equity comes from; they simply want to know that there *is* equity there, and they need to be convinced that you intend to pay back your loan. It's really as simple as that.

Later on in this book, we'll recommend that you start attending investor groups in your local area. If and when you do, you'll encounter these same terms and strategies, in more or less the same way we've presented them here. Most likely, you'll wonder why no one has ever told you about them before.

Good question. But this probably isn't the right place for us to launch into our tirade about the near-complete lack of practical education in our public schools. For better or worse, you have to learn this kind of thing from experience—and from books like this, and from peers and mentors, and wherever else you can pick it up.

Someday, we'll write another book about our theories on education.

How to Use Equity Lines of Credit

Equity lines of credit are readily available today to anyone who owns stocks or real estate, including your home. A line of credit is issued by the lender, and you get a checkbook and a credit card to access the line. These automatic-access accounts are very helpful for real estate buyers who lack substantial personal savings because they allow you to move quickly when you see a good deal. You simply write a check that is used as your escrow deposit.

As with so many other mechanisms in the investing world, however, there are dangers inherent in lines of credit. If you don't have the ability to pay them back, they can ruin you.

How might this happen? Well, all lines of credit feature adjustable, rather than fixed, interest rates. As of this writing, interest rates are relatively low. But these rates can be adjusted every month, and, if they go up, the cost of your past borrowing goes up, too. While this doesn't normally result in a rapid change in your monthly payment, the impact of gradually rising interest rates can sneak up on you.

Eventually, you can find yourself in a *negative amortization* situation. Simply put, a negative amortization occurs when your payments on the loan are less than the monthly minimum required to pay off the loan. In theory, depending on the terms of your loan, the lender has the right to "call the loan" and seize and sell your collateral—which means foreclosure, in the case of real estate collateral. More likely, since your loan is secured by real estate, the lender will simply let the loan increase in size, on the assumption that your equity is increasing faster from appreciation. So while foreclosure is an extreme example of what could happen through misuse of a line of credit, it is something that any borrower should understand and make allowances for.

Is the risk inherent in lines of credit worth the reward? You have to answer this question for yourself. Frankly, we use lines of credit all the time, but we tend to be aggressive investors. Especially in the real estate market of today, opportunities don't last very long. You need to have the ability to *move quickly* in order to take advantage of good deals that may come your way. At the same time, you shouldn't do things that take you out of your own risk tolerance or (if things go badly) put pressure on you that you're not prepared to deal with. You need to figure out your own way to participate in the real estate business.

Seller Loans

Seller financing, in which the seller makes a loan to the buyer to help close the sale, is very common in the real estate industry.

Typically, the seller takes back a second mortgage on the property (after the bank's first mortgage) in order to help the buyer finance the purchase with less cash. The buyer of a home can normally obtain a loan for 90 percent of the assessed value of the home (thereby achieving a 90 percent loan-to-value ratio), and the buyer of an investment property can expect to borrow 80 percent of the purchase price (an 80 percent loan-to-value ratio). The remaining 20 or 10 percent can usually be made up from a seller-financed second mortgage, but sometimes the lender requires more cash from a buyer.

In addition to the traditional type of seller financing, in which the seller takes back a second mortgage, it is also possible to get the seller to subordinate a small loan that is financed to a second mortgage from another lender. (*Subordinating* simply means putting the loan "in line" behind another loan. A first mortgage has first call on the asset; a second mortgage has second call, and is subordinated to the first.) Here's how this typically works: you (the buyer) obtain a new first mortgage for 80 percent of the value of the property. At the same time, you get a line-of-credit second mortgage for 10 percent of the financing from a conventional lender. This arrangement makes the seller's financing, in effect, a third mortgage, subordinated to both the first and second mortgages.

Since the seller is confident of the value of the property (having just established it by means of the sale to you), the third mortgage is probably not seen as a big risk. If the seller doesn't need all the cash from the sale to buy another property, it can also be a good investment.

This leaves you, as the buyer, with 100 percent financing, which at today's historically low lending rates is a great way to tie up property, even in a hot market. True, you will probably have a negative cash flow from the property because you are carrying so much debt on it. In such a case, you're betting that the property's appreciation will more than cover your negative cash flow and that you can afford that negative cash flow until you have the cash to pay down the debt or you can find another investor willing to share the equity with you in return for covering the negative cash flow. (See Chapter 14, "Partners, Partnerships, Equity Sharing, and Syndications.")

It is always a good idea to get to know the seller of any property you buy and to find out what she intends to do with all of the cash she is getting from the sale. In most instances, the seller won't need all of the cash for the next property she is buying, because she will be financing the new property. The financing leaves the seller with cash to invest, and most people (surprisingly) have no idea what they are going to do with that cash. We have found long-term investors for some of our other properties who have been sellers to us at one time. These people may have a good initial feeling about you because you purchased their property at a price that was acceptable to them. They now have money to invest. If you can find them a good short-term investment, it is a good way for them to test the waters with you again. Once the next investment goes well, it allows you to continue to build a good relationship for future investments together, either as a pure lender or as an equity partner.

Hard-Money Lenders

We call them hard-money lenders. Others call them loan sharks. To us, "loan shark" is too harsh a term, because hard-money lenders play an important role in real estate. They fill a financial void where traditional lenders fear to tread.

Hard-money lenders loan money based on the "hard asset" that is used as security. The primary difference between hard-money lenders and traditional lenders is that the former will loan you up to 100 percent of the appraised value of the property. Sometimes, a hard-money lender will even loan you *more* than 100 percent of the value, if you have developed a good relationship with the lender or if you've completed some improvements to the property since the appraisal that the lender feels has enhanced its value.

For example, consider a run-down property that an investor buys at a discount price. The investor gets a first mortgage on the property from a conventional lender. The balance of the cash that she needs to close and fix the property is advanced by the hard-money lender. Once the property is rehabbed, a new appraisal is performed, and the hard-money lender may loan additional money against the new equity.

The other difference between hard-money lenders and banks is that hard-money lenders charge a much higher interest rate. This is how they earn their unsavory (and we think undeserved) reputation as loan sharks. The truth is, while there may be a bad element in the hard-money lending industry, you simply find out who those people are and stay away from them. You learn to deal only with those lenders who are recommended by other people you know in the industry, and you set about building a good working relationship with them.

As we said earlier, hard-money lenders play an extremely valuable role. They fill a financing void: between traditional lenders and those people who have great potential to build wealth in real estate, but don't have all the money they need to take advantage of the opportunities they find.

To find hard-money lenders in your area, we again suggest that you attend a local real estate investment group meeting. Other alternatives are to run an ad in the newspaper or to call some of the advertisers in the "money to lend" section. When you find a potential source, *check it out*, and check it out thoroughly. If you are in a small town, for example, check your source's reputation in the large metropolitan area that is closest to you. He may have a track record there (good or bad) that you should know about.

Getting Started Strategy No. 8: Create Powerful Partnerships

We will explore partnerships more extensively in Chapter 14. For now, keep in mind that partners are a big source of OPM. Some partners will be active with you in your real estate deals, and some will be very passive—simply looking for a higher return on their money than they can get at the bank. It will take you a while to develop these partner contacts, but once you do, and once you begin to make money for them, others will seek you out.

As you learn more about real estate and partnerships, you will hear horror stories about partnerships. People are likely to tell you that partnerships *never* work. That is certainly true for some people, but it may not be true for you. (It hasn't been true for us.) Much of it depends on you and how you deal with others. In our experience, partnerships that make the whole greater than the sum of the parts can be very rewarding, both financially and psychologically. Keep open to the opportunities of partnership, and, again, don't be dissuaded by someone's opinion.

THE WEALTH-BUILDING CHECKLIST

☑ **USE THE POWER OF OPM TO MAXIMIZE YOUR RETURNS.** This is one of the most important lessons in this entire book. If you haven't grasped this powerful, central concept, we urge you to go back and read that section of the chapter again. "It takes money to make money," as the old saying goes. Well, that's true enough—except that in real estate, it doesn't take *your* money to make money. You can (and should) use other people's money (OPM) to create leverage, and gains, for yourself. You use their money, your property appreciates, and *you get to keep the appreciation.* Nice work if you can get it—and you can.

☑ **ESPECIALLY WHEN YOUR CASH IS LOW, USE NON-CONVENTIONAL FINANCING TO GET A FAST START IN REAL ESTATE.** Again, use other people's money (OPM). See if your seller will take back any paper. (In the 1980s, when interest rates were extraordinarily high, some well-heeled sellers, tempted by 12 percent, 30-year notes, took back *all* the money, knowing that they probably wouldn't do as well elsewhere.) Look into resources like hard-money lenders—who may have a bad reputation in some quarters, but who actually serve an invaluable role in making some worthwhile deals happen.

☑ **CREATE POWERFUL PARTNERSHIPS TO EXTEND YOUR REACH AND ABILITIES.** We're once again going to tell you to listen hard to people and ignore all the bad advice they give you. If someone tells you that "all partnerships are a disaster," that person is probably telling you more about herself than about partnerships. Unless you're superrich and have every skill known to man, you're going to have to engage in partnerships of one kind or another. Spend your time checking out potential partners—and then spend your time making the partnership work. Communicate!

CHAPTER 4

Creating Your Real Estate Master Mind Group

Aclassic motivation book, *Think and Grow Rich*, brought to our attention the concept of building a personal "master mind group." The author, Napoleon Hill, describes a business strategy that centers on the idea of building a strong group of people who will serve as your counselors and advisers, and who will help you over the years as your career progresses.

We both believe strongly in the merits of this strategy, and we've incorporated it into many aspects of our lives. In the real estate world, for example, we have expanded upon the concept to include a broader network of people who collectively can achieve a common goal of business referrals.

It has worked for us, and we suggest that you try it on for size. Your group will probably start small and then grow over the years. Most likely, some members of your network will drop out for their own reasons. In other cases, you'll find a way to drop them. What's important isn't how *big* your group is at any one time, but rather, how *effective* it is for you.

If you are just starting in real estate investment, building your master mind network may be one of the most important things you do. It will not only energize *your* business, but it will also create synergies within your group—and helping other people is also good for you, in the long run.

Getting Started Strategy No. 9: Find Your Real Estate Niche and Learn How to Exploit It

The first step in building your master mind network is to discover your real estate niche and then to exploit it by becoming the best in that niche. Maybe your reaction to this prescription is to say, "But I don't *know* what my niche is!" Don't worry about it. You're reading this book. You'll attend a couple of real estate investment classes, if you haven't already. You'll do your homework, in the sense of talking to people who are already in the real estate business. It won't be very long before you start to find your way. You will gravitate toward the type of real estate that is right for you and that takes full advantage of your particular talents.

Look back at Chapter 2, which described a number of ways to make money in real estate. Check off the ones that appeal to you the most. Usually one or two will jump out at you as the most interesting, and those will certainly be the place to start your investigation. Don't worry about closing off options prematurely. You can always circle back to some other aspect of real estate. In fact, over the years, you most likely will find that what you like to do best changes, either because you get bored with the status quo or because new opportunities present themselves to you. In many cases, these opportunities will come to you from within your own master mind network.

It's all about *finding* that niche and *exploiting* it. In several towns in Florida, a company puts the following message in huge black letters on bright yellow billboards: "WE BUY UGLY HOUSES," followed by a phone number. Yes, we got a good laugh when we first saw those distinctive signs. Then we got intrigued. The pitch was certainly memorable, but did it work? We looked into it, and it turns out that it *does* work. The company gets a steady stream of calls from people trying to unload "ugly houses." One interesting aspect is that the person reading the billboard gets to define the word *ugly*. Sometimes the calls came from people with really unattractive houses. Other times, it was the circumstances of ownership that were ugly, like a bitter divorce, and the owners just wanted to get out of their house. In all cases, the big yellow sign with the offbeat message seemed like a real answer to the problem at hand.

"We buy ugly houses" is a marketing campaign that perfectly illustrates our strategy of finding a niche and exploiting it. When you see the sign, there is *no question* in your mind what these investors' niche is. They buy houses that other investors might turn up their noses at. They probably do a higher-volume, lower-margin business. They probably don't ask a lot of questions or put much of a burden on the seller. Somehow, those four words on the billboards convey lots of information and generate tons of leads.

Clearly, this is a creative concept. Unfortunately, we can't just tell you to get a similarly clever idea and let it go at that. Not all of us can come up with a four-word phrase that makes the phones ring off the hook. (We certainly have never done that in our own businesses.) The good news, though, is that you don't *have* to be that clever. You just have to be sensible, focused, and *diligent*. You have to find out what type of real estate you want to become an expert in, get that process going, and then, once you have set the business up successfully, repeat the process.

Building Your Master Mind Network

Once you have determined your niche, you want to begin to build your real estate network. Your network will consist of people who can make referrals to you for the kind of real estate you are looking for.

Why would they do *that*, you ask?

Easy: because they hope to get something in return. Not everyone will get something in return, of course (it doesn't always work out that neatly), but things do tend to even out over the long run. I scratch your back; you scratch mine. As Zig Ziglar, the master motivator and sales trainer, always says, "If you want to become successful, all you have to do is help a lot of other people become successful."

This will be true of your master mind network. You should approach it with the explicit goal of creating a group that works for all its members, not just you. If people see that the group works for them, they will become more involved with the process, and the resulting success will reward everyone.

Make a list of people you know who are very active in real estate but who don't do exactly what you do. Here are some people you will probably have on your list:

Real estate attorneys
Real estate brokers
Builders
Accountants
Real estate investors in a niche different from yours

Mortgage brokers

Bankers

Insurance agents

Real estate investor group leaders

Repair people

Just scanning this list, you can see that some of the people on it have a direct interest in real estate, and others do not. The key to your group's success is not so much *what* its members know (although you will need some experts), but *who* they know. So contacts are key. Equally important is personal attitude and drive. You want to find people who are motivated and who want to get business themselves. Master mind and referral groups work best when all the people in them work together to create business for everyone.

Once you have started developing your list of the types of people you want in your group, start filling in real names for your contacts. For instance, let's say you start with an attorney. Most likely, you'll decide that you want a lawyer who specializes in real estate transactions. But if your niche turns out to be buying homes in probate, then you'll probably want to find the probate attorney who has the biggest practice in the area.

Once you have a person penciled in on your list, you should make an appointment with him to talk about your real estate investments (or dreams). The first thing you're likely to find is that some of the people (probably starting with the attorney) will want to charge you for their time. Don't let this discourage you, even though it's obviously not where you want the relationship to wind up. Consider it a business expense. Say, "Fine, I'll take an hour."

During that hour, of course, you are going to pick the person's brain for every relevant piece of information he can provide.

Meanwhile, you are going to convince him that he wants to help you get the kind of business you are looking for, because you are going to send him business yourself. That one hour of legal time will more than pay for itself with the first referral that comes your way from that attorney. True, some of your contacts won't materialize into referrals for a while, and others will *never* pan out. That's OK. You have to work at it. People who don't add to the success of the group will be dropped from your referral network, and a new person in that category of referrals will go in their place.

As you can see, a referral group is only as good as its members. It's powerful only if the members of the group are willing to make referrals and otherwise help one another. Sometimes this has to be made very explicit. Some referral groups, for example, meet on a monthly basis, with each person in the room standing up and giving a brief talk (no more than five minutes!) about what type of referrals he or she is looking for from the group. By so doing, you remind one another of your respective specialties—and of your commitment to helping one another out.

Finding Your Group Members

The best way to find members of your referral group is through a referral from someone else—in other words, using the network to build the network.

Another smart place to look is among people whose actions have already signaled that they are happy to join groups of people for a common business cause. A real estate investors' group is a good place to start. You can find out when and where such a group is meeting near you by doing a Google search for "real estate investors' group" for your city, or by looking in your local newspapers under "group meeting announcements."

We've already mentioned these investors' groups. They are a great place to go to learn about the industry and to meet like-minded people. And while you're on the lookout for people to add to your personal group, you may well come across people who have property to sell that you might be interested in, or who might want to go in with you on a particular property.

Another good place to build your master mind group is your local chamber of commerce meeting. This group represents a mix of all types of businesses, all of which are dedicated to growing. Consider becoming actively involved in this group—for example, by joining the new members subcommittee, where you will meet representatives of companies that are new to the area and may either need properties or have real estate to sell. Growing companies mean change, and change is often an opportunity to make a sale.

Sponsoring charity events in your area is a great way to make contacts and help a good cause. As lead sponsor, you have the opportunity to come in contact with leaders in your community who can help refer business to you. Many charitable groups make a point of getting behind their sponsors' businesses, because they know that if they do, it will be far easier to persuade the same people to sponsor the event again the following year. If they understand that you're always on the lookout for referrals, they'll do their best for you.

Getting Started Strategy No. 10: Use the Tools of the Trade to Build Your Master Mind Group— and Your Business

We told you about the very successful Florida-based real estate buyers who trade in "ugly houses," and how they use billboards as their method of reaching new clients. But not everybody has such a clear and powerful concept, and not everybody can afford that type of highly visible marketing campaign. Nevertheless, there *are* marketing tools that you can use to grow your real estate business. For example:

1. *Use investor business cards.* You should prepare investor business cards that state your niche or specialty. They don't have to be expensive, but they should *look* professional. Your local copy shop or office-supply store should be able to do an adequate job. (Ask for samples of its best work.) Consider putting your picture on the card. People like to do business with people they identify with, and there is no better way to achieve that relationship than to put your picture on the card. Some people will remember your face better than your name.

2. *Develop your 30-second "elevator speech."* An elevator speech is simply the briefest possible accurate statement about what you do for a living. Imagine that you have someone's ear only for the (short) duration of an elevator ride. What message do you want that person to walk out of that elevator with? Ideally, the message will be both informative and provocative. You want to get the main idea across and to imply that there's a lot more that your listener needs to know about you. What will get people *interested* in you? Sparking interest is the first step in bringing someone into your referral network—or, at the very least, creating a new business opportunity.

3. *Create an investor Web site.* Building your own investor Web site is another step that might help your investment business. There are two possibilities, which you can pursue simultaneously if you have the time and the money.

One is an "internal" Web site specifically for use by your referral network, allowing each member of the network to post referrals for one another and providing a quick method of communication. The other is external, aimed at promoting your investments business itself. If you have a specialty in small motels, for example, you could create a site that tells what you do and the advantages you offer. The challenge is to get people to *visit* that site. One good way to do so is to send an e-mail to a selected list of motel owners (which you can purchase from a marketing database vendor) that includes a link to your site. A surprising number of people click on these "embedded links" and wind up at the sponsoring sites.

Make sure that when people wind up at your site, there's information there that's useful to *them*, not just to you. Make it worth their while to come back to your site—and to tell other people about it. At the same time, don't get paralyzed by complexity. The cost of tinkering with Web sites has dropped in price, and there is nothing wrong with starting out with a template site that has just basic information and adding more material later. The key is to *get started*, and not wait till you have the money to add all the latest bells and whistles to your Web site.

Getting Started Strategy No. 11: Master the Seven Principles of Building a Successful Master Mind Group

There are no hard-and-fast rules for building a successful master mind group, but the following seven principles should get you off to a quick start:

1. *Always refer outsiders to members of your group*, and then tell the member in question that you gave the referral so that she can follow up. Telling the member is an important point. That tells the member you are working for

her—a fact that might not come up in a conversation with the person you referred. It also lets the member contact the source directly, without the lead falling through the cracks as so many leads do. Remember, giving referrals yourself is the best reinforcement of the behaviors that you want everyone else in the group to adopt. The more you give, the more you get, because the other members will start to view you as someone who puts money in their pockets. Once you get to that position, you can bet that they will always be happy to take your call.

2. *Always act on the referrals you get.* Be known as someone who follows up quickly and does a great job. Even if you don't generate any business this time, if you help the referred person, that person will reciprocate someday, in some way. We all love to talk about the great service we get—so make sure that you are the one they are talking about!

3. *Communicate the outcome to the person who gave you the referral.* Most people don't do this, and yet we all want to know what happened to our referral. It's simply human nature. Going back to the person who gave you the referral gives you another opportunity to speak with that person and lets him know that you are a professional that he should always deal with. The use of e-mail has made this quick and easy, but don't forget that personal conversations often create better opportunities. Many times, it is in the casual part of a conversation that someone says something offhand—something that the person might not think or choose to bring up in an e-mail—that can be most helpful to you. Take the time to make a call or visit sometimes. Lunch is always a good idea.

4. *Write those thank-you notes.* Your mother always told you to write thank-you notes, and now you're learning why. They are considerate, and they keep you in touch. As you build up income from your business, you can also include a little gift—or, better yet, a referral for that person.

5. *Share your success stories with your other network members.* Your master mind group members have your best interests at heart, or they shouldn't be in your master mind group. Tell them when someone has sent you a referral and it worked out well. Without exaggerating, heap praise on the other person, and make it clear how much you appreciate that person and what she did for you. The other members will get the idea, and will want to be part of the story.

6. *Network with networkers.* This may sound like simple common sense. But the truth is, some people are far better at networking than others, and those are the people you want in your group. Look for people who are self-starters and who come across as successful, outgoing people. These will be your biggest source of business.

7. *Constantly upgrade your network.* No matter how hard you try, things won't always work out. If someone isn't helping you, start looking for a replacement. There are lots of people out there who would love to help you, if you ask, and those are the people you need to look for in building your investment business. Keep upgrading your group until you have built a finely tuned master mind referral machine.

THE MASTER MIND GROUP CHECKLIST

☑ **FIND YOUR NICHE AND LEARN HOW TO EXPLOIT IT.**
You will build your master mind group around your
own specialization, seeking out and adding the kinds
of individuals who can complement your own interests and skills. So concentrate first on figuring out
where you fit into the bigger picture. Which corner of
the industry will you specialize in? How will you
acquire the necessary skills? Who can help you apply
those skills once you've acquired them?

☑ **USE THE TOOLS OF THE TRADE TO BUILD YOUR
MASTER MIND GROUP—AND YOUR BUSINESS.** One of
the most important aspects of building a powerful
master mind group is being able to express clearly (1)
what you do and (2) how that's different from what
your competitors do. Develop your "elevator speech"
(even though you'll probably never deliver it in an
elevator). Make it memorable. Make your investor
business card memorable, too. Use Web sites to (1)
reinforce the power of your master mind group and
(2) get your name known out there in the world. In
both your internal and external Web sites, be sure to
include things that are *useful* to the visitor. Above all,
get going. Once you have a path charted, stop making
excuses and go for it.

☑ **MASTER THE SEVEN PRINCIPLES OF BUILDING A
SUCCESSFUL MASTER MIND GROUP.** Referrals are
gold. Treat them as such. Refer as much business as

possible to other members of your master mind group, and tell them you've done so. When they refer business to you, *follow up* on those leads, and let the referrer know the outcome. Write thank-you notes, and—in the context of the master mind group—publicly recount and celebrate the referral story. Finally, keep a constant eye on the quality of your group. It takes a networker to network, so surround yourself with people like that. Keep looking for opportunities to upgrade the group by replacing nonproducers with producers. It will pay off for everybody!

PART 2

Mastering the Real Estate Investment Process

CHAPTER 5

Making Your First
Real Estate Investment

Your first real estate investment should be your home, if you don't already have one.

Now let's complicate things. If you already have a home and have built up equity in it, consider moving to a bigger home and converting your existing home to a rental. By making this move, you will be improving your portfolio position by upgrading to a higher-value home. Your existing home will probably be a good rental, unless it is very expensive. If you don't want to convert your existing home to a rental, consider either selling your home or refinancing it and using part of the money you generate to fund your real estate investing business. If you decide to sell, use a small portion of your proceeds on the sale as a down payment on another home that you can live in, so that you can benefit from the appreciation.

Maybe the scenario we just described struck you as unsettling, because it involves change. Yet change is exactly what you need to embrace right now in order to reach your goals. And although you may not have thought of it in just these terms, change is the main reason why you bought this book. So get ready to embrace it!

The reason you start your investment program with a home is that there are many advantages to home purchases that you won't have with other properties. For example:

1. *Your down payment will be lower.* In the current lending environment, you can structure no-down-payment—or at least *low*-down-payment (10 percent or less)— options on your home. Quite a few lenders are offering 80/10/10 plans. This means that they loan 80 percent of the purchase price with a first mortgage, provide a 10 percent equity line of credit, and require a 10 percent down payment. (In future chapters, we'll show you how to get that last 10 percent for a down payment, if you don't have it.)

2. *The interest rate you pay on your home is always lower than what you'd pay on an investment property, so this keeps your monthly payment lower.* Lock in the best 30-year, fixed-rate mortgage you can. If you later decide to convert the house to a rental, you will have a greater chance of generating a positive cash flow right from the beginning with your longer-term mortgage at the lower interest rate.

3. *More financing is available for owner-occupied housing than for any other category of real estate.* This means that there is more competition for your business. It also makes financing much easier to qualify for. In later chapters, we will show you ways to increase your borrowing ability, but buying a home will be your best opportunity.

4. *The resale market is typically strongest for residential properties.* There are always more people looking for homes than

for any other type of real estate, so your chances of unloading the property when the time comes are relatively good.

5. *There are tax advantages to selling your home without paying capital gains tax.* This gives you more profit to reinvest in your real estate business. (See Chapter 15 for specifics.)

For all of these reasons and more, your home should serve as the foundation of your real estate plan. As you will see, this will probably mean more moves for your family than either you or your spouse would like, because, if you follow our advice, you will continue to move into better and better homes over the years. Maybe this is the first time someone has suggested to you that you can make more by spending more. It may sound strange, but it's true. Yes, you do have to keep the payments in line with what you can afford, but the more you build up in equity, the more you can afford the next time you buy. Meanwhile, of course, you'll be living in style and enjoying your lives more.

Why Buy Today?

If you have never owned a home, consider making the move *now*. Given the favorable interest-rate environment, your opportunity is the best it has been in years, and the best it is likely to be until the next economic cycle. This could be a long time, since the last time we had rates in the 6 percent range was about 30 years ago.

In many major markets across the country, double-digit appreciation has made home buying a very smart move indeed. Even in the vast majority of "softer markets," home appreciation still beats inflation by several percentage points. Appreciation, combined with low down payments, means positive leverage that works in the homeowner's favor.

Mastering Real Estate Investment Strategy No. 1: Use Positive Leverage to Maximize Your Return

The great secret of real estate—the secret that will make you rich—is positive leverage. We've already introduced this principle, but let's look at it a little more closely. The median price of an existing home in 2005 was approximately $219,000 (see www.Realtors.com). A 10 percent down payment on that property would be $21,900. Now let's assume that the property appreciates by 14.7 percent—the same rate at which property values nationwide grew between 2004 and 2005.

Here's the key point to remember: that appreciation applies to the *total value of the home.* In our example, the annual appreciation for one year would be $32,193. Compare that return to your cash investment of $21,900 (the down payment) rather than to the total value of the home, and you have an annual rate of return of 147 percent on your invested down payment. Obviously, very few investments yield that large a return. While your appreciation isn't likely to continue at that rate year after year, even half of that 147 percent rate would yield you a 70 percent return on your invested dollar.

Of course, this simple illustration doesn't take into account your monthly payments, taxes, and insurance, but these costs are somewhat offset by the fact that you aren't paying rent somewhere else. In addition to the high rate of return, you also get to deduct the interest you pay from your federal taxable income, and when the time comes to cash out of your real estate holdings, you will pay no tax on your first $500,000 of capital gain. And then, of course, there are the intangibles. You and your family have a home of your own—the American dream. You have a safe base of operation for all of you.

In addition to all of these advantages, common sense tells you that you have to live *somewhere.* If you rent, you will pay and pay, and wind up with nothing. If you buy, you will ultimately have a nest egg of your own, free and clear after you've paid off your mortgage. For that reason alone, you should take the plunge and buy a home as *soon as you can.*

Some home-buying processes change over the years, but most do not. In this chapter, we share home-buying strategies that have stood the test of time and can be adapted to a great variety of situations.

Mastering Real Estate Investment Strategy No. 2: Remember That Location Is Paramount

There is an old axiom in the real estate business that the three most important considerations are *location, location,* and *location.* It's true. Always buy in the best neighborhood you can afford.

Your first step in the buying process is to establish how much home you can afford to carry, in terms of monthly payments. Obviously, this is a combination of price, mortgage rate, and the size of your down payment. Once you have established that number, you are far better off buying the smallest house in an expensive neighborhood than buying the biggest house in a lower-priced neighborhood.

The logic behind this is that the higher prices in the expensive neighborhood will tend to pull the price of your home up as they appreciate. If homes in the lower-priced neighborhood lose value, by contrast, the value of your home will drop along with them, even if it remains the best in the area. In a poor neighborhood, at some point, your home may become difficult to sell because of the decline in values. We have heard some real estate horror stories over the years, and plummeting prices were almost always the result of a particular neighborhood's declining in value. This is why location is most important.

Mastering Real Estate Investment Strategy No. 3: Buy the Least Expensive House on the Street

Another great home-buying strategy is to buy the least expensive house on the street. As a rule, this allows you to realize more gain from any home improvement or remodeling, since you will be less likely to overbuild for your neighborhood.

Neighborhood amenities are another important considera-tion. One of the most important is the reputation of the school district. Avoid buying into a neighborhood in a weak school dis-trict, if you can. While you cannot do anything if the quality of the schools in your neighborhood slips over time, knowingly buying into a neighborhood with weak schools is a mistake.

Mastering Real Estate Investment Strategy No. 4: Confirm Your Neighborhood School with the Central Administration

As a result of overcrowding and other considerations (including, for example, racial balance), school systems are sometimes com-pelled to redistrict. When you're buying a home, therefore, don't assume that the school right down the street is the one that your child will attend. Call the school system's central office, give it the address of the property you propose to buy, and find out which school district that house is in. Access to specific schools can be very important to future buyers, so being in the right district can dramatically affect your future resale value.

Everyone has his or her own tastes and preferences when it comes to homes, so we won't presume to tell you what sort of house to buy. But to maximize the return on your investment, here are some guidelines to consider.

Mastering Real Estate Investment Strategy No. 5: Consider Resale Value When You Buy

It is important that you buy the kind of home that will appeal to the largest number of buyers. An unusual home with a unique design may look good to *you*, but, when it comes time to sell, that offbeat look may turn off potential buyers. Selling a home invokes the law of averages. So keep in mind when you buy that unusual designs will limit your market and potentially hurt the resale value of your home.

You should also consider other factors that affect potential resale value. For example, there is a bigger market for four-bedroom homes than for three-bedroom, and a bigger market for three-bedroom homes than for two-bedroom. Also, the greater the number of bathrooms, the better the resale value. Having two bathrooms is now considered almost a necessity, and an extra half bath (a powder room) helps both while you live in the house and upon resale.

Mastering Real Estate Investment Strategy No. 6: Hire a Property Inspector

Before you close on any home, be sure to have it inspected by a professional. Yes, home inspection is another cost, but having an expert evaluate the home you are buying for structural and other problems is a cheap form of insurance. Even if you are qualified in this area yourself, it is best to bring in an outside expert. We all get caught up in the excitement of buying a new home, and that excitement can cause us to overlook things that might normally be glaringly obvious.

The problem is that mistakes when buying property can add up quickly, and they can get *very expensive.* So let someone who is unbiased represent your interests in this part of the process. If that person finds problems, insist in the contract that the seller pay for the cost of the repair.

Consider buying a home warranty. Remember, once the deal closes, it's hard to get any money back, so a home warranty will at least cover you for the unexpected. If you are using a Realtor, ask her to suggest a reputable home inspection company and a home warranty company. If you are buying on your own, check in the Yellow Pages for national companies that have a local presence in your area. Remember, a warranty is only as good as the reputation and stability of the company you are buying it from.

Mastering Real Estate Investment Strategy No. 7: Have a Buyer's Broker Represent You

Buyer's brokers are a relatively new way to buy real estate. Historically, the vast majority of real estate brokers have worked for the *seller.* This has created hard feelings and some unhappy results. Today, many brokers are happy to take on buyers as clients and represent them. If you're buying, our recommendation is that you work with a buyer's broker, who will be looking out for your best interests.

As a rule, we suggest that you find the most experienced real estate professional available to represent you. Because brokerage fees are generally the same throughout the industry (that is, they're generally not based on the broker's level of expertise), it doesn't cost you any more to work with the best.

An experienced and successful broker will know a great deal about the market and how much you should pay for a home. He can help you negotiate to get the best price. The broker will also have contacts with experienced lenders, title companies, insurance companies, and real estate lawyers. Using proven professionals will make your buying experience smoother and more successful.

Where do you find the best brokers? Start with the local Board of Realtors. When you are buying, ask for a list of brokers in the area who have an Accredited Buyer Representative (ABR) designation. This designation is sponsored by the National Association of Realtors and can be used only by agents who have received special training and been certified in buyer representation. Then ask for the names of the top five buyer's brokers on that list, based on sales volume. Interview each of them, and pick the one with whom you are most comfortable. Yes, this takes some time, but it will definitely pay you back.

When you are selling, use the same type of process to find the most successful brokers. Frequently, this is determined by sales volume in the area. If the person has a professional designation like GRI (Graduate of the Realtors Institute), so much the better.

Shopping for a Mortgage

Why is it that people who will drive across town to save money on a toothbrush won't shop for financing on a $100,000 home? It doesn't make sense. Given the wide disparity in mortgage costs today, you simply cannot afford *not* to shop for the best deal. By doing so, you will save yourself many thousands of dollars over the life of your mortgage.

Mastering Real Estate Investment Strategy No. 8: Use the Four Best Ways to Shop for a Mortgage

There are several ways to shop for your financing, and we recommend that you use a combination of all of them. Start by looking in the local newspaper. Most papers print a weekly summary of mortgage rates in your area, and this summary includes most of the information you'll need in order to start comparison shopping.

Then start calling national banks that have a presence in your market. Simply pull out the Yellow Pages and start shopping. Tell each bank the approximate size of the mortgage you are looking for, and it will tell you about some of the basic financing plans it has available. Even if you don't ultimately do business with a particular bank, this will give you a window into the competitive rates and terms.

The third strategy is to shop online. There are now some excellent sources for mortgage shopping, and the offers we have seen have been good. Two sources to start with are www.lendingtree.com or ELoan.com. Online companies like these will ask you to complete an extensive credit application, which they send out electronically to the lenders they work with. Based on the application and your credit report (which they will obtain), you will get specific offers from those lenders that qualify you for the loan.

The fourth shopping method is to use a mortgage broker to represent you. Make sure you are working with a broker who represents multiple financing sources, rather than one who's simply a captive broker for a single lender. You want the broker to use her expertise and to shop for your loan by submitting it to several lenders.

Understand that using a mortgage broker costs you money. That is the way mortgage brokers make their money, and there is nothing wrong with that. On the other hand, the fee you pay is likely to come in the form of higher interest, and, depending on how long you keep the property, that cost could add up to a lot. Compare the interest rates quoted to you before you make a final decision. Ask each of your lenders or brokers to specifically quote you the annual percentage rate (APR) on the loan. The APR is a special qualification that adds all of the fees you pay on the loan to the interest to give you an interest rate that can be compared on an apples-to-apples basis. Remember that even a quarter of a point over the life of a 30-year loan can amount to a lot of money, so *bargain down those rates.*

If you find that you are having trouble getting a loan, it may be because of something in your credit report. If you are turned down for a loan, you can get a free copy of the credit report that the lender used to make its determination. Make sure you order the report to see if there is a problem, and also to determine if the report is even accurate. In Chapter 10 we discuss your credit rating, and how to build the highest possible one for yourself. It takes some work to improve your credit score, but it is worth it.

Mastering Real Estate Investment Strategy No. 9: Explore the Fixed-Rate Mortgage

While shopping for a mortgage, you will learn about fixed-rate and adjustable-rate mortgages with a variety of time spans attached to them. Simply stated, the interest on a fixed-rate loan stays the same over the life of the loan, while that on an adjustable-rate loan changes at different stated intervals of time. As a rule, we favor the typical 30-year fixed-rate mortgage in low-interest-rate environments. But there are plenty of other factors to consider, including your anticipated length of residence in the property.

Consider this scenario: When you are buying a home in a low-interest-rate environment and rates are rising, get a fixed-rate mortgage, or at least one that gives you the option of fixing the rate at a later date. For example, as of mid-2005, it is possible to get a 30-year fixed-rate mortgage at around 6 percent. With a five-year adjustable-rate mortgage, however, you may be able to snag the loan for just over 4 percent. If you are *sure* that you will keep the property for no more than five years, then the adjustable-rate loan may be the way to go. If you are not sure, it's probably better to get a fixed-rate loan and eliminate your exposure to future interest-rate hikes.

If you get a fixed-rate loan and rates go down, you can always refinance at a later time. If you get an adjustable-rate mortgage and rates rise, not only will your monthly payments increase, but there is a chance that if rates rise substantially, you might not qualify for new fixed-rate financing, and you would be stuck in a mortgage with rates going up every year. That can be a painful situation, and it's one that you should go to great lengths to avoid.

Over the years, there have been many games played with adjustable-rate mortgages, including "teaser rates" (extremely low rates tied to an index that increases your interest rate in a year) and "balloons" (mortgages that simply end after a short period of time, requiring you to pay them off and get new financing). Be very careful about taking on one of these loans, particularly if you think you may live in the home for more than a few years.

Why? Because balloons have a way of coming due at the most inopportune times. If you can't pay off the balloon or refinance, you may lose your property.

Mastering Real Estate Investment Strategy No. 10: Save with a 15-Year Mortgage

If you can afford the higher monthly payments (about 25 to 30 percent higher), consider a 15-year mortgage instead of a 30-year mortgage. For the relatively small increase in payments, you will pay off your loan in *half the time*, and therefore pay *half the interest*. This can add up to an amazing sum over the life of the loan.

If you are unsure about being able to make the higher payments consistently, get a 30-year mortgage that allows you to make additional payments to reduce the principal. Make sure that all prepayments are applied to reduce your principal—in other words, that extra payments don't just count as an interest payment or a regular payment. With this type of loan, you make an extra "principal only" payment whenever you can, without the pressure you might feel from a 15-year mortgage—and you'll still be able to knock months or years off the mortgage, depending upon how much you are able to contribute each month.

If making extra payments on a 30-year fixed mortgage becomes a problem, you can simply skip the extra payments. One caution, though: people who begin to skip the extra payments often find it difficult to get back into that good habit. That's just human nature. So we recommend that if you go this route, you make those extra payments as consistently as possible.

Another idea is to pocket the payment difference between the 15-year and the 30-year mortgage. In other words, go ahead and get the 30-year mortgage, but take the additional payments that you would have made on the 15-year mortgage and use that amount to fund an investment program. By so doing, you gain diversification, and you don't have everything tied up in real estate. Put the investment payment on an "automatic draft," which simply means working with your brokerage firm or bank to have a certain amount of money taken out of your checking account each month and used to purchase shares in a mutual fund or other investment vehicle.

Which of these three options is best? That depends on your personal circumstances and your level of self-discipline. The main point, though, is that you *do* have options.

Mastering Real Estate Investment Strategy No. 11: Concentrate on Resale Potential Rather Than Age of a Property

The debate will never end about which type of home is better: new construction or an existing residence. The truth is, there is no definitive answer. It is likely that on a square-foot basis, a new home will cost you more, because building costs have gone up in recent years. On the other hand, modern amenities found in new homes, such as larger interior spaces and upgraded kitchens and bathrooms, are appealing and will also work to your advantage when it comes time for you to sell the property.

Our suggestion is that you look at both older and new homes. You'll have an up-close look at the advantages and disadvantages of each, and you'll quickly develop your own preferences. There is no one right answer for everyone, so take the time to look at a good number of homes and pick what *you* like best.

We've already mentioned the pros and cons of "sweat equity." If you're handy, this is an excellent way to build value, and it's the equivalent of having a second job or starting a small business. This argues for buying an existing home with cosmetic (not structural!) flaws. But if you can't imagine anything worse than spending your evenings and weekends working on a fixer-upper, a new home is probably the best choice for you.

Mastering Real Estate Investment Strategy No. 12: Never Fall in Love with a Property

Almost without exception, it's a bad day when you fall in love with a property and decide that you simply *have to* have it. (It's an even worse day when your spouse does so.) When situations like this develop, try to keep your emotions under control. Step back and look at the deal from a distance. Emotional attachment to a property is likely to *cost you money.* You'll pay too much or you'll overlook expensive problems, or both.

Mastering Real Estate Investment Strategy No. 13: Get a Second Opinion on Price

Another strategy to counter the effects of the "buying bug" is to make your contract contingent on your getting an appraisal for at least the amount of the purchase price. By getting your own appraisal, you are bringing in a third-party expert who will tell you if you are over-paying. You may still want to go ahead with the deal, but taking this important step can keep you from making a big mistake.

You have two choices when it comes to appraisals. You can hire a designated expert appraiser, or, if you are working with a Realtor, you can have that Realtor run comparables on other properties in the area and see what they sold for. For a typical residential property, your Realtor can do a perfectly adequate job. The more unusual or expensive the property is, though, the more you may want to spend extra money to get another opinion. The appraisal clause gives you the opportunity to get the opinion of someone else whom you feel comfortable with before you are fully bound by contract, and before you put your deposit at risk.

Mastering Real Estate Investment Strategy No. 14: Use a Lease Option

If you can't come up with the down payment for a home or you can't qualify for a mortgage, try to get an "option to buy" on a home that you can rent. Negotiate with the owner. Try to convince her to let some of the rent you pay be credited toward a future down payment if you decide to purchase the property.

Options to buy are a lot more common than you might think, and they can be a good way to build future value, even if you are still forced to rent for the time being. (See Chapter 16 for a full discussion of options.) Once the credited portion of your rent equals the down payment required to qualify for a loan, you can (but don't have to) exercise your option to buy the property. Lenders look more favorably at buyers who have a solid record of paying the rent on time and who are trying to buy the home that they have been living in for a year or more.

Mastering Real Estate Investment Strategy No. 15: Be Cautious When Buying a New Home from a Builder

We hate to dampen anyone's enthusiasm for buying a new home. At the same time, we have to warn you to keep your eyes open.

Brand-new homes come with particular reasons for caution. For example, when you are looking at a builder's model home, you need to keep in mind that what you see there is the *best possible version* of what you'll get. The reality is likely to be something less than this vision of perfection.

Let's face it: there are all kinds of builders out there. There are honest developers who will go overboard to make sure you get everything you want. And there are crooks out there, too. And there's a third group that you also have to watch out for: builders who are stretched too thin financially and can't finish what they've started. To guard against this possibility, cover yourself with a good contract that spells out in detail exactly what you are going to get when everything is built, and don't forget to include deadlines for completion of various aspects of the home. When you start building a house, it is worth your time and money to hire a real estate attorney to review all of the builders' documents. Make sure you use an attorney that specializes in real estate, to ensure that he is familiar with the process and contracts involved.

We have known far too many people who have been stuck when builders overcommitted and could not meet their delivery dates. These buyers had to live with parents and friends while they waited for their homes to be finished. Consider putting a performance penalty into your builder's contract. After a reasonable grace period, the builder starts *paying you* for every day she delivers the home late. This is another good reason to involve your attorney. He can serve as your "tough guy" in the negotiation, so that you can maintain a positive relationship with your builder.

New homes in larger developments can have special problems. If you are buying in the early stages of a development project, *do everything you can* to check out the developer and her track record. If the developer runs into financial problems, you and your neighbors could end up with unfinished streets, pools, golf courses, or clubhouses.

To check out builders and developers, go to the local home-builders' association in your area. Additionally, you can check for complaints with the local Better Business Bureau and do an online search for articles on the builder or developer.

Mastering Real Estate Investment Strategy No. 16: Read the Survey Carefully

When you get your financing, your lender will almost certainly require a survey of the property you are buying. If you are using seller financing, the seller won't order the survey, but make sure you order one for yourself. In either case, *review the survey*. The survey basically tells you who owns what, so it's not something you can afford to make a mistake on.

Don't count on the lender to do the review. We have seen lender-accepted surveys with numerous encroachment problems that no one discovered until years later. While the lender should also be concerned with the survey, in most cases it is just building a paper file. If a problem develops, you will have to solve it, so spend the time now to read the survey and make sure.

Most people never even meet their surveyor, and that's not smart. You paid good money for this expert (yes, the bank makes you pay for it), so make a point of talking to him one-on-one. Don't be afraid to ask the surveyor if he sees any potential problems with the property.

Make sure you understand your survey so that you can head off any problems after you have purchased the property. We once bought a piece of property that had a driveway extending onto the neighbor's property. That little item never came up in the first survey. Fortunately, we had great neighbors, and there was no problem—but there *could* have been.

Mastering Real Estate Investment Strategy No. 17: Have Your Title Company Delete Exceptions in Its Title Commitment

Your *title* is the evidence of your legal right to your property. You can buy something called *title insurance* that supposedly limits your exposure to a "clouded" (i.e., disputed) title.

Unfortunately, title insurance isn't what most people think it is. In fact, it *doesn't* insure your ownership against all title problems. It insures your ownership only against title problems for which the title company has not listed an exception. And guess what? The title company will list every exception it can possibly think of. If you accept a policy with all of the exceptions in place, it will be *your* problem if one of them arises.

Make the title company delete any exceptions you don't like. If it won't do that, shop for another title company. By the way, while you are shopping, make sure you are dealing with a large, reputable company, not just anyone who will write a policy. Title insurance won't do you any good if the company has gone out of business when you need to make a claim.

Title exceptions are becoming a common part of the buying process. Do not rely on your real estate agent to help you in this area, since it is very rare for real estate agents to read the policies. The reason? They are not trained to do so, and in most states, the buyer will need a lawyer to render an opinion on such a policy. Please read your policy carefully, and make sure you understand what the policy covers. If you don't, ask your lawyer for help.

Mastering Real Estate Investment Strategy No. 18: Ensure a Profit on Your Property When You Buy It

At the beginning of this chapter, we cited the age-old tenet about the importance of location. We'll end the chapter with another long-standing real estate maxim.

You make your biggest profit on a property when *you* buy it. In other words, if you structure a good deal at the front end, you are likely to sell at a good profit. This means that the *price* you pay for any property, and the terms on which you buy that property, will probably determine how successful you are in selling the home for a profit down the line.

Of course, you may get lucky. You may enjoy added appreciation for other reasons, but you should consider that just icing on the cake. Focus on structuring a good deal from the beginning, and chances are that you will be the richer for it later. If you don't feel comfortable with the price going in, *don't buy the property*. Go find a deal that you *are* comfortable with.

THE HOME BUYER'S CHECKLIST

☑ **BUY, DON'T RENT.** Use the power of positive leverage to start building your real estate nest egg. Stop paying rent (which makes someone else rich) and start deriving the benefits of home ownership today.

☑ **BUY TODAY.** Interest rates are as low as they've been in 30 years—and as low as they're likely to be for another 30 years. Buy now, and get into the game.

☑ **BUY SMART.** Buy the best location and the least expensive house on the street. Make sure you know which school district the property is in, and whether that's considered a good district. Don't fall in love with any property—especially quirky properties that may have limited resale potential. Use experts (buyer's brokers, inspectors, surveyors, etc.) to increase your margin of safety. Be wary of hidden defects in older homes, but be equally wary of the dangers that dishonest or undercapitalized developers can pose.

☑ **USE SMART MONEY.** Comparison-shop for your mortgage, just as you would for a car or any other major purchase. Know when to go with a fixed-rate mortgage, and when to go variable. Consider a 15-year mortgage or other sort of "forced savings" plan.

CHAPTER 6

How to Determine a Good Deal

One of the hardest things to learn in the investing process is how to figure out what constitutes a "good deal."

This is true whether you are the buyer or the seller. Often, this issue manifests itself (painfully) when the parties start second-guessing themselves and stop being able to make a decision. The result? They get very frustrated with the investment process and start missing opportunities. Or maybe they overreact and rush into a deal that they should have moved more slowly on.

Or, perhaps most frustrating, they keep reexamining their past actions. Did they pay too much? Did they sell too soon? Did they forgo a golden opportunity by failing to pull the trigger? When this happens, they fall further down the well of indecision and frustration.

How do we know this? Because we've been there. Unfortunately, it's just part of the learning process. If you remain an investor, it will be because you ultimately learn (as we have) that *investing is a type of game.* Sometimes you win; sometimes you lose. Most of the time, though, you're happy to *be in the game,* giving your skill and your luck a chance to prove themselves. Most people, sad to say, never give themselves that chance.

One key point to remember is that a "good deal" is very often in the eye of the beholder. As a result, both parties can walk away from a successfully completed deal thinking that they got a good deal—and they can both be right! Why? Because a good deal is not necessarily a "win/lose" situation, in which one party's loss is the other party's gain. In many cases, either the two parties have different goals and objectives or their timing is different, and so everyone's most important needs can be met. And having been there, too, we can honestly say that few things feel better, in a business situation.

About a year and a half ago, we saw a 26-acre property for sale. It had two older homes on it and about 800 feet of frontage on a nice little lake. This pretty little tract of land sat across from two of the most exclusive developments in the county, and it was listed for $2,000,000. We noticed the property because we drove along the road every day. The more we saw it, the more we liked it, but it felt a little too big for our personal use. In addition, we were heavily involved in building a new financial software package at the time, and we were not interesting in jumping into a new real estate project until the software was completed and on track. So, because the timing wasn't right and our attention was focused elsewhere, we didn't do anything about the property. We just kept driving by it.

Now, when you love buying real estate and you drive by a property that you really like every day, it can really begin to *get* to you. And this piece of real estate was getting to us, particularly because it had two features that are absolute gold in real estate: a great location and waterfront. Finally, we couldn't take it any more. We called the Realtor and told him that we were interested and wanted to make an offer. But the Realtor advised us that the owner had just started the process of rezoning the property into six lakefront lots that she planned to offer for a total of $4 million, when completed.

We were crushed. As we saw it, we had just lost $2 million of profit that we could have realized if we had just followed our instincts. Well, losing $2 million (even when it never really was your money to begin with) really hurts. It hurt so bad, in fact, that we did a very foolish thing: we bought the property for the full price without the lots even being finished. The seller thought we were nuts. The Realtor thought we were nuts. And if the truth be known, we weren't too sure, either. What we *did* know was that the property was one of the most prime pieces in the area. In the worst case, we thought, we could build our own houses on them and live happily ever after—or perhaps sell the houses after we built them if someone made us an offer we couldn't refuse.

Note that we *fell in love with a property*. As we explained in the last chapter, that is a very dangerous situation to put yourself in. You start seeing opportunities that may not be there, and you stop seeing problems that definitely *are* there.

Fortunately, as it turned out, our gut feeling was right. The lots proved to be the best lots in the area. And although we had absolutely no idea at the time we bought the property about how we would market the lots, we came up with a unique marketing plan—with the help of the Realtor who had sold us the property and who became an ally—that gave them an air of prestige and seclusion, creating a residential conclave on the lake. Ultimately, we didn't build our houses, after all—but we doubled the prices again, and we now have contracts on five of the six lots, which will bring a total sale price of more than $8 million in less than 12 months.

We relate this story not to celebrate our good luck (for which we are thankful), but to show two things. First, a "good deal" is determined by many factors, not the least of which is being in the right place at the right time. Second, if you don't get in the game, being in the right place at the right time won't help you a bit.

Perspective is also important. There is not one piece of property that we have sold that isn't worth more today than it was when we sold it—and most of them are worth a great deal more. So in one sense, you could say we were pretty dumb to sell those properties when we did. And maybe we were. But in each case, time and perspective are different. At certain points in time, we needed to sell the property to raise money for other ventures outside of real estate. At other times, we sold a property to free up funds to buy another property that seemed to present greater opportunities. The point is, you can't second-guess your decisions because you are always looking at an investment based on your reality at that moment. If you don't learn that lesson very soon in the real estate business, you will make yourself very unhappy. So here's a basic rule: no second-guessing yourself!

By the way, do you think the person who sold the property to us was unhappy? Well, she wasn't. She was happy because she got her full $4 million asking price, and $2 million in extra profit without doing much of the work she had anticipated having to do. How do we know she was happy? Because several months after the closing, she let us put a second mortgage on the property, so that we could go do another business deal—and she loaned us the money secured by property that she was comfortable with.

So here's another useful rule: Always remember the people you buy from, because they tend to have all of your money.

Someday, they may prove to be excellent investors with you in other ventures.

How Do You Determine a Good Deal?

So the definition of a "good deal" changes from moment to moment and depends on multiple factors, many of which may be entirely unrelated to real estate. (Where is your money at the moment? Where is your attention? What's competing for your time?) That being said, there are some fundamentals that determine whether or not a proposed transaction is a good deal. Simply stated, there are three approaches to determining the value of a property at any point in time, and you must understand and be able to determine these three different kinds of "values": (1) cost, (2) market, and (3) income.

After discussing these three traditional approaches to determining value, we will also explain our own approach, which we call *enhanced value.* This is the value you bring to a given transaction because of your own knowledge. It's the intangible "secret sauce"— the wisdom you bring to the table about what can be done to the property to make it worth more. It is this kind of knowledge, we argue, that leads to true and lasting success in real estate.

THE COST APPROACH

The *cost approach* to value is based on what it would cost someone to duplicate the property in question, if that person were starting from scratch. Simply stated, you first determine the total square footage of the property—call it a house, for the sake of this example. Then you multiply that number by the square-footage cost for new homes in the area, also taking into account any sorts of special improvements that might add value to the property. Then deduct for depreciation: how much does wear and tear on the property detract from its value, compared to a brand-new version of the same property? Add in the value of the land in an unimproved state, and you'll have an approximation of the "cost value" of the property.

At first glance, this approach may seem easy enough, but it requires several different kinds of specialized knowledge. For example, what is the cost of new construction in the area? Yes, there is an average number, and that number is easily obtainable, but averages can play tricks on you. Deducting for depreciation, too, is an area of subjectivity. You can do it by age, of course, but some properties definitely wear faster than others.

Lot value is also a variable. While the values of lots in some neighborhoods may have little difference, values in other neighborhoods can have a great deal of difference, depending on where the lot is located relative to any amenities.

But the fact that these are variables, with some subjectivity built in, should not deter you from learning the process. The best way to do so is to work with an appraiser and learn how he evaluates a property. Find an experienced, highly recommended expert, and hire him to provide you with your first appraisal. The trick here will be to get the appraiser to explain how he does what he does. He will have gone through the process often enough that it seems intuitive, but with a little prodding, he should be able to articulate how he's making the appraisal. For example, ask him to give you comparable numbers for the area and to tell you how he has determined cost and appreciation. Ask him to show you how he looks at both depreciation and different kinds of improvements. How does he look at local land values—how fast are they changing, and what should one be looking out for?

Even one paid appraisal, in which you carefully go through these questions one by one, will allow you to learn the area and peg values to various improvements. After that, you should be able to "ballpark" the cost approach far better than other beginning investors who haven't gone through this informal apprenticeship program.

THE MARKET APPROACH

The *market approach* is the one most commonly used to appraise residential real estate. It is also called the "comparable" or "comp" approach, and it is used by most Realtors, using a tool called the Multiple Listing Service, or MLS.

Simply put, the Realtor uses the MLS database to generate a list of homes that have sold in your area over the past six months, and you compare your proposed purchase to the properties on the list. Again, you would use specifics to adjust the value of your target property up or down. If your target property has more square footage, you could award it a higher value than the other homes you are comparing it to. Additions or deductions could also be made for other subjective factors, such as location relative to amenities or condition of the property.

While the comparable approach requires some subjective determination on your part, it is easy to pick up once you start viewing the properties.

THE INCOME APPROACH

The *income approach* is the most fact-based appraisal approach because it is based simply on the numbers. Start with gross income; deduct for vacancies, debt service, and expenses; and you get the net income for the property. Once you find the net income, you compare it to the return you are willing to accept and "back your way into" the purchase price you can pay.

For example, if you are an investor and you want a 10 percent return on your investment, you multiply your net income by 10, and that gives you the most you can pay for the property and still achieve the desired rate of return.

While it's true that "the numbers are the numbers" and the numbers don't lie, the numbers can still be abused in ways that can get you into trouble. Investors often make the mistake of getting the numbers to say what say what they want them to say— usually in the direction of buying that property that they've fallen in love with. For example, instead of assuming some vacancy factor (which is pretty realistic!), they tell themselves that they can keep the property 100 percent occupied, and therefore they don't have to build a vacancy discount into their calculations. They eliminate a management fee, telling themselves that they'll handle the task of managing the property themselves. Why is this unrealistic? Because it values their time for management at zero, and that is simply not a true picture of the situation.

In short, be realistic when you use the income approach, and use real numbers. If you bend the numbers to justify your purchases, you are unlikely to be happy with the results.

While the income approach is excellent for larger properties, it is difficult to use with many residential properties because prices have gone up faster than rental income. You may find that after you take out all of your expenses and debt service, you have a negative cash flow. In that case, no matter what multiplier you use, the property won't have a value with the income approach. Unfortunately, you won't get many sellers interested in selling you their property at a negative price, either.

If you buy properties with negative cash flow, you will wind up using either the cost or the market approach to justify your price. You will have to give extra value to your estimates regarding appreciation of the property, and of course that gets very unpredictable and speculative at times.

From experience, we can tell you that negative cash flow payments *wear* on you, as each and every month you write a check out of your income from other sources. It isn't fun, and it's one of the two major things that people don't like about real estate investing (the other is property management). The upshot is, either you learn to live with the reality of writing those checks every month, or you structure your transactions to avoid negative cash flow. In later chapters we will discuss ways to do this, but the easiest is to add more cash up front and take on less debt service. If you don't have the cash yourself, then you have to come up with an investor who can help you solve the problem.

So there you have it: the cost, market, and income approaches to appraising the value of a property. In many cases, a skilled appraiser takes the results of all three approaches and puts them together, assigning the highest weight to the approach she considers most accurate for the property. It takes years of training and experience to get this right, but there's no reason why you can't get comfortable with and begin to use all three of these appraisal tools.

THE ENHANCED VALUE APPROACH

"Enhanced value" is our fourth approach to an appraisal. You won't see it in any textbook because it's *our* approach. It is the value that will either cost you the most money or make you the most.

What is enhanced value?

It is the true opportunity. It is the distinctive viewpoint that you, and only you, can bring to the transaction—the viewpoint that "sees" beyond the normal approaches to value and renders them almost irrelevant.

Donald Trump has it. It was the enhanced value approach that Trump used when he took the thirteenth hole of the Trump National Golf Club in Westchester County, New York, and spent $7 million creating an artificial waterfall on it—thereby making it a featured and talked-about attraction, known by golfers worldwide. That hole, with its endlessly talked-about water feature, is one of the most photographed spots in golf. It makes people want to play at the club, and buy memberships.

Enhanced value is what you will work to envision, and create, in your real estate career. Maybe your vision won't embrace $7 million waterfalls. Maybe it will be limited to the ability to envision what a tumbledown shack will look like after your labor has transformed it. The scale and scope of your vision don't really matter much; what matters is your ability, developed over time, to see what could be there when you've finished enhancing the value of a given property. The longer you are involved in real estate, the better you will get at this, and the more exciting and financially rewarding the business will become for you.

THE GOOD-DEAL CHECKLIST

☑ **DON'T GET PARALYZED BY SELF-DOUBTS.** Like most other business activities, real estate can and should be thought of as a game on a large scale, using real stakes. Too many people get stuck in their own ruts and fail to make a move. Get in the game, and trust your skill and luck.

☑ **DON'T SECOND-GUESS YOURSELF.** In real estate, you have to take your best shot, and then move on. Think of it this way: almost every real estate sale that has ever been made has been a "dumb" one, in light of the subsequent appreciation of the property. But all those sales *weren't* dumb, or at least didn't appear to be so at the time. Make your best deal, and move on— keeping in mind that the person you bought from (or sold to) may be a strong prospective business partner in the future.

☑ **USE THE TRADITIONAL TECHNIQUES FOR VALUING PROPERTY—ALONE AND IN COMBINATION.** Professional appraisers use three approaches—cost, market, and income—to put a value on property. Work closely with a high-quality professional to learn how this is done. Learn how combining these three different techniques can add new dimensions to your ability to spot a good deal where others might not see it.

☑ **USE THE ENHANCED-VALUE APPROACH TO SEE VALUE THAT ISN'T THERE YET.** The real geniuses in real estate develop the ability to see the *potential* value in a property, and then work to realize that potential.

CHAPTER 7

How to Write Money-Making Contracts

The Big Print giveth, and the little print taketh away.

One of the basic principles taught in contract law is that not all contracts are created equal. There are "standard contracts." And then there are "standard buyer's contracts," "standard seller's contracts," and everything in between. Of course, you won't actually *see* contracts labeled that way; they will just be drafted to benefit the side of the contract doing the drafting.

This is extremely important stuff. A novice investor can give up all of her positive cash flow—or, worse, lose her shirt—just because of the way a contract is drafted. Despite this fact, very few people take the time to understand their rights and to learn how a document should be structured to give them maximum safeguards.

Yes, we have seen millions of dollars' worth of real estate bought and sold on a verbal agreement, but that doesn't make this the best way to operate. The downside risk is too great. The truth is, *all* real estate investors should understand how to write a contract, and how to use specific language to get what they need out of the deal. Even if you use a lawyer to draft your contracts, your lawyer may not always think about the transaction the way you do. Remember, lawyers are trained in the law, not in creative deal making. So while their work may be legally correct, it may not get you the property you want, on the terms on which you want it.

This chapter is a bit of an odd duck, in the sense that you won't see anything like it in most real estate books. Why? Because it is advanced material, addressed to the serious investor—one who is willing to spend the time needed to understand the structuring of a contract. You should consider doing this; it may be worth a fortune to you.

Mastering Real Estate Investment Strategy No. 19: Learn the Rules of Contract Drafting

In order for a contract to be enforceable by a court, there are certain required elements that have to be included. These are

1. Competent parties
2. Legal description of the property
3. Offer and acceptance
4. Consideration
5. In writing (for real estate)

In addition to these basic elements, other terms and contingencies that one or more parties feel are important to protect their interests may be included. These additional elements aren't required for the contract to be enforceable in a court, but they may control the contract's life, or even what the involved parties can do in the future.

In most states, there is a contract form that has been approved for use by that state's Board of Realtors and the State Bar Association. This is the contract that the real estate agents in your area will tend to use, and you should definitely get a copy of it to review. When you are purchasing a single-family home or a small investment property, in most cases you can be reasonably confident about using that form to protect your interests—although with an addendum containing clauses that we will discuss later. But, if you are buying and selling more expensive and complicated properties, you will want to design your own contracts: one for buying and one for selling. This will enable you to include all potential terms and conditions that are to your advantage.

On the surface, most "offers to purchase" (also known as sales contracts) look the same. The reason is that there are certain basics that have been accepted by the courts as being required elements of such a contract. In addition, as a result of custom and past practices, other items may be considered the norm in certain parts of the country. For example, in Florida, the seller generally pays for title insurance. In other states, the buyer does.

Does this mean that you're obligated to write your contract according to these customs? Absolutely not. You are free to draft your contract in any manner agreed to by the parties involved. In fact, agreement is one of the essential elements of a contract.

For now, though, let's focus on the required elements.

1. *Competent parties.* The parties signing a contract must have the legal right to do so. Minors, for example, have not reached the age of competency to sign a contract and must have a guardian to act on their behalf. If you enter into a contract with

a minor, the courts say that you have a *voidable contract*— in other words, a contract that the minor can get out of, but you are bound by.

Corporations can present another competent-parties problem. A purchaser of property held in a corporate name or partnership name needs to determine that he is dealing with the right party. If that individual has not been approved by the corporation's board of directors, the transaction may be voided at some date in the future. Imagine your surprise when, after purchasing a bargain investment, you discover that the transaction isn't valid because you dealt with the wrong party!

2. *Legal description.* Legal descriptions are very important because they state exactly what you are buying. If the description is incomplete, you don't have a legal right to the items that were left out.

The sad truth is that many people are very careless about legal descriptions. In many cases, buyers simply copy the description the broker put on the Multiple Listing Service form—a form that was written with the seller's interest in mind. Don't let this be you! Be careful to get a precise, comprehensive legal description of what you think you're buying.

3. *Offer and acceptance.* This simply means that for there to be a contract, some sort of agreement must have been reached. This is the part of the contract that tends to be most heavily litigated after the fact. Why? Because in many cases, contract phrases are unclear. One party thinks a certain phrase means one thing; the other party knows it means something else. Off they go to court.

This is why real estate sales contracts must be in writing and must be signed by all parties. This isn't a guarantee, by any means, but it can serve as strong evidence of the parties' intent.

4. *Consideration.* There must be sufficient consideration for a contract to be valid. Sometimes people misunderstand this to mean that there must be money on the table, but that is not necessarily so. In most cases, consideration is simply the enforceable promise of the parties to buy and sell. Thus, you will often see the phrase, "for ten dollars and other good and valuable consideration."

5. *Legality.* The contract must be for a legal purpose and must be executed legally. In other words, it can't be based on fraud or misrepresentation, or it will not be enforced in court.

Another aspect of legality involves the free will of the involved parties. A contract signed by a person with a gun held to his head will not be recognized as valid, even if all the other elements are present.

6. *Writing.* In real estate, the bottom line is that the contract must be in writing and signed by all parties. Some states will require witnesses as well, so you should be aware of your own particular state's requirements. Yes, you can close a deal on a handshake, but if you have to go to court to enforce the deal prior to closing, you will have to have the contract in writing.

The Style of the Contract

Almost all contracts today are preprinted, in part to make them look like they are "standard" contracts, not favoring anyone. Although it's often convenient to follow the form of these standard contracts, you certainly don't have to do so slavishly. If you don't like something in the contract, change it by writing the modified language in the margin of the standard form.

Another way to change the terms is to use an *addendum* to the contract, generally prepared as a separate page and referenced in the contract ("see Addendum A"). The addendum allows you to change any clause or phrase in the contract, and *the changed version takes precedence.* This strategy is useful when a buyer presents you with a contract on her form. The addendum mechanism (which we'll describe in detail at the end of this chapter) is simple to use and allows you to regain some degree of control.

Adding the Right Clauses

As we go through this chapter, we will analyze various additional clauses that you can use in your contracts. We will review clauses that are beneficial to the buyer, those that are beneficial to the seller, and neutral clauses. Getting the right clauses in your contract depends on at least three things: your *knowledge* of those clauses, your negotiating ability, and the relationship between you and the other parties. So let's start with the knowledge base: what you need to know about clauses.

PURCHASE PRICE

There are numerous formats for stating the purchase price, deposit, and balance due. Based on our experience, the following format works best, because it explains both the flow of money and how it adds up.

The total purchase price shall be
payable as follows: $_____

a)   The deposit shall be held by

_____

in the amount of $_____

b)   Subject to new ( ) or assumption ( )
     of a mortgage with

_____

       Interest rate _____% payable
       $_____ per month with
       an approximate balance of $_____

c) A mortgage and note to be held
     by the seller at _____% interest
     payable _____ monthly for
     _____ years in the amount of $_____

d) Other _____
     _____ $_____

e) Balance to close $_____

                        TOTAL: $_____

CREATIVE DOWN PAYMENT CLAUSES

The formal structure of the document is one aspect of a contract. The other is the creative clauses that you may add to the contract, either by having them preprinted on your own contract form or by means of an addendum to someone else's contract. Let's look at some examples.

The first clause has to do with the down payment. One frequently overlooked fact is that a down payment does not have to be made in cash. Cars, boats, stock, mortgages, and various kinds of services can serve as down payments. We just made an offer on a property by typing up a note and mortgage on another property we own. The seller had wanted a substantial deposit because we were asking for a long inspection period (imagine that!). We didn't want to have cash tied up, so we suggested a mortgage on other real estate. The seller was comfortable with the property, so that made our proposal easier.

How do you write such an offer? First, refer to item d in the purchase price clause form we just presented. In that space, you could write the type of property and refer to a complete description elsewhere, or you could simply state "see addendum." In either case, you would state the value of the item in the right-hand column.

In an addendum, you could use the following phrase:

Down payment to be in the form of _____
having an agreed-upon value of $_____.

Mastering Real Estate Investment Strategy No. 20: Protect Your Purchases with a Financing Contingency Clause

"Location, location, location" is the most important factor in real estate—but "financing, financing, financing" isn't far behind. With the correct financing in place, a property will work for you and provide income and growth. With the wrong financing, a property can cause a strain on your finances and place a major burden on you.

A friend of ours who teaches real estate around the country once suggested that he would buy any property you wanted to sell, for any price, if he could just name the terms. Sounds crazy, right? How could he do that? Well, if you carry the idea to an extreme, his terms might be "nothing down and nothing per month for 100 years with a balloon payment at the end." The seller would almost certainly get the property back at the end of that 100-year period (because the balloon payment would be so high), but the buyer would have gotten the use of it for nothing for a century.

Obviously, no seller in his right mind would ever make such a deal. But the example does show the importance of financing and how you structure your deal.

The following is the basic financing contingency clause used in contracts:

This contract is contingent on the buyer receiving a firm commitment for a loan in the amount of $_____ at an interest rate not to exceed _____%. The buyer shall apply for said loan within _____ days from the acceptance of this contract and receive a commitment no later than _____ days from said date. Should the buyer be unable to obtain such commitment or waive this contingency, then, at the option of either party, the contract may be cancelled and the deposit returned to the buyer.

As a seller, looking at this clause presented to you, you might want to make the clause more restrictive by limiting the number of days for the buyer to make his loan application and getting the loan commitment to a shorter term. You also might want to say that the interest rate on the loan will be market rate. This language would lock the buyer into the transaction if *any* loan was available, as opposed to one that had the low rate that he wanted.

From a buyer's standpoint, you would want as long a term as possible to shop for the mortgage, so that you don't lose the deal if the shopping takes longer than expected. You might use this type of clause:

This contract is contingent upon the buyer obtaining a new mortgage on the property in the amount of $_____, the terms of which must be to the satisfaction of the buyer in his sole discretion.

This type of clause gives you, as the buyer, maximum flexibility. If you do not like the terms of the loans that are available for whatever reason, the contract is null and void. From just this one illustration—buyer and seller looking at financing contingencies—you can see the battle that can go on in contracts. The bigger the deal, the bigger the battles.

While real estate is normally purchased with institutional financing, sellers are frequently asked to help finance all or part of the transaction. If the sellers don't need all of the cash from the sale, they are frequently willing to provide at least part of the financing to the buyer. This is particularly true when the other investment alternatives that are available to them in the marketplace are producing low yields.

As a buyer, you may want to draft a financing clause in your purchase contract that actually states the terms that will later be used in the mortgage carried back by the seller. By doing this in the contract, you avoid surprises and lock in terms that are more favorable to you. If you do not stipulate the terms in your sales contract, you will, at best, be forced to use standard language that is neutral to all parties. The following are examples of clauses that you might use to structure a contract to your advantage.

The mortgage to be carried back by the seller shall be automatically assumable. The mortgage shall contain no prepayment penalty and shall allow for a 30-day grace period on late payments.

This clause helps you to sell the property to another buyer using the seller's financing you arrange. The clause also eliminates prepayment penalties, which cost you money.

The mortgage shall look only to the property as collateral for the mortgage and shall not be entitled to a deficiency judgment.

This clause eliminates personal liability for you as the borrower. It is called nonrecourse *financing. We always try to negotiate this, and it isn't as difficult to obtain from private lenders as you might think. Remember, we are using this mechanism in the context of seller financing, and the seller has just sold you on the value of the property. Is she now going to say that she doesn't think it's worth that much, so she needs more collateral? That would be very unusual.*

Mortgagor shall have a first right of refusal at any time the mortgagee desires to sell the mortgage and note at a discount.

This clause means that you have an option to buy the mortgage if the seller decides to sell it. If the discount offered is good, you can make some extra money if you buy it back—and it did not cost you anything to get this clause included.

Note, though, that this option will be thrown in only if and when you ask for it—and, of course, if the seller agrees to it. Sometimes you get these clauses accepted, and sometimes you don't. It's almost always worth a try. As you learn more about options, you will learn that it's usually smart to ask for an option on something, because you're likely to get it and because it may be worth something in the future and these little profits here and there add up over time. We know Realtors who represent buyers who always ask for a future listing if the property is sold within a certain number of years. These options, set up at a time when the buyer is obviously pleased with the Realtor's work, can amount to a nice nest egg in the future.

Mortgagor shall be permitted to miss one monthly loan payment per year, with said amount being added to the final payment.

We used to call this the "Christmas clause." We don't see it as often as we did a few years back, but it is a nice cash-flow clause, and it gives you a payment break. The Christmas clause may be starting to make a comeback. Recently we saw a mortgage company offering this in new mortgages. It was trying to differentiate itself from other lenders, and this clause really didn't cost it anything.

Mortgagor may substitute collateral at any time of equal or greater value of the property.

This clause gives you the flexibility to move the mortgage to another property. The property that had the mortgage can now be refinanced to give you cash, or sold free and clear to give you cash flow.

Mortgagor may have released from the mortgage parts of the property proportionally to the principal paid.

This is one example of a release clause. If you don't have a release clause, you have to sell the entire property (or at least pay off the entire mortgage) if you want to sell any part of the property. When it comes to development land, release clauses are a practical necessity.

The mortgagee agrees to subordinate his interest to any future mortgage placed on the property by the buyer.

This is a very important clause, as it allows you to go out and get new financing at better terms or to get a construction loan if you are developing the property. Any time you can get a lender to subordinate her interest to that of another lender, you free up equity that you can borrow against for other purposes.

Creative financing clauses are used to help you solve a problem. Don't overuse them, or you will make negotiations unnecessarily difficult. Try to get as many of the clauses in your contract as you think you need—and as you think the other party will agree to. Ultimately, developing your negotiating skills through real-life bargaining will determine your level of success.

Mastering Real Estate Investment Strategy No. 21: Diffuse Balloon Mortgages with Extension Options

Creative financing—in particular, seller financing—frequently involves something called *balloon mortgages*. A balloon mortgage has a long-term amortization schedule, but the payoff is much sooner. An example would be a mortgage with payments structured in accordance with a 20-year amortization schedule, but with a balloon in 5 years. In other words, all the principal is due at the end of the fifth year.

As noted in earlier chapters, the problem with balloon payments is the uncertainty of what will happen when the balloon comes due. Who knows what the world will look like in five years? What if interest rates are such that financing is not available or is too expensive? As with most challenges in the real estate field, the time to deal with this situation is *before it occurs*—and the best time is during the contract stage. A clause should be added to the contract regarding seller financing, and then restated in the mortgage, that allows you to extend the balloon when it becomes due if you are unable to find satisfactory financing. The following balloon clause will help you accomplish this:

> In the mortgage taken back by the seller, there shall be inserted the following phrase: in the event, in his sole discretion, that the buyer cannot find adequate or acceptable refinancing upon the due date of this mortgage and note, the buyer reserves the right to extend the payment date for

a period of _____ years. The borrower, at his option, may make a payment of $_____ on the principal amount at any time without prepayment penalty. The terms and conditions of the remaining mortgage will stay the same.

The lender may accept this clause as is, or she may add a penalty payment for each year you want to extend the mortgage. Most lenders don't really want to take the property back and go through foreclosure, so extensions of between six months and a year are commonplace. Lenders *do* want their money, though, so the farther out you try to extend the loan, the more they are likely to ask for in return.

Mastering Real Estate Investment Strategy No. 22: Avoid Personal Liability with an Escrow Deposit

The amount that a buyer should put down as a deposit on a deal depends on many details, including the value of the property and present market conditions. Naturally, your objective as the buyer is to put down as little money as possible and to tie up the property for as long as possible.

The first rule of deposits is that you *never give the deposit to the seller*; instead, you give it to either a third party or (preferably) your own attorney or escrow agent. The reason is obvious: in case of a dispute, it is much easier to get your money back if the seller does not have it. You are a lot less likely to wind up in court—although that's where you *will* wind up if there is a serious dispute.

The deposit may be made in any number of ways, including a promissory note, stock, a check, a draft, and so on.

> The buyer hereby places $_____ in escrow with _____ to be used as a deposit on this contract upon acceptance by the seller. Upon approval of all documents requested for review, the buyer hereby agrees to place an additional sum of $_____ on deposit. Should the buyer default on this contract, the seller shall retain the deposit as his complete liquidated and unliquidated damages and have no further rights pursuant to this contract. Should the seller default or otherwise be unable to complete the sale of this property, the buyer shall receive an immediate refund of all deposits hereunder and will thereafter be allowed to pursue any and all remedies granted to him by way of the seller's actions under this contract.

Note that the wording of this language restricts your liability, as the buyer, to the amount of the deposit. This is important because it keeps the seller from suing you for specific performance, which would force you to buy the property. It also prevents the seller from trying to get damages for items unrelated to the deal. For instance, a seller might say that because you didn't close on the contract, he was unable to close on another property, and that cost him money, which you now need to make good on. Avoid these potential problems by clearly limiting your liability to the deposit and nothing more

Mastering Real Estate Investment Strategy No. 23: Create "Outs" in Your Contracts

In simpler times, the consensus was that you needed only one "out" in a contract. But with the ever-increasing tendency to litigate, courts have been taking some strange views on getting out of transactions, which argues for including more than one contingency.

The following are clauses that can be used by a buyer to create potential "outs" in a contract. These clauses are frequently referred to as "weasel" clauses. We don't like that term because of its bad connotation. The truth is, there are very legitimate reasons for having contingencies in a contract, and you need to find ways to include them.

> The offer is contingent upon the inspection and approval of the terms of sale by the buyer's attorney to his sole and discretionary satisfaction within _____ days.

> This offer is subject to the inspection and approval of the following:
> 1. All existing leases and addendums, either written or oral.
> 2. A copy of the underlying mortgage.
> 3. A certified survey showing the actual location of the building on the property.
> 4. A statement from all appropriate regulatory bodies that the building meets all code requirements for use and occupancy as an office building.

> The buyer shall have thirty days from the delivery of the aforementioned items to accept or reject them as satisfactory. The buyer shall be the sole judge of the adequacy or deficiency of the documents and, if denied, shall terminate the contract with all deposits to be returned to the buyer.

Clauses 1 through 4 in the second example show the kinds of things you might request to review prior to a closing. Each could be modified to fit the situation. You will also note that these clauses can be used as delaying tactics. Statement 4, for example, asks for a statement from a regulatory body. Requests of this type, while important, can also tie up the property because they take so long to get.

Mastering Real Estate Investment Strategy No. 24: Specify Time Limits in Contracts

The control of *time* is an integral part of any contract negotiation. As a buyer, you want to limit the seller's time for reviewing the contract and acceptance. If you give her too long, she may shop your contract for other offers, or she may just postpone making her decision, for whatever reason. In either case, you want to limit her ability to stall, because stalling makes it less likely that you'll get the property.

If the property that you are purchasing is in town and the seller can be contacted without delay, it is not unreasonable for you to put a time limit on your contract acceptance of from 12 to 24 hours. If the seller is out of town, you have to consider the time period between her getting the contract in hand and notifying you of her acceptance. Given the widespread availability of overnight delivery services, a two-day turnaround is not unreasonable.

> The seller shall have until _____ o'clock on _____, 20__, in which to accept the offer or the contract is automatically void.

By specifying a specific time frame for action on the other party's part, you create urgency in a situation where there might otherwise not be any.

Mastering Real Estate Investment Strategy No. 25: Add Performance Requirements to Your Contract

Sellers of income-producing property are notorious for making representations about the income and expenses of the property that are not in line with reality. Simply put, they exaggerate the positive and minimize the negative. Occasionally, real estate brokers will put together what's called a "broker's reconstruction" of the property, summarizing what they believe the property would return with proper management, but there's a lot of guesswork in most such reconstructions.

So big surprises can crop up once the buyer takes possession. Frequently, the buyer will discover, much to his dismay, that the income he receives is lower than what was projected and/or that the expenses are higher. To avoid this problem, or at least to minimize its impact, a buyer can use what is referred to as a "performance clause" to force the seller to "put his money where his mouth is."

> Performance clause: The net operating income of the property after all expenses, including debt service, shall be no lower than $_____ for the first six months of operation of the property. Should the net operating income (NOI) be less than said amount, the payment due to the seller on his mortgage will be reduced by the difference of the two numbers.

As you can see, the practical effect of this performance clause is that if expenses are greater or income is lower than is indicated by the seller, the difference will come out of the seller's pocket. If the seller suggests that this is unfair, since she will be unable to control the expenses after selling the building, the objection can be resolved by placing the management of the property in the hands of a third party. If the seller continues to balk at this clause, it may be an indication that she has exaggerated something good (or minimized something bad) about the performance of the property.

Mastering Real Estate Investment Strategy No. 26: Review All Leases on a Property Prior to Settlement

When buying rental property, it is extremely important to review all the leases on the property. You need to specifically request that the seller provide an estoppel letter from each of the tenants, stating that no written or oral promises have been made outside the lease. The estoppel letter "stops" the tenants from raising any such issue at a later date.

You should review each lease carefully, especially to make sure that you are not getting tied into a long-term lease that could affect the value of your property. For example, if the lease called for two five-year renewals, for a total of ten years at a fixed rent, the value of your property would not increase for ten years (at least based on the income appraisal approach) because the income isn't increasing.

By reviewing the leases and other rental documentation, you will be able to determine more accurately whether or not the seller has been forthcoming in the income statements that he has given you.

> The seller hereby agrees to deliver to the buyer within fifteen (15) days of the acceptance of this contract, all leases presently existing against the property. Included with the leases shall be a breakdown of all tenant revenues, including rent rolls and rental applications provided by the tenants. The seller shall further submit to buyer an estoppel letter signed by the existing tenants stating that no oral or written promise other than the lease agreement has been made by the owner regarding leased property. Upon receipt by the buyer of the aforementioned documents, he shall have thirty (30) days to review the same and accept or reject the property based on his satisfaction with said documents.

Although it is not completely necessary, it is a good idea to have the sellers assign all the leases to you at closing. Even though leases run with the land, it is generally a good idea to have documentation showing that the seller has put the leases into your name. The following clause inserted in your contract will solve any potential problem:

> The seller hereby agrees to assign any and all tenant leases to the buyer at settlement.

Mastering Real Estate Investment Strategy No. 27: Demand "Guarantees" on Financial Representations

Frequently, sellers of rental property tell prospective buyers tales of the ease with which new and better tenants could be obtained for the property and how the rent could be increased if someone spent just a little more time in active management of the property. In most cases, this is simply the seller's puffery: if it were that easy, she would have done it herself.

These sales pitches do, however, present an opportunity to the buyer. If the seller is representing that the property can easily be rented, then she should be willing to back up her words with her money. The following clause covers any vacancies that may exist at the time of the closing for a period of one month. If you are unable to find a tenant within the month, the seller will have to pay for that month's rental.

> If a vacancy exists in the property on the day of settlement, seller hereby agrees to deposit out of seller's proceeds one month's rental per vacant unit in escrow. The money shall be held in escrow until the vacancy is filled or thirty (30) days have expired, whichever shall occur first.

Mastering Real Estate Investment Strategy No. 28: Avoid Outstanding Lease Payments

Make the seller collect on any outstanding lease payments before closing. Unfortunately, once a seller signs a contract to sell a property, he starts to forget about the property—particularly about any problems like unpaid rent. So it is very important for you to keep the management burden on the seller and keep him involved in the property. If a tenant has not paid her rent, for example, place the burden of collection (and possibly eviction) on the seller.

> The seller agrees to deliver possession of the property to the buyer at closing with all leases current. In the event any lease payment is outstanding, the seller agrees to deposit in escrow for the benefit of the buyer the sum of $_____ for each vacant unit to cover the cost of any rent and eviction proceedings.

Mastering Real Estate Investment Strategy No. 29: Employ Closing Extenders

There are times, when you are buying an investment property, when the longer you can delay the closing, the better off you are. The property is tied up, and you will receive all appreciation and equity built up during this period. The only disadvantage would be the delayed tax benefits or lost cash flow.

There is a fine line that determines how far you can push the seller with extensions. Some won't be in a hurry and won't care. Some will. Push them beyond their comfort zone, and you will probably wind up losing more concessions than you win.

Another reason to try to include a delay clause is simply to protect yourself if you encounter unforeseen problems in getting your money together.

If the buyer is unable to complete the purchase of the property within the stated period of time, he may extend the contract by paying in escrow to the seller an additional $_____. The contract may be extended for up to _____ additional periods for a similar payment. Upon the closing of the property, all additional payments made shall apply to the purchase price and down payment.

Mastering Real Estate Investment Strategy No. 30: Keep Your Option to Sell Open

One of the joys of purchasing investment property is the opportunity to resell the property for a profit *prior to actual settlement.* And this does happen—particularly in a seller's market. To create this possibility, the buyer should always write his contract in the name he wants to close in, plus the phrase "and/or assigns," or should allow for assignments in the contract. In some instances, failure to put the word *assignment* or *assigns* in a contract would prohibit the buyer from doing so.

The buyer is hereby given full rights to assign this contract and all rights, duties, and obligations thereunder to another party.

This statement is a pretty aggressive version of an assignment clause, and some people believe it is better to go this route. We prefer the following less hard-nosed version, simply because it seems to generate fewer arguments:

John Smith and/or assigns

In a seller's market such as we have now, some sellers (particularly developers) try to restrict assignments, in part because their construction lender doesn't want to create an overheated market. They worry that if values become overinflated, people may back out of contracts, leaving the developer and lender with a lot of unsold inventory. Another potential problem is that prices may fall as the market settles, and lenders will get stuck with fore-closures when investors stop making payments.

When you find yourself working in this kind of active market, you can contract for your properties in the name of a limited lia-bility company and then sell the shares in the company to a buyer if and when you find one. This strategy avoids the assignment problem altogether, as the name of the contract owner (the com-pany) never changes.

Mastering Real Estate Investment Strategy No. 31: Increase Deductions with Written Tax Allocations

When purchasing investment property, one of the key advantages is the tax-advantaged depreciation that flows through to the investor.

Depreciation is based on an allocation of the property's value between the land and the building, with the cost of the building being the basis of depreciation. The more dollars you can shift to the cost of the building and away from the land, therefore, the greater your depreciable base. Having a contract stipulate this allocation can be very helpful in the event that (1) the Internal Revenue Service audits you, and (2) it becomes interested in this question of allocation.

Simply put, the IRS has only two things to go on. One is prop-erty tax records, which break out land and building. The other is the contract between the buyer and the seller. In most cases, unfortunately, buyers and sellers don't take the time to stipulate the allocations. As transactions become larger, though, this can become an important issue, and a clause should be inserted to protect the buyer.

> The buyer and seller do hereby agree that the purchase price of this property is to be allocated as follows:
>
> | | |
> |---|---|
> | Land | $_____ |
> | Building | $_____ |
> | Equipment and personal property | $_____ |
> | Other | $_____ |
> | Total | $_____ |

Mastering Real Estate Investment Strategy No. 32: Use Outside Property Inspectors

Unless you are an expert in construction, you need to have your proposed purchase inspected by a qualified engineer prior to closing. Some people think that this is a needless expense; we think they're very wrong. We know of several vacant buildings now in litigation that cannot be occupied because of structural defects. We have seen single-family homes purchased with foundation cracks, sill damage, and roof problems. No, an engineering inspection is not a guarantee that no problems exist, but good inspectors usually give a warranty on their inspection, which means that you and they are covered if you encounter a structural problem after you take possession.

> This contract is subject to the receipt of a satisfactory report by a qualified engineer regarding all heating, air conditioning, electrical, plumbing, structural systems, and roof. The

report shall be deemed satisfactory at the sole discretion of the buyer.

Mastering Real Estate Investment Strategy No. 33: Ask for a Preexecuted Mortgage Satisfaction

If the seller is taking back financing on the property, the buyer will make periodic payments to the seller for a certain number of years. At the end of the payout period, the seller must terminate the mortgage transaction by delivering to the buyer a satisfaction of mortgage. Unfortunately, although sellers should be cooperative in submitting the satisfaction, often they are not. A buyer who has made payments on time for a 10-year period suddenly finds that the seller, for some unknown reason, is unwilling to draft a satisfaction of mortgage and convey it to the buyer. And without that document, you won't be able to sell or refinance the property because there will be a cloud over the title.

To head off this predicament, have the title company or escrow agent draft a "satisfaction of mortgage" at the time of closing. Specific instructions are drawn up that detail the terms of payments on the mortgage and that direct the escrow agent, upon notification that the buyer has met her obligations, to convey the satisfaction, which is signed and ready for recording, to the buyer.

> The buyer hereby agrees to complete all the terms of the mortgage carried by the seller herein stated. Payments will be made directly to _____ as called for in said mortgage agreement. Upon the completion of said mortgage payments, the escrow agent hereby agrees to transfer a satisfaction of mortgage hereby prepared, signed and notarized for recording and recorded directly to the buyer.

Mastering Real Estate Investment Strategy No. 34: Itemize Personal Property That Is Part of Purchase

There have been numerous stories (some funny and some not) about the misunderstandings caused by the disposition of personal property in the case of a home purchase. Refrigerators, stoves, dining room lamps, and antiques have all been points of confusion and conflict. Huge amounts of money and time have been wasted because a buyer and a seller had a final disagreement over an item of personal property.

The best way to avoid any such dispute is for the buyer to draw up a list of the personal property to be conveyed with the real estate. Depending on the importance that the purchaser places on the items, the list may include photographs of the items in question. Why? Well, we've been involved in several situations where the contract called for a refrigerator to be sold with the property. In between the sales contract and the closing, the seller took out the modern, double-door, ice-making refrigerator that was in the property at contract time and replaced it with an old, dilapidated, single-door refrigerator. It became a problem at the final inspection.

Window-unit air conditioners are another source of contention between buyers and sellers. The buyer tends to think that air conditioners are attached to the property, and the seller tends to feel that since all he has to do is unscrew the hinges and remove the units, they're his. The same problem tends to arise with draperies and curtain rods. Even though the draperies may be custom-made for the particular home, the seller sometimes wants to take them with him, rather than leave them behind for the buyer. All of these problems can be avoided by structuring a clause within the contract to cover personal property, and attaching a list of the agreed-upon items.

> The buyer and the seller mutually agree that the inventory attached as Addendum 1 of this contract is a complete list of all items to be conveyed with the property. Said inventory is to remain in the property when conveyed without substitution. All property will be delivered to the buyer in good working order on the day of closing or will be replaced at the seller's expense.

Mastering Real Estate Investment Strategy No. 35: Shift Cash Expenses to the Seller

In today's high-cost world, closing costs can eat deeply into a buyer's cash. A buyer, therefore, should try to shift as many of these costs to the seller as possible. The primary reason for this, of course, is to save money. Another almost equally important reason is to protect your supply of cash. What you pay at closing for expenses and prorations is always added on top of your down payment as a cash requirement. The less cash you lay out, the greater the odds that you'll have the cash needed to make a down payment on *another* property.

The clause for a buyer would be

> The seller shall pay for all closing costs and transfer fees.

In lieu of this clause (which for obvious reasons can be difficult to negotiate), a buyer should stipulate specifically what he wants the seller to pay for. By doing it this way, you have a greater chance of getting the clause accepted without controversy.

> The seller shall pay for documentary stamp tax and intangible tax on the deed and mortgage, including recording fees and title insurance.

Another alternative, when the seller is carrying some financing, is to recognize that you, as the buyer, will probably have to cover some of the closing costs. At the same time, you want to conserve your cash. To accomplish this end, you can agree to pay some of the closing costs, but *let the seller advance you the money.* The amount advanced will simply be added to the mortgage that you are agreeing to pay (assuming that the seller is taking back a mortgage). This is really not as unreasonable as you might at first think. The money will not come directly out of the seller's pocket. Instead, it will come from the first mortgage proceeds.

> All buyer's proration and closing costs will be paid by the seller at closing but will be added to the seller's purchase mortgage amount.

Mastering Real Estate Investment Strategy No. 36: Generate Cash with Rebates for Repairs

If you put $3,000 down on a house and the seller rebates $3,000 to you at settlement for repairs and redecorating, what is your down payment? Zero!

This technique can be used to generate nothing-down transactions. Sellers are often amenable to the idea, especially if you are giving them cash from other sources, such as new financing. The practical result for the seller is the same as taking $3,000 off her purchase price, which most sellers are expecting to reduce to some extent in any case. The result to you is $3,000 more cash in your pocket. Remember: *less cash required is better than a lower purchase price.*

> The seller shall rebate to the buyer at settlement $_____
> to be used for redecorating and repairs at the discretion of
> the buyer.

Mastering Real Estate Investment Strategy No. 37: Get Pest Inspection on Improved Property

All property purchased with improvements on it should be inspected for termites, carpenter ants, and other destructive pests. The cost of an inspection is ridiculously low compared to the damage that may exist—and that isn't likely to be discovered until the buyer takes title. Naturally, if wood damage is found, the buyer will want to shift the cost of correcting the problem to the seller or, at his option, have the right to get out of the contract. The following clause provides the buyer the maximum protection.

> The seller, at his expense, shall provide to the buyer a report
> dated within ten (10) days of closing conducted by a certi-
> fied pest inspector that there are no visible signs of infesta-
> tion or wood-destroying organisms. The report must be to the
> complete satisfaction of the buyer. If infestation is indicated,
> the buyer has the option of canceling the contract or the prop-
> erty shall be treated and repaired at the expense of the seller.

You will note that the clause provides for the seller to purchase the report. In some cases, we change this clause when we are the buyer. In other words, we get our *own* report. When we do this, we meet the inspector at the property and walk through it with her. It costs a little more when you do it this way, but you can learn a lot about the property when you go through it with the inspector and see it through her eyes.

Mastering Real Estate Investment Strategy No. 38: Place the Burden of Title Insurance on the Seller

Depending on the purchase price of the property, title insurance can become a big expense. As a buyer, this is an additional expense that you want to shift to the seller; otherwise, you will have to come up with another expensive item out of your limited cash.

In addition, you will also want to protect yourself against title defects on the property. There are basically two ways to achieve this: through title insurance and through an updated "abstract," or history of the property's title. Title insurance is generally considered better, because it is a form of insurance and will pay you cash if you suffer any damage. The following clause places the burden of the cost of the title insurance policy on the seller, and at the same time forces her to clear up any defects prior to closing.

At least ten (10) days prior to closing, the seller shall provide, at his expense, an owner's title insurance commitment for a policy to be paid at closing by the seller. In the event the commitment shows that a defect of title is present, the seller shall have sixty (60) days in which to remove the defect. If the seller is unable to cure the defect within said time, the buyer may cancel this contract and have all earnest money refunded to him or allow the seller additional time to cure the title. Seller agrees that if the title is found to be unmarketable, he will use all diligent effort to correct the title defects within the stipulated time, including the bringing of any suits to quit title.

Mastering Real Estate Investment Strategy No. 39: Get the Property Surveyed

Just because a property is for sale and presently occupied does not mean that it complies with the present zoning and building regulations. Frequently, sellers over the years have made unauthorized additions to the property, including the building of additional units that have not been approved by zoning.

A buyer who purchases a property based on the expectation of having three rental units, only to discover later that the property is zoned for only *one* unit, will experience a painful gap between the expected income and the real income from the property.

In addition to zoning and occupancy issues, other problems may crop up. For example, the seller may have built his fence a foot over onto the neighbor's property, or vice versa.

In the worst case, an adjacent neighbor may have gained ownership of part of the property through "adverse possession," meaning that an uncontested encroachment has led to a de facto transfer of ownership. To be properly protected, the buyer's contract should include certain warranty language regarding zoning and public and private restrictions.

> The seller hereby warrants the property is not in violation of any zoning ordinance or other governmental regulation. The seller further warrants that there are no encroachments or liens against the property that are not of public record.

Mastering Real Estate Investment Strategy No. 40: Make Your Contract Clauses Survive Closings

After settlement or closing, the deed and mortgages are recorded, and they take precedence over the terms that were in the sales contract. The contract is said to have merged into the deed. All the clauses that you carefully drafted for your protection are of no effect if they were not put into the deed and mortgage instruments by the settlement agent.

To keep your contract clauses alive, insert the following clause. This is not a guarantee that the courts will uphold your position, and you may want to review it with an attorney. The best solution is to ensure that your closing instrument contains a repeat of the clauses in your contract that were important to you. This clause is just insurance against that not happening.

> This contract and all of its terms shall survive the passing of legal title and will not merge with the deed.

An alternative to the broad language in this clause is to tie it to a specific clause that you want to survive enforcement after closing. In this case you would add, "This clause shall survive passing of legal title and shall not merge with the deed."

Mastering Real Estate Investment Strategy No. 41: Use Default, Severability, and Binding-Agreement Clauses

The thought of going through a lawsuit is enough to make most people sick to their stomachs. And with good reason: in many cases, the only true winners are the attorneys. Nevertheless, you might as well face the fact that lawsuits are unavoidable at times and that you need to construct your contracts for maximum protection.

As a buyer, you want to limit your liabilities as much as possible to the earnest money deposit—that is, to your down payment.

> In the event the buyer defaults, the seller shall retain the earnest money deposit as complete liquidated and unliquidated damages and all rights arising from this contract are hereby terminated.

Should the seller default, the buyer may want to force a sale instead of walking away from the transaction and losing out on the deal she so carefully put together.

> In the event the seller shall default under the terms of this contract, the seller recognizes the buyer's right to sue for specific performance and/or damages. In the event a suit is instigated, the prevailing party shall be entitled to court costs and reasonable attorney's fees.

The last sentence of the preceding paragraph is important because without it, the buyer will probably have to pay his own attorney's fees and court costs. This could become an example of winning the battle but losing the war if the case drags on and the fees mount up.

If you are the seller in a transaction, you may want more than the earnest money deposit. You may want the courts to enforce the sale.

> In the event the buyer defaults under the terms of this contract, the seller is entitled to retain any deposits paid on the contract as well as to recover any amount by which his actual damages exceed the deposit. The seller may, at his option, sue for specific performance. The prevailing party in any action under this contract shall be entitled to reasonable attorney's fees and court costs.

One technique frequently used to impose hardship on an opponent in a lawsuit is to bring action at a location far from where he lives. This increases travel costs for the opponent and forces him into unfamiliar territory where he has to deal exclusively with strangers. To minimize this risk, you should state where any litigation will occur, if litigation becomes unavoidable.

> For any and all legal action arising out of this agreement, proper jurisdiction and venue shall rest in the County of
> _____, State of _____.

> In deciding the legality of any part of this contract, interpretation shall be construed under the laws of the State of
> _____.

The principle of *severability* is also important to both the buyer and the seller. Severability means that if one part of the contract is found illegal, or for some other reason is voided by a court, the rest of the contract can still be preserved. If you do not use a clause like the one that follows, the entire contract would be void if one clause is found to be illegal.

> Should any provision of this contract, in whole or in part, be found invalid for any reason, the remainder of the agreement shall remain valid and enforceable.

Finally, consider including a "binding agreement" clause. There have been numerous instances where both buyers and sellers have attempted to get out of a contract by pleading ignorance of what they were doing. Even though ignorance of the law is no excuse in a criminal action, courts tend to be much more lenient in civil cases, particularly if strict enforcement would result in someone's losing a property. To protect yourself, you should clearly state your willingness to enter into a binding agreement and put the other party on notice that he may need an attorney.

> **Warning!** The parties are hereby cautioned that they are entering into a binding agreement that creates certain legal

rights and duties. Each party is advised to seek the option of a competent attorney as to the matters stated in this agreement.

Mastering Real Estate Investment Strategy No. 42: Use Penalty Provisions to Ensure Timely Property Possession

If for any reason the seller is unable to deliver possession to the buyer on the day of settlement, she should be considered a tenant from that point on and pay rent.

For each month, the seller should be willing to pay an amount equal to 1/12 of the principal, interest, taxes, and insurance, plus 1/12 of 10 percent of the buyer's down payment. While this total amount may be higher than neighborhood market rents, it's a fair percentage based on the value of the property. After all, didn't the seller set the value of the property?

> The seller hereby agrees to deliver possession of the property to the buyer at closing. If the seller is unable to deliver possession on that day, the seller shall be charged $_____ per day for each day he holds over. An amount equal to _____ days shall be withheld from seller's proceeds for said payment.

Mastering Real Estate Investment Strategy No. 43: Conduct a Final Inspection

In some states, a mandated walk-through, or final inspection, of the property is conducted immediately before settlement. A notation is made as to the items that are not working, and a reserve can be established to pay for those items. In other states, the walk-through is not conducted automatically. To properly protect your interest as a buyer, you should stipulate that all items should be in working order as of the date of settlement, as evidenced by your personal walk-through of the property.

> Seller warrants that all heating, air conditioning, plumbing, and electrical systems are in good working order at closing. In addition, all appliances now on the premises, unless specifically excluded in this contract, will remain on the property and be delivered to the buyer in good working order on the day of closing. A walk-through of the property will be conducted by both the buyer and seller for the purpose of determining the operation of these items. Any item not working will be repaired by the seller at his expense. An amount of $_____ will be held from seller's proceeds at settlement until all such work is complete.

If you are the buyer, make sure that an adequate amount is withheld to cover repairs. It is much easier to collect before the closing than after. When in doubt, ask for more than you think is necessary to cover the cost.

If you are selling the property, you want to avoid the problems of warranties and representation. In this case, you want to use the following:

> The property is being sold in an "as is" condition, and the seller makes no representation or warranties about the property or its contents. The condition was taken into consideration in determining price.

Mastering Real Estate Investment Strategy No. 44: Insure against Property Damage

Most states have now adopted a law stating who bears the burden of loss should a property burn down prior to settlement. In some states, that person is the seller, and in others it's the buyer. Check and see where the responsibility lies in *your* state and make sure that you are adequately protected under the contract. Another sure way to protect yourself is to see that a clause is inserted stating that the burden will rest with the other party.

> If the property or improvements thereon are damaged by fire or other casualty prior to the settlement date, the loss of said property shall be borne by the seller. The buyer shall have the option of either proceeding with the contract, taking the property in its present condition, along with insurance proceeds, or canceling the contract and receiving a full return of the deposit that has been made. The seller agrees to maintain full fire insurance and property/casualty insurance on the property for a value no less than the present contract price through settlement date.

Mastering Real Estate Investment Strategy No. 45: Disclose Professional Relations

Unless otherwise disclosed between the parties, a real estate agent represents the seller. Consequently, the agent has to represent the seller's interests. Many sophisticated buyers, therefore, hire brokers to represent them directly. This is an acceptable practice and, has been approved by the National Association of Realtors. So that all of the parties are clear as to the responsibilities of the agents, a clause should be inserted in the contract stating whom the agent represents.

> The seller is hereby advised that _____
> real estate company is representing the buyer as his agent.

In order to keep from having to pay the buyer's agent from proceeds outside the settlement, resulting in a higher down payment to the buyer, a clause can be inserted into the contract that stipulates that the payment to the buyer's agent will come out of the down payment money the buyer has put up. Some sellers may resist this, but in fact this is the same procedure used to pay the seller's agent.

> All real estate commissions are to be paid from the net proceeds of the sale. The buyer's agent is to receive a _____% real estate commission.

Mastering Real Estate Investment Strategy No. 46: Change Contract Terms with Addenda

As noted earlier, an addendum is an addition to a contract. It allows you to add or otherwise modify an existing contract without crossing out or retyping the original contract. For negotiating purposes, it allows you to take a contract that has been submitted to you using someone else's form (and presumably favoring that person's interests) and convert it to your advantage.

The addendum should be referred to within the original contract ("see addendum" or words to that effect). The addendum should be physically attached to the original contract, and, if it runs for more than one page, both parties should initial and number each page.

You should be aware that in contract law, typed words take precedence over preprinted words, and handwritten words take precedence over typed words. This is based on the theory that handwriting better reveals the intent of the parties.

Note: In some states, the signatures may need to be witnessed. Check with a local attorney for proper requirements.

ADDENDUM

This addendum entered into this _____
day of _____, 20__, is hereby attached
and/or made a part of that certain real estate purchase contract dated _____, 20__, by and between
_____, hereinafter referred to as
"Purchaser," and _____, hereinafter
referred to as "Seller."

This addendum shall through its execution be binding on
the parties hereto having the same force and effect as the
real estate purchase contract. The addendum shall take
precedence over any and all conflicting terms as stated in
the real estate purchase contract to which this addendum is
a part and it shall take precedence over any previously executed addendum.

The terms as hereby agreed to are as follows:

The undersigned by the execution do hereby agree to be
bound by the terms herein and shall extend upon their
respective heirs, executors, administrators, representatives,
successors, and assigns.

WITNESS	PURCHASER	DATE
WITNESS	PURCHASER	DATE
WITNESS	SELLER	DATE
WITNESS	SELLER	DATE

THE CONTRACT-WRITING CHECKLIST

☑ **MAKE THE CONTRACT WORK FOR YOU.** Preprinted contracts tend to look as if they're graven in stone and not subject to amending and rewriting. Nothing could be further from the truth. Whether you are the buyer or the seller, you have the right to try to amend the contract in your favor.

☑ **CONTRACTS CONSIST OF (A) BASIC ELEMENTS AND (B) OTHER COMPONENTS.** A real estate contract must meet six key criteria to be enforceable (competent parties, legal description of the property, offer and acceptance, consideration, legality, and in writing). Beyond these six elements, there is an almost infinite variety of concepts that can be added through special clauses and addenda.

☑ **CLAUSES CAN BE ZERO-SUM OR WIN/WIN.** Some clauses favor either the buyer or the seller, so that when one "wins" through the addition of a clause, the other loses. Other clauses can create advantages for both parties. The trick, as a negotiator, is to get as many of both as possible into your contract.

☑ **USE CLAUSES TO (A) INCREASE YOUR FLEXIBILITY, (B) SHIFT EXPENSES AND LIABILITY TO OTHER PARTIES, AND (C) PROTECT CASH.** Whether you are the buyer or the seller, your goal in contract writing is to give yourself more flexibility (including plenty of opportunities to get out of the deal, if necessary) and to shift expenses and potential liabilities either to the other party or to third parties (e.g., insurance companies). At the same time, you want to take flexibility and options *away* from the other party, if that suits your interests. Finally, unless you're in Donald Trump's tax bracket, you need to *protect your hoard of cash* to maintain flexibility going forward.

☑ **USE THE CONTRACT TO HEAD OFF PROBLEMS BEFORE THEY ARISE.** The time to solve problems in real estate is *before they start.* The more detail and clarity you build into your contract, the more likely it is that everyone's needs will be met and that expensive lawsuits and settlements can be avoided down the road.

CHAPTER 8

The Art of the Deal: Negotiations

Real estate mogul Donald Trump called negotiating "the art of the deal" and used that phrase as the title of his first book. Country music legend Kenny Rogers sang, "You've got to know when to hold 'em, and know when to fold 'em."

They were both right. Negotiating is an art that has to be learned. And one of the key elements is knowing when to hold onto your position and when to wait for a better deal. Between those two extremes a lot of money is made and lost.

It's true that to a certain extent, negotiators are born, not made. To some degree at least, the ability to hammer out a good deal is a God-given talent that some people are blessed with, and some aren't—just as a few of us are blessed with a 95-mile-an-hour fastball, and most of us aren't.

But that *doesn't* mean that you can't improve on what you have and get better than you are, no matter what your level is at this moment. Even the greatest pitchers have a pitching coach, and Donald Trump learned about real estate deals at his father's knee. So education and training can help you get better at whatever you do—including negotiation.

This chapter focuses on skills taught to us by our own mentors. We're also going to discuss some lessons taught to us in the School of Hard Knocks, when someone more skilled than we were "ate our lunch" at the table. Hey, it happens to the best of us. Sometimes, if the other side is *very good* at what it does, you don't even know it has happened. And sometimes, you're happy that you learned something new—even if it was at your own expense.

Mastering Real Estate Investment Strategy No. 47: Understand That "No" Doesn't Always Mean No

If you want a great lesson in negotiating, spend a day with a five-year-old. They are the *best*. First, they are fearless, because they're too young to have been burned very often. Second, they are very much into themselves, because neither their parents nor their teachers have been able to break them of the habit of being what they want to be or getting what they want to get.

If a five-year-old wants a piece of candy, he isn't going to ask you just one time and take your first "no" as the final answer. No, indeed! He will ask you until you say "yes," or at least make a counteroffer that sounds acceptable.

This is the first rule of negotiating. "No" is just the beginning. "No" is the first step in finding out exactly what the other side means and how that position can be viewed in a positive light.

You might as well face it from the beginning: negotiating is the process of getting rejected. In fact, it is the very process of rejection, bad as it sometimes feels, that gives you the opportunity to find out what the other side really means. If you hate rejection, get over it—or find someone else who handles it better and can be your negotiator in your stead.

This isn't necessarily an admission of failure. Many times, we have used third parties to handle negotiations for us because they can often say and do things that you can't say or do for yourself. Additionally, if you use another person as a middleman negotiator, that person can always bow out if things don't go well, and you can ride in on your white horse and save the day for both sides. The point is that you need to understand the process, recognize your skills or lack thereof, and create an environment of negotiating that works for you—no matter who's actually running the process.

Mastering Real Estate Investment Strategy No. 48: Control the Playing Field

In football, as in most sports, there is something called the "home field advantage." In fact, much of the football season is played with one eye on getting into a position where your team will have the home field advantage in the playoffs.

The playing field in real estate is equally important. *You want to control the context, and the process, as much as you can.* One of the most skilled negotiators we know is an attorney whom we have dealt with on many occasions. Sometimes he is on our side of the transaction, and (unfortunately) sometimes he is on the other side, representing himself or one of his companies. When he negotiates, he always tries to control the playing field by being the first to introduce the contract to be used in the transaction.

He isn't overly aggressive about it. On the contrary, he is pointedly helpful, always offering to manage the process of creating the contract document. Very few people turn down his offer. Why? Because it is expensive for them to go hire an attorney, because drafting contracts is also time-consuming, and because in some of the complicated transactions he is involved in, it is very difficult to structure contracts both creatively and in a legally enforceable way. So, most people readily relinquish that responsibility.

When they do, they give up a lot. While the contract isn't the only element of control in a real estate transaction, it is an important one. Frequently, it defines the terms of the deal, and if you are the one who originally defines what things mean, then you start with a big advantage. In the last chapter, we learned that if a contract claims to be a "standard contract," the first question to ask is, *What kind of "standard"?* Is it a standard buyer's contract, a standard seller's contract, or something else entirely? You learned in the last chapter that there's a big difference. Here is one example, from a contract that favors the seller:

The buyer shall be given 15 days to inspect the property.

But suppose the inspection clause reads as follows:

The buyer shall be given 60 days to conduct a property inspection by an inspector of his choice. In the event the buyer determines that the property fails the inspection, at his sole discretion, then buyer and seller shall have 90 days to correct any deficiency.

Well, it still looks reasonably fair. After all, 60 days doesn't seem like too much time to arrange for an inspection, especially in a busy market. But the buyer actually has *150 days* (i.e., 60 + 90) just for the inspection process. The drafter of the contract has in effect created a five-month option on the property for the buyer, where he can control what happens to the property without having any money at risk. In today's real estate environment, five months is an *eternity*. You can control the property and ultimately keep it, flip it, or walk away. This flexibility is gained just by setting the table to your advantage.

Some of you may be thinking, "Well, I would *never* sign a contract like that!" And maybe you wouldn't. But the reality is that it happens all the time. First, in most cases, the "60 + 90" issue (or the equivalent) never even gets red-flagged in the discussions. Most people, even lawyers, read contracts very quickly, and a simple, boring clause like this tends to get lost in a multipage legal document. Second, the inspection clause doesn't *sound* particularly one-sided, because the language says, "The buyer and the seller are given this time." Hey, that's fair, isn't it? Not really—but it sounds fair enough.

Even if the party objects to "60 days," she will probably demand only that it be reduced from 60 days to 30 days. If our attorney friend was in the deal and the issue was raised, he would quickly volunteer to change it to 30 days, adding something like, "No problem at all; it's just the *inspection* we're talking about here." In the process, he'd make you (the seller) feel slightly foolish for even raising the issue. And henceforth, you'd feel that much more uncomfortable about raising other issues in the contract, including far more important issues.

Here are several other ways to control the playing field in a real estate transaction:

1. *Meet your counterpart in your office.* In your office, you control the environment and the administrative staff. But as with all rules, you'll find that there are times to make exceptions. Sometimes you may want to meet in the other party's office so

that he is more comfortable. It depends on the situation. It is part of the art of negotiating.

2. *Control the production of any documents in your transactions.* This includes contracts and leases. As we've already said, controlling the workflow controls what the document says at the outset. Of course, it's likely to get changed as the negotiations go back and forth, but at least the contract and other documents *start out* the way you want them to. Following this rule will cost you out-of-pocket money, because in most cases it means that your attorney will be doing the drafting and you will be paying the bill. But concentrating on these relatively small amounts of money is a huge mistake, especially if it means giving up control of the contract process.

3. *Control the closing.* All other things being equal, you want to hire the closing agent and name the place of closing. This is *not* to imply that either you or the closing agent will do anything underhanded. What you are trying to do is control the environment, making it easy to move a transaction along. If people are stressed because of their environment, they are more likely to be argumentative, even on small points.

A closing by its very nature is adversarial. By custom, the parties meet in the same room, each hears the financial picture from the other side, and anything one party dislikes necessitates a shift of money from one side of the table to the other side. We don't like these types of closings. We often try to arrange separate times for the buyer and seller to sign documents—or, at a minimum, arrange separate rooms. Yes, this sometimes results in delays, when the other party has a problem that needs our input. To counter this, we tell the closing agent how to get in touch with us if needed.

4. *Control who inspects the property.* If you hire the inspector, you know that she is going to be looking after your interests.

When possible, we always try to be present when any inspections are done, so that we can hear the informal comments about the inspection. Sometimes the inspector will know the property, or at least the area, and by talking about it will give you extremely valuable information.

5. *Control who conducts the property survey.* The survey shows you encroachments on the property. If you are writing the check and talking to the surveyor directly, you will find out more than if you don't speak to him. Encroachments, even small ones, can be a thorny problem, because they most often involve your direct neighbor. Common sense tells you that you don't want to start off on a bad footing with your neighbors if you don't have to. If there is an encroachment, have the seller clean it up before closing, because she will be moving. Let her be the bad guy.

6. *Control who writes the title policy—particularly the exceptions in the policy.* We've already addressed this challenge. Title exceptions are what the title company says it isn't covering. If you don't read these exceptions and get the company to delete them from the policy, you aren't buying much coverage. Title companies have been at this a long time, and their data centers know what to exclude. Don't let them do it.

7. *Control which lender is used and which financing terms are acceptable.* The buyer chooses the lender, of course, but the seller can affect the terms by eliminating language favorable to the buyer in the contract. For example, if the contract says, "subject to the buyer getting financing at the prevailing rate," you as the buyer are much more locked into the deal than if the contract says, "subject to the buyer getting financing on terms acceptable to him at his sole discretion."

8. *Control the type of deed to be issued.* A "general warranty" deed conveys the most rights, so as a buyer that is what you

always want the seller to give you. A "quit claim" deed conveys the fewest rights—for example, it doesn't even warrant that the seller owns the property. Make sure you are getting the type of deed you want and need.

Mastering Real Estate Investment Strategy No. 49: Use a Partner to Head Off Pressure Responses

Let's imagine that you're sitting at the table facing the other party in a real estate transaction, and a serious problem pops up. What next? If you are the decision maker on your side, you may feel compelled to make a decision right there on the spot. If you're an old hand in the industry and are experienced at negotiations, you may do fine under this kind of pressure. But the less experienced you are, the more it can cost you, because you aren't conversant with all of the moving parts of a transaction. If you are up against a skilled player, she will know exactly how to put you into a position of making a decision at exactly the most inopportune time for you.

Successful real estate players like Donald Trump conduct their negotiations themselves. Why? Because they have been in business so long that they know where they can go with a particular transaction, and they can think on the spot. (They also recognize that their presence alone may have a positive influence on the negotiation.) If you don't have this kind of experience and stature, your best course of action may be to say, "Let me check with my partner."

It doesn't matter what kind of partner you're referring to. Maybe it's a business partner, or your spouse, or just an associate whose advice you value. The point is, you need to buy time, to get a little extra time to think about what was just offered or rejected, and maybe get that partner's advice.

You can also use this strategy to turn the tables in your favor. For example, you could say, "Well, that seems reasonable enough, but I really need to discuss it with my partner. So let's go ahead and put it in writing, and I will take it to him to discuss."
See how you have changed the playing field? You have required the other side to put its position in writing, and you have bought yourself a period of time to think about this new position—*without the other side being able to change its mind easily.* If you're a buyer, this move is almost always to your advantage because you can effectively take the property off the market for at least that period of time.

Mastering Real Estate Investment Strategy No. 50: Use the Power of Silence

"You can hear a lot by listening," as the legendary Yogi Berra is supposed to have said.

This quote reminds us that *listening is one of the most important aspects of negotiating.* Normally, the more you talk, the more you lose, because you give the other side more and more information about your true bargaining stance, and that rarely helps you get the best deal.

There are some very bright people on our staff whom we *never* take to a negotiation, because there is no telling what they will say. Their disclosures are innocent and well intentioned, but they tend to hurt our negotiating position. Think about it. Assume you're buying a property. What signal does your team send when one of its members says, "Oh, we have the *perfect* furniture for this room!"? It tells the other side, loud and clear, that you have already mentally bought the property and moved in. As soon as this has been said, you can forget about negotiating, because the seller *knows* you'll back down.

Sellers also often give away the store by giving little hints about what is happening in their lives—if you can get them talking. We were once negotiating to buy a house. In talking to the wife of the couple who owned the property, she happened to mention that she was going away that weekend. When we asked where, she said she was flying up to see her husband, who had already moved on to his new job. Then and there, we knew that the sellers were likely to be very flexible in their negotiations because we knew the couple was now living apart. The point is, always be cautious about what you are saying and mindful about the information you may be giving to the other side.

When in negotiations, try thinking of yourself as a *counselor*. Your job is to be open and to ask questions in a warm and friendly matter. Act as if you are going to try to help the other side with its problem—because, in fact, you *are*. Listen to the other side's comments, and ask friendly follow-up questions. The more you can learn, the more likely it is that you can formulate an offer that will work both for you *and* for them. Approaching negotiations in this vein is more fun, often more successful, and personally more rewarding. And if you meet this same party in another transaction, that deal may prove even more successful.

Mastering Real Estate Investment Strategy No. 51: Employ Take-Away Options

The most successful strategy we use, in almost all types of negotiations, is the "take-away." Frankly, we debated about whether to include it in this book, because it works so well—and there's some chance that some of our opponents will read these pages. We decided that we couldn't leave out such a powerful strategy.

The take-away is used when a negotiation has reached a stalemate, or the other side is being unreasonable. When the other side says something like, "I wouldn't even *consider* that offer," your first response should be, "I understand exactly how you must feel." (This is a softening statement that sets up what is to follow.) Then you should continue by saying something like, "We appreciate your time, and we hope we can work together sometime in the future," or some other appropriate sort of comment. At that point, you can wait for the other side to respond, or you can just begin to pack up to leave. Whatever you do, *keep quiet.* Why? Because the next person who speaks . . . *loses!*

What you normally hear, after the silence, is a retraction of some or all of what the person just said. If you don't hear such a retraction, you'll know that the speaker was serious about his (unacceptable) position, and you might as well move on. Either way, you have the information you need: either to resume negotiations or to go to the next deal. You can't win them all, and time is money. The sooner you find out whether or not you're in the game, the better.

Mastering Real Estate Investment Strategy No. 52: Use the "Columbo Close"

You may recall the television series *Columbo*, in which Peter Falk played the role of a detective who appeared to be a bumbler. In fact, the bumbling was a tactic. When interviewing a suspect, he'd ask lots of questions, then, when he was finished, he'd get up to leave. But when he was almost out the door, he'd turn and say, "Ah, just one more question." And that question would always turn out to be the zinger. The suspect, thinking the grilling was over, would be caught off guard. The tables were turned.

In negotiations, the "Columbo close" can be used in a similar fashion. Imagine you're in the final phase of your negotiation. Everything seems to be done. Then, in your best Peter Falk voice, you casually ask, "You know, I was just *wondering* if . . ."

You'll have to fill in the rest of the sentence. Maybe it's, "You know, I was just thinking, if you don't mind—could we make the inspection period 90 days, instead of 30? I really would be more comfortable, if that's OK with you."

Or maybe, "You know, if we increased the price I pay you for the property, but you agreed to pay all of the closing costs, it would save me having to pay cash out of my pocket, and you'd get the same net cash from the sale. That works for you, doesn't it?" And you'll be amazed at how often it *will* work for them.

Mastering Real Estate Investment Strategy No. 53: Use a Conversational Approach

Everyone ultimately develops his or her own style of negotiating. Some people are reserved, some are loud, and others fall somewhere between the two extremes. It really doesn't matter which style you use; you just have to determine what works best for you.

One style that works for many people is a conversational approach, centered on questions that are used to determine the seller's objectives in relation to price, terms, and timing—the three factors that will determine the deal. We have found that questions starting with "would you" or "could you" work best because they convey consideration and thoughtfulness.

For example, if the seller says he wants 20 percent down, and that amount doesn't work for you, your response could be, "Well, would you consider breaking that up for me, with 10 percent down and a note for the balance in two years at 8 percent?" Or, "Could you break that up for me, and take 10 percent now and the balance in a note at 8 percent?" If you ask the question in a nonthreatening manner, it's likely to be received that way by the other party. He may still say "no"—but if he does, he will often say *why*, and that answer will give you more information as to what he is trying to accomplish.

The more you can find out about what the other side needs, the better you can structure the deal to meet those objectives instead of simply getting into an unproductive cycle of offer and counteroffer. You may ultimately find that there is no good deal available for you. Well, again, the faster you find that out, the faster you can move on to something else.

Mastering Real Estate Investment Strategy No. 54: Use Your Star Negotiator

There is a common assumption among many authors of real estate books that you should handle your own negotiations. We don't agree. The person who should negotiate your deal is the one who is most likely to bring about a success. Sometimes that is you, and sometimes it isn't.

Earlier, we pointed out that great negotiators (like great athletes) have a gift. You want the best person on your team—your star negotiator—making your arguments for you. If that's you, *great*. If it isn't, then find the best person in your network of professionals to do it for you.

We consider ourselves to be very good negotiators, after years of experience in many different circumstances. But we're well aware that there are many situations where there are better people for the job. Sometimes we use people who have a relationship with the other side of the transaction. Sometimes a development deal we are doing requires a credible expert—on, say, environmental problems—to explain our stance on that issue to the other side. The point is, if for any reason you feel that someone else can negotiate better than you, be humble and wise enough to admit it and bring that person in. Your goal is to *bring about a successful deal*, and that may mean that you do nothing but find the deals and turn them over to someone with the skills to represent you in the rest of the transaction. *Don't lose focus on your deal-making objective.*

Mastering Real Estate Investment Strategy No. 55: Never Negotiate against Yourself

One serious mistake in negotiation is to make decisions on behalf of the other party. For example, suppose you are preparing to make an offer that you think is realistic. But then you think, "Uh-oh, the seller's not going to accept that!" Then you raise your offer even before the seller hears it. Before you say that you would never do something that foolish, let us assert that everybody does it, and often for an honorable reason: we tend to put ourselves in the other person's shoes. Well, try not to do that if it leads you to negotiate against yourself. Structure your offer based on what works for you, and let the seller make up her own mind. You may be pleasantly surprised.

Another time this comes up is when you make an offer, and the seller doesn't do anything in response—so you make another offer. Don't bid against yourself! Get the other party to counter, even if it is for full price. At least if you get a full-price counter, you can bind the contract with just your signature. Remember, time is money. If the other party doesn't counter and you make yet *another* offer, you're wasting a lot of time.

Mastering Real Estate Investment Strategy No. 56: Don't Fall in Love with the Deal

If you fall in love with the deal, it is going to cost you. The motto for negotiations is, and always will be, he who cares less, wins.

There are many reasons to fall in love with a deal. Sometimes we fall in love with the property. (We've warned you about that!) Sometimes we get wrapped up in a deal because we have told people we were doing it. Sometimes we fall in love with a deal because we have already spent the profits, at least in our mind's eye.

Don't fall victim to these kinds of mistakes. The best deals you make are the ones that you have carefully analyzed and structured to meet your needs. If you depart from the script because you "want to do the deal," you're almost sure to make mistakes. We have done this ourselves, and it has been expensive.

Negotiating is an art. It requires a solid knowledge of your product and your goals, and the ability to think on your feet. Some of you will be very good at this. All of you can get better; it just takes practice. And it helps a great deal if you can learn to *enjoy the process* as you go.

THE NEGOTIATIONS CHECKLIST

☑ **DON'T TAKE REJECTION PERSONALLY.** Learn to deal with the word *no*. It's nothing personal. The word *no* is often followed by the word *because*, and the words that follow *because* often tell you what you need to know in order to succeed.

☑ **DO WHAT YOU CAN TO CONTROL THE PLAYING FIELD.** The home-field advantage is real. You want to control both the context and the process, if possible. One way to do this is to take on (or have your lawyer take on) tasks that are either burdensome or complex. The person who controls the text of the evolving agreement, for example, holds a lot of power.

☑ **DON'T GET STAMPEDED.** If you start feeling pressured—say, in response to a new offer that has just been put on the table—*resist that pressure.* Say that you'd like that last offer in writing, so that your partner can review it. It doesn't much matter who your partner is, or even if you have one. You need to buy time and (most likely) get some outside advice about this new offer.

☑ **LISTEN MORE THAN YOU TALK.** People love to talk about themselves. Use that fact to your advantage—and meanwhile, refrain from talking too much yourself.

☑ **USE "TAKE-AWAYS," THE "COLUMBO CLOSE," AND "WOULD-YOU'S."** Every negotiation is different. Each has its own rhythm and takes its own twists and turns. Get familiar with a range of negotiating tactics, and use them when they are helpful. The goal with all such tactics should be to either (1) close the deal, or (2) find out that there's no deal to be had.

☑ **NEVER NEGOTIATE AGAINST YOURSELF.** It sounds too obvious to dwell on, but everybody does it. Put your best offer together, and give the other side a chance to respond to it. Don't second-guess yourself before the other party has even had a chance to respond. (Again, you'll be wasting your valuable time.)

☑ **NEVER, NEVER FALL IN LOVE WITH A DEAL.** It's the same idea as "never falling in love with a building." Don't let a deal get its own momentum. It doesn't matter if you've got an ego stake in making it work. If it can't work, *let it go.* The deals you fall in love with tend to get very expensive.

CHAPTER 9

The Successful Closing

According to Yankee legend Yogi Berra, "It ain't over 'til it's over." He probably wasn't talking about a real estate transaction at the time. But he *could* have been.

It would be nice to think that once you've gotten your offer accepted and a contract signed, your work is over. But believe us: you're not even halfway home. Believe us: you are about to face an extraordinary array of legal, economic, and even psychological land mines, all hidden just below the ground in front of you, and all seemingly designed to blow up this great deal you've just put together.

If this cold, hard view of reality puts you off, all we can say is, "Get used to it!" It's an integral, inescapable part of the real estate business. From the day your offer is accepted until the day you walk out of the closing room—either as the nervous buyer or as the relieved seller of that property—about a million things can go wrong, and most likely some of them *will* go wrong.

What's the answer? Well, again, toughen up. And in the meantime, use a checklist like the one we present in this relatively short chapter. A checklist does three good things at once. First, it minimizes the chances that you'll make a dumb mistake and forget something entirely—and believe us, it happens! Second, it increases the odds that you'll do everything in the right sequence, which in a complicated deal can pose a challenge. And finally, it also gives you at least *some* reassurance that you're at least *partially* in control of the process.

Over time, after you've been through a number of closings, you'll probably come up with your own checklist, one that's tailored to reflect your particular needs and tastes. When that day comes, great! Meanwhile, feel free to use ours. Whatever wisdom is in there is hard-won wisdom—and you're welcome to it.

Mastering Real Estate Investment Strategy No. 57: Use a Buyer's Checklist

One reason why we like checklists is that we don't like surprises. Of course, no two real estate transactions are ever *exactly* alike, so every transaction includes its little surprises. The point of the buyer's checklist is to anticipate (and, to the extent possible, control) the major elements, and "quarantine" the surprises to the minor elements. Maybe you've come across the notion of the "critical path," which is how operations people plan complex production processes. At any given point in time, asks the critical-path expert, what's the most important thing to be worrying about? What's on the critical path at the moment, and what's not on the critical path?

The buyer's checklist grows out of that same way of thinking. What do I have to be worrying about *right now*, if this deal is going to go through? What do I have to worry about next?

Here are a dozen fundamental building blocks that should serve as the core of your checklist. (Many of them contain more than one element, as you'll see.) As soon as you discover something new and useful to you, add it to your list:

1. *Assemble your financial information and keep it updated.* We'll cover this at length in the next chapter. For now, suffice it to say that wherever you get financing, your lender is going to want to know everything in the world there is to know about your personal finances. It's your job to make sure that your potential lenders are thinking about you in the right ways. This means (a) making sure that today's picture of your creditworthiness is complete and accurate and (b) taking steps to make tomorrow's picture look even better. We'll have lots more to say about this in Chapter 10.

Every lender you deal with is likely to require many of the same items from you. So after you put together the file for your first loan, keep everything you provided in a single file, and keep it updated. (That way, you can pull it out in a hurry, when a good deal presents itself.) The file should include at least the following:

A. *Your last two years' federal tax returns.* Rudimentary? Yes, unless you can't lay your hands on them in a hurry. Why not make five copies of each now, and make a habit of making copies as soon as they come back from your accountant—or, if you fill out your tax forms yourself, make five copies before you mail them?

B. *Your verification of employment.* This is really easy to get on short notice—until the day it isn't. Here's a bad scenario: maybe there's only one person in your company who can generate this information, and on the day you need it, he or she goes on vacation for two weeks. Get it now, make copies, and file them away.

C. *Your current financial statement.* Once you go through the painful process of preparing your financial statement, take the small amount of extra time that's needed to make extra copies and file them with the other key papers just mentioned. True, almost every lender uses a different form, and you'll probably have to fill out a different form every time you start the loan-application process. But the differences among these forms are really at the margins, so having several copies of an up-to-date version on hand (or several copies of *several* up-to-date forms on hand) will be a great help.

2. *Apply for your loan.* Sometimes this goes quickly; sometimes it doesn't. Above all, you want to minimize the chances that a snag will occur and prevent your deal from closing. Quickly narrow down your process to two lenders (more than that is just too much work) and let them bid against each other for your business. In this day and age, loans are a commodity, and there is a very competitive market for your business. Again, see Chapter 10 for more details on loans and lenders.

The lender you choose—or more often, the lender who chooses you—will control many other aspects of your deal, including the choice of the property appraiser, surveyors, and title insurance agency. This puts you in a difficult situation: you don't really control the process (even though the lender may try to *say* that you do), but you need to exert some influence over these vendors to make sure that things turn out the way you want them to. For example, in far too many cases, we have had problems with closings because the appraiser's preliminary valuation was too conservative. In those cases, we've tried to influence the appraisal (i.e., bump it upward) by supplying additional facts. Maybe the property has unique attributes that have been missed or undervalued. (One appraiser overlooked the entire third floor of a residence we wanted to buy, transforming it from a five-bedroom to a three-bedroom home!) Maybe there are "comps" (comparable sales statistics) out there that support a higher valuation for the property. You can't be pushy, but you certainly can be helpful in an energetic kind of way.

3. *Order title insurance and check for exceptions on the policy.* Title insurance protects you against problems of clouded ownership. We've mentioned this in earlier chapters. Most people overlook this step, and it's almost always a mistake. If you read the fine print on your title insurance, you are getting insured "except for the exceptions." So it's a *very good idea* to read what those exceptions are. (In our experience, if anything goes wrong, it will be covered by one of those exceptions.)

And if it hadn't just happened to us as we were writing up this chapter, we might not have included the following, seemingly obvious caution: *confirm that the legal description of the property is correct.* If it isn't (and it wasn't, in the case that we're now in the process of trying to resolve), your insurer may wriggle off the hook of having any financial obligation.

4. *Review the survey for encroachments and easements.* Encroachments are past actions by neighbors that give them a physical presence on your property—for example, a fence that takes a turn and winds up on your side of the property line. Surveys turn up these kinds of encroachments. Another thing to watch out for is *easements,* a guaranteed right of access that a previous owner has granted to somebody. Sometimes it's a utility company that needs access to its poles; other times, it's a neighbor's sewer line that goes under your property to get to the down-

hill sewer main. In both cases (encroachments and easements), you'll know about them only if you study your survey carefully.

What you do next can be decided only on a case-by-case basis. If the fence is only two inches over the line, you may decide not to worry about it. If it's ten feet over the line, that's probably a different story, and you probably want to correct that degree of encroachment—i.e., insist that the seller get the fence moved before the closing. This isn't simply being fussy or unduly territorial. In some states, neighbors can actually gain legal possession of those parts of your property through a process called "adverse possession" if you don't do anything about the encroachment for a certain number of years.

Again, study and understand your survey. If you can't understand it, sit down with the surveyor and have him go over it with you. If you go through this process a couple of times, you'll quickly get used to reviewing surveys, and you'll head off a lot of heartaches at your closings.

5. *Order hazard insurance, including any special policies that might be required, such as flood, hurricane, or earthquake insurance.* Specialty insurance like flood and earthquake insurance is getting more and more expensive. In Florida, they have had to set aside special funds to provide homeowners with this insurance.

Insurance companies don't want to insure against hurricanes and floods. On the other hand, very few lenders will loan money in the absence of such insurance—and if the property is in a hurricane or earthquake zone, you definitely need the relevant insurance. So check ahead of time to make sure that it is available.

In this book, and in other books and articles we've published, we *strongly endorse* the purchase of ample insurance to protect your assets. If you're going to cut a corner, don't cut it here—the stakes are simply too high.

Even after you make the right decision (that is, to buy all of the insurance you need), you still must be vigilant. Case in point: an insurance company that we dealt with for many years neglected to set up the flood insurance that we thought we had purchased on the property. Someone made a mistake. There's no benefit from pointing fingers, but the closing agent thought the insurance policy was bound, and we thought we had a verbal confirmation that the policy was in effect. We didn't discover that it *wasn't* until a hurricane was bearing down on us—and, of course, once a hurricane is on the way, no more flood insurance is going to get written for a while.

No, we didn't get wiped out. But the story could have ended very badly, and we certainly spent a lot of anxious hours unnecessarily. Be vigilant!

6. *Get a termite inspection, and then buy the policy that covers treatment.* Termites are more or less of a problem depending on where you live. (And we use "termites" to cover all kinds of gnawing, destructive insects.) In Florida, for example, you *have* to have the insurance, because sooner or later all untreated homes will be infested with termites. Even if your home *is* treated, you may get a termite infestation—but at least in that case you are protected from what can quickly add up to thousands of dollars' worth of damage.

7. *Read the deed.* Maybe you think that the deed (the official document that details the transfer of ownership of the property from the seller to you) won't present any problems. And most of the time, you'd be right. But on the rare occasions that you're *wrong*, it can be a disaster.

We recently went to a closing that seemed pretty straightforward. While we were going through all the paperwork and other bureaucratic steps, we took a moment to read the deed—at which point we noticed that the description of the property didn't match what we thought we were buying. Left out of the description was a small strip of land that clearly went with the property. But if that strip—the *water frontage*, by the way, which made the property as attractive as it was—had continued to be omitted, it wouldn't have been conveyed from the seller to us. Yes, we could have sued, and we probably would even have won. But lawsuits are expensive and time-consuming—and *your time is valuable.*

8. *Read the mortgage (deed of trust) and the note.* Yes, it's easy enough to nod your head in agreement when someone (like us, for example) advises you to *read everything.* Obviously, you should read everything you're signing, right? But the simple truth is, you frequently don't have enough time. In many cases, you get the documents at the very last minute. Sometimes you don't even see them until *after* closing. This is one circumstance in which an attorney can be very helpful, because lenders and closing agents tend to be a little more responsive to their requests. (They don't want to go to court, either.) If you can't read everything (and very often, you can't), focus on the items on this checklist. If you can't even read everything on this checklist, focus on the mortgage and the associated note. That's where the big money is.

9. *Review the HUD One settlement sheet for errors.* This is also known as the closing statement. Very likely, this one will make you very angry, because it's chock full of what we call "bogus charges"—little fees that drive you nuts, such as application fees, processing fees, fees for supervising the processing of the processing fees, and so on, and so on. You get the idea. Check this sheet for huge errors (to your disadvantage), write the checks for what you have to, and move on.

10. *Verify anything that might be especially important to you.* We recently bought a property that was on the water and had a dock. The dock was a major reason that we wanted this prop-

erty, and we wanted to expand its size to accommodate our growing flotilla of adult water toys. Well, neither the lender nor the seller cared a hoot about that dock. But we had enough experience to be able to list everybody else who *might*: the state's relevant regulators (environmental protection *and* environment quality), the county, the city, and the subdivision, all of which had rules that came to bear on the size and use of a dock.

If you don't check things out, you're likely to be very surprised, in the negative sense of the word. If you don't know enough to list the relevant parties off the top of your head, go hire somebody who does.

11. *Build your contact list.* As you commission (or get access to) all of the relevant reports and inspections ordered, put together a running list of everybody who has participated in the process. Get phone numbers and e-mail addresses for *everyone.*

Why is this important? All of these documents are controlled by people who have their own agendas and problems. If one of them has a daughter whose soccer game conflicts with your closing schedule, your closing is going to lose every time. Keep after these people, where possible and appropriate. Keep them on task. Keep putting your requests in writing, and keep following up with confirming phone calls. And by the way, be respectful and polite, even as you are cracking the whip. As our mother/grandmother was fond of saying, "You can get more with a little honey added."

12. *Do your final walk-through.* Your final walk-through should be done just before closing—no more than a day before closing, in fact. On that walk-through, it's very likely that everything will look as anticipated. On the other hand, we've encountered last-minute roof leaks, vandalism, and even squatters who weren't supposed to be on the property at all.

Any problems like this give you the right to insist that the property "close in escrow." This means that everyone signs the documents, but neither title nor money changes hands until the seller either resolves the problem or gives you (the buyer) enough money to resolve the problem.

We honestly hope that the list we just walked through won't turn you off from the real estate business. What we are trying to do is give you a balanced picture of what a closing can look like— and how to increase your odds of participating in a *successful* closing. Good things in life rarely come easily. Success in real estate requires hard work and vigilance. A checklist is a good way of *focusing* that hard work and vigilance.

Mastering Real Estate Investment Strategy No. 58: Use a Seller's Checklist

So far, we've focused almost entirely on the perspective of the buyer, which in fact is the viewpoint that predominates in this book. Why? Because we're guessing that the prospective buyers are reading this book, and also because the seller is getting *out* of a set of obligations, whereas the buyer is assuming them. The buyer needs more help in almost every case.

But much of the same advice we offered to the buyer also applies to you as the seller: make sure the deed conforms to the property, and so on. You are not attending the closing hoping that it will fail; therefore, just like the buyer, you want to do what's necessary to make it succeed.

That being said, you as the seller have some distinctive opportunities and obligations, which we should look at now. First and foremost, your job is to move things along *as fast as possible*, so that you can get your money out of this particular property and get it out working for you again. We are amazed at the number of sellers who don't seem to understand this principle and who allow closings to be delayed, to the buyer's advantage.

As we have discussed before, time is money. In many cases, the buyer (especially if he is a seasoned investor) will try to stretch out the closing. Every day he can stretch out the closing, he is enjoying an interest-free option on your property. For that reason alone, time is working against you. You therefore need to exercise care in the contract phase to (1) make sure that time periods are shorter and (2) make clear that if the deadlines are not met, the contract can be voided at your option.

Hold inspection periods to 30 days on all properties ranging from a single-family house up to a quadraplex. (Bigger properties may require more time.) Require the buyer to file a loan application within 7 days, and to secure approval within 30 days. These are not unreasonable deadlines, although they will require people to move at a faster pace than they may find comfortable. Remember, if they don't meet your deadline, then you have the right, but not the obligation, to cancel the contract.

This can definitely work to your advantage. In some fast-moving real estate markets, you can get backup contracts beyond the one you signed, and potential buyers may be persuaded to start bidding against each other. For those of you in markets where this has not occurred, this may sound surprising, even unlikely. But in hot markets like California and Florida, backups and bidding wars are getting more common. Recently, for example, a property we were trying to acquire had several backups waiting with higher offers than our contract, and everyone was hoping we would stumble. (In fact, had we wanted to, we could have sold our contract to some of the backup people at a nice profit, but that wasn't our game plan for this property.)

Your most important worry, from a seller's standpoint, is whether the buyer can get the loan. Once you find that out, the process will move more quickly, but you do need to watch for this. If there is a problem, you need to be ready to help the buyer get the loan. This is where your contacts come in, and it may be that you need to refer the buyer to one of them to get the transaction done.

As a seller, be prepared to lend a hand if for some reason the appraisal comes in low. In rapidly moving markets, appraisers are generally the last to accept the fact that prices are moving faster than they think. This is particularly true if the appraiser is the lender's appraiser (and more and more lenders are using their own). It is in their interest, of course, because if you help them meet the cost of the property, they don't put themselves at risk of an overappraisal, and they reduce the chance that they will get stuck with the property if they ever have to foreclose.

The lender's appraiser will also want to make sure that she doesn't get her lender hung out on an overvalued property. If she does, she isn't likely to get any more business from that lender. Once she gets blackballed by the local lenders for overappraising property, she will have a hard time getting back into the club— and lenders, of course, are the appraiser's bread and butter.

Closing can be an interesting experience, to put it mildly. If you aren't attentive to the details, you can lose a lot of money. As boring as the process is, it's actually full of (hidden) drama, because the stakes are so high.

Inevitably you will see things on your closing statement that you didn't agree to and don't like. Some are legitimate, but you've forgotten about them, and it doesn't feel good to be reminded.

Some are outright stupid, like overnight express charges when the title company charging them is in the same building as the lender. (That one always gets us going!) Sometimes our wives tell us we should just let this kind of stuff slide, but for whatever reason, we can't. So pick your battles. Sometimes the little ones are worth fighting; sometimes they're not.

The bigger the transaction, the harder you will want to try to control the closing itself. On multimillion-dollar properties, we always try to close at our attorney's office, but often that isn't possible. If it isn't, then you should have your attorney present, and he should have his staff on standby. Most likely, some of the lending papers will need to be changed, and your attorney will have to work with the lender's attorney on the spot to make the changes. If this doesn't happen, the closing is delayed—and sometimes the deal falls apart forever.

Here's your motto going into the closing: *If it is important to get the deal done, get the deal done.* Say it before you walk in the door. Say it again when you hit those trivial, annoying, inevitable bumps in the road.

THE CLOSING CHECKLIST

☑ **DEVELOP AND USE A BUYER'S CHECKLIST.** There are least a dozen major things that you need to attend to, mostly in advance of the closing, that will make the transaction go more smoothly. Be vigilant! Take care of business!

☑ **DEVELOP AND USE A SELLER'S CHECKLIST.** This is a shorter checklist, even given the overlaps between your list and the buyer's list. Basically, you want to keep the process fast, and (when appropriate) to look for ways to keep the transaction on the rails. If you're willing and able to take back money, and that will keep the deal on track, make the offer at the appropriate time. (Have your lawyer in the room.)

CHAPTER 10

How to Borrow Money

You've probably seen ads on TV for books, videos, or seminars that will tell you how to "buy real estate with no money down."

This is indeed possible, and, in subsequent chapters, we'll tell you how it's done. You should understand, however, that not all real estate can be bought "nothing down," and if you have cash available for a down payment, you shouldn't miss out on making some money just because you have heard you should always buy "nothing down." This is a trap that some people get caught up in after they go to a "no-money-down" real estate seminar: they leave thinking that if they put cash down on their next purchase, they have somehow failed. They haven't.

Yes, there are many advantages to using "nothing down" and other creative financing strategies. And, yes, we try to use as little cash as possible to buy property. On the other hand, we want to keep an open mind for all options and focus on what is really important: *return on investment* (ROI).

Which brings us to the subject of lenders. No matter what kind of down payment you use, you most likely will have to deal with lenders (banks and other institutions) for the balance of the purchase price.

Lenders come in all shapes and sizes. They are a strange breed: they always want to loan you money when you *don't* need it; and when you *do* need it, they're suddenly hard to find. And just when you start to get comfortable with one, it will tell you that, because of some obscure regulation (maximum loan restriction to a borrower is common), it can't lend you any more money.

If you are going to be successful in real estate, you will have to learn how to court lenders, and you will have to learn to work with them. You will need to understand they are, in fact, under fairly tight regulatory controls, and you will have to work within those confines. The sooner you take a cooperative attitude toward your lender (being proactive, getting the lender what it needs in order to get your loan processed), the faster you'll get your project funded, and the quicker you'll be moving on to your next project.

The purpose of this chapter, therefore, is to help you understand the elements of the lending process to help move you quickly toward your first loan.

Who Are the Lenders?

The primary lenders on real estate are

- Banks
- Savings and loans
- Insurance companies (for commercial loans)
- REITs (primarily for large projects)

- Mortgage companies
- Pension funds (primarily for commercial loans)
- Private investors
- Hard-money lenders

If you are dealing with single-family properties, you will be working primarily with mortgage companies, banks, savings and loans, private investors, and hard-money lenders. As you move into bigger projects, you begin to encounter some of the bigger lenders we have listed, but don't worry about that now—unless, of course, you plan to jump into that arena from the very start.

The Two Ways of Dealing with Lenders

When dealing with lenders, you basically have two choices: you can deal directly with the institution's loan officer, or you can hire a mortgage broker to act as a go-between. The broker will charge you for this service, but if you're new to real estate investing, it may well be worthwhile. Even if you're experienced and have multiple deals to your credit, the time savings alone may make it worthwhile to engage a mortgage broker. We've said it before, and we'll keep on saying it: *time is money*. When you consider using or not using a broker, don't forget to figure in the cost of your time when you're making your calculations. We recommend that you *don't* make a hard-and-fast rule about dealing with brokers; instead, take it on a case-by-case basis.

In our own business, we've done it both ways: we've worked with lenders directly, and we've also worked through mortgage brokers. Yes, like everyone else, we like to save brokerage fees— but not if it costs us money in other ways. Here's your decision rule: get your deal financed quickly, and move on to the next one.

Mastering Real Estate Investment Strategy No. 59: Order a Free Credit Report

Whatever method of financing you ultimately choose, you will need good credit to get it. The way it works is simple: you apply for a loan, and the lender runs your credit report through one or more credit-reporting agencies (also known as "credit bureaus") to see if you're a good bet. If the credit agency says that you have a bad credit history (that is, that you have a track record of not meeting your obligations), your financing options will be limited. So let's devote a few pages to credit: getting it, and getting it on your terms.

First things first: check your credit to see if it is good, and if it's not, *clean it up as fast as you can.* Credit and credit scores have become so important today that it is extremely important that you stay on top of them. Since we are very active in real estate, we maintain a continuous open file on both our individual credit reports and our corporate reports. Why? Because the credit-reporting system is deeply flawed. The reporting agencies make mistakes all the time. You can run a report one minute and get one picture of your personal or corporate credit status, and then run it again literally a minute later and get a totally different picture. Believe us; we've done it. It's an unsettling experience.

Here's a case in point: a friend of ours spent a *whole year* correcting and improving his report—only to buy a new report one day and discover that all the mistakes that he had corrected over the course of the previous year had somehow crept back into his current report! Fortunately, he had kept copies of all the previous reports and correspondence, so he was able to get it properly fixed fairly painlessly. But frustrating? You bet.

The more you learn about credit reports and scoring, the more likely it is that you will get annoyed with the whole system and its erratic results. Well, we hate to say this, but the best advice we can offer is, *get used to it!* The system is what it is, and you have no choice but to deal with it. The best thing you can do is (1) learn the rules of the game and (2) play by the rules as best you can.

Thanks to a recent change to the Federal Fair Credit Reporting Act, you are now entitled to a free copy of your credit report once a year from each of the Big Three reporting companies. To meet this mandate, the three national consumer reporting companies have set up a central Web site and a single toll-free help number. To order your report, click on www.annualcreditreport.com, or call 877-322-8228. You can also write for a report at

Annual Credit Report Request Service
P.O. Box 105281
Atlanta, GA 30348-5281

We recommend that you call or go online. (It's just easier, as a rule.) If you write, you will need to provide your name, address, social security number, and date of birth. If you have moved in the last two years, be sure to include your previous address.

As noted, the law allows you to get one free report annually from each of the Big Three reporting companies: Equifax, Experian, and Trans Union. Here are their individual phone numbers and Web addresses:

Trans Union Corporation
800-916-8800
www.tuc.com

Experian National Consumer Assistance Center
888-EXPERIAN (888-397-3742)
www.experian.com

Equifax Credit Information Services
800-685-1111
www.equifax.com

Some people recommend getting one every four months so that you can keep an eye on things more often than once a year. The problem with doing that is that you get only a partial picture. We take a different approach: we order them all at once, so that we can perform a complete check of our whole credit picture. If you do it this way, you can compare the reports side by side and examine any differences that may show up. This is important because you never know which service a lender is going to pull from, so you need to make sure that they are all accurate. Another advantage to doing all three at once is that you can do it at the same time every year, thereby making the process nearly automatic. ("It's June 15—time to order up the credit reports.")

As we've already noted, reporting agencies make a lot of mistakes in the maintenance of consumer credit histories. It is all too common for someone who has never paid even a single bill late to discover that his or her credit report has negative entries that don't belong there. There are a lot of reasons why this happens, but the bigger point is, it's your job to set the record straight. Since the quality of your credit report determines your ability to borrow, you absolutely have to ensure that your credit report is 100 percent accurate and reflects your true credit history.

But that's not all you should be thinking about. You should review your credit report not just to look for mistakes that may have been made by the credit bureaus, but also as a means to help you gain (or regain) some perspective on your overall financial picture. When we review our own credit history, we sometimes find entries that are completely accurate, but that simply represent previous credit that we had forgotten about. For example, you will occasionally notice an open line of credit that you didn't remember you had. Well, assuming you no longer want it, *close* it. This is important, because if you have too many open lines of credit, that can hurt your chances of gaining any additional credit in the future—*even if you haven't tapped your existing lines of credit.*

This happened to a friend of ours when, because of a heavy travel schedule and lots of reimbursable airline tickets, he tried to raise his corporate credit card limit. His bank said no. Why? Because the credit agency added up all of his existing and largely untapped lines of credit (corporate *and* personal) and decided that he was a bad risk. "What if he decided to run up all those cards and lines at once?" the logic went. "He probably couldn't meet his monthly obligations." No matter that he had a spotless payment record up to that point! (Our friend kept the low-ceiling credit card—discussed later—and found another bank that was willing to issue a card with a higher limit.)

This is one good reason why you have to beware of the store credit cards that offer "10 percent off your purchase when you sign up for our credit card!" Too many of those 10 percent offs, and you may be setting yourself up for a difficult time in the future. In fact, your overall credit score may be lowered enough that you'll have to pay higher interest rates when you set out to borrow *big* money. So that "10 percent off" can be costly, in the long run.

Now that you can get your credit report for free, *do it*. No excuses! You simply can't afford not to. Don't take chances in this realm. You would be amazed at how many people with very modest, mostly inactive credit histories have had their lives thrown into turmoil because of negative entries that erroneously showed up on their credit reports and went unchallenged and uncorrected. Here's the rule: *Do not allow any more than 12 months to go by between reviews of your credit history.* You need to be able to catch any mistakes, close any unneeded lines of credit, and perform "preventive maintenance" in as timely a fashion as possible.

Mastering Real Estate Investment Strategy No. 60: Understand Your Credit Rights

If, after reviewing your credit report, you determine that it contains inaccuracies (particularly inaccuracies that reflect negatively on your credit history), then it's time to spring into action. Specifically, you want to dispute the entries directly with the credit bureau.

There are several ways you can dispute inaccurate information on your credit report. One is to utilize the bureau's own dispute form, which will be included with the copy of the report you receive. Another is to initiate a letter on your own to the agency, telling the bureau that you are disputing a specific entry. Finally, you can file a dispute online or by calling the bureau's customer-service department.

Once you initiate the dispute of an item on your credit report, according to the provisions of the Fair Credit Reporting Act, the bureau has 30 days to either verify the claim or remove the inaccuracy. While the credit bureaus are usually very good at removing verified inaccuracies promptly, don't take anything for granted. Make sure you request a copy of your revised credit report showing the mistake corrected. You are supposed to get this follow-up report free, as well.

If 30 days pass and you haven't heard anything about your case from the bureau you are working with, contact it again. The agency representatives will probably be very apologetic, and you should find your case resolved quickly at this point. If that does not happen, however, then you should send the agency a certified letter that demands a resolution to your case in your favor, as well as proof of that resolution, within seven days. Mention in your letter that if you do not hear from the agency within that time, then your next course of action will be to contact the Federal Trade Commission (FTC) to file a formal complaint. Then *follow through* on that course of action, if necessary. You can reach the FTC at 202-326-3650 or at www.ftc.gov.

Mastering Real Estate Investment Strategy No. 61: Have Negative Entries Removed from Your Credit File

Be very diligent about resolving any inaccuracies as quickly as possible. There is nothing worse than having your all-important credit hamstrung by negative entries that don't belong to you. Review your report, make note of inaccuracies, and get moving on eliminating them.

According to the Fair Credit Reporting Act, negative information more than seven years old is not supposed to appear on your credit report. If you find there is such an entry, then contact the credit bureau immediately about having it removed. You will be given a case number, and your dispute will be handled in much the same way that a dispute over inaccurate entries is treated.

There is one exception to the seven-year rule that should be noted. Bankruptcies may remain on your credit report for up to 10 years, so if you have a bankruptcy reflected on your credit report that is older than seven years but not older than ten, then its appearance on your report is not a violation of the FCRA. However, if ten years have passed since the bankruptcy, and it is still reflected on your credit report, then by all means be as proactive as you can about having the entry removed.

Being proactive is important. The people who staff credit bureaus are no different from most of the other service people we encounter in an average day. They tend to be individuals who view themselves as overworked and underpaid, and they look at their job chiefly in terms of the paycheck it provides. As a result, you must ensure that you are keeping a *very close watch* over the investigations taking place with respect to your credit report. Do not allow the credit bureau to be lax. Don't let it take longer than 30 days to respond to your dispute. *Stay on top of it.* Feel free to contact the credit bureau via telephone or e-mail to get an update on your situation.

We suggest going to the trouble and limited expense of making your follow-up inquiry via certified letter. If you send certified letters, you have a record of your correspondence with the credit bureaus. This will be important should it become necessary to prove (1) that you contacted them, and (2) when you contacted them. And in our experience, getting someone to sign something saying that he got your letter tends to have a wonderful focusing effect on that person. You tend to go into the right slot in the in-box.

One way to make your credit file appear more positive is to use your right to provide information regarding mitigating circumstances that may surround any of the negative information in your file. The only thing your credit report reflects is the cold, hard facts—such as that your payments on one of your accounts fell behind 60 days. You have the right to augment such an entry with whatever information you can about the circumstances surrounding the late payments that may serve to soften the blow of the information itself. For example, were you unemployed during the period you fell behind? Were you living out of the country during that period, and the creditor's bills never reached you? Make certain any relevant information like that makes it into your credit file. No, its appearance in your file will not change your credit score, but it could make a difference to a prospective employer or other entities—such as apartment-leasing companies—that use credit reports as a first screen.

Mastering Real Estate Investment Strategy No. 62: Know Your FICO Score

You may not know it, but there's something called a "FICO score" that determines how much you will pay in interest on any loans you take out. In fact, this single number, which is determined by the Fair Isaac Corporation (hence the acronym), affects almost every aspect of your financial life. It is the single most important financial factor that people will judge you on. It can determine whether or not you qualify for an apartment, and even whether or not you get a particular job. For our purposes, the higher your FICO score, the lower the interest rate that you will have to pay for mortgage money.

Most people don't know their score (or even know that it *exists*). But to succeed in real estate, you have to (1) understand your FICO score, (2) do everything you can to get it up as high as you can, and (3) *keep* it that way.

Your FICO score is based on your spending habits, where you live, how much you make, and how much you owe. The score ranges from 720 to 850 as the highest, and 500 to 559 as the lowest. Why is this important? Because a person with a low FICO score can pay as much as 3.5 percent more in interest (at current levels) than a person who has a high FICO score. On a $100,000 loan, that would mean an extra $515 per month in payment. You can see why it's important to work to improve your score.

Mastering Real Estate Investment Strategy No. 63: Improve Your Credit Score

Your first step toward improving your FICO score is to get a copy of it, either by getting a copy of your credit report, as previously discussed, or by going to www.MyFICO.com and getting it directly from the Fair Isaac Corporation for a small charge.

Let's say that, after reviewing your FICO, you decide you want to improve it. Here are five good ways to do so:

1. *Build credit, if you don't have any.* No, this doesn't mean you should run out and buy everything you can on credit. But if you've never established a line of credit, that works against a high FICO score. The solution: apply for one or two of the major credit cards like MasterCard, Visa, or American Express. If it's your first such card, you may have to play by some stringent rules that are imposed by the bank. No matter; it's important. And remember, *the point of getting these cards is to show that you can use credit responsibly.* You should use the cards, and you should pay them off in full every month. We do *not* want you to use this credit-building process as an excuse to go into debt.

2. *Make all of your credit payments on time.* It is better to pay the minimum amount on time than to pay more late. Being late on your payments by even one day can begin

dropping your FICO score and cost you in higher interest rates in the future.

3. *Keep your debt-to-credit ratio as low as possible.* This means that the total debt on your cards should be as low as you can keep it, compared to the credit limit allowed. Maxed-out credit cards lower your score.

4. *Don't try to get a lot of credit at once.* In other words, don't run right out and try to get multiple credit cards as soon as you've finished this chapter. Lots of activity at one time makes credit people nervous. Their computers think you must have a cash-flow problem, and they lower your score.

5. *History helps.* The longer you have credit with people, the more you look like a good risk. So once you get a card, keep it. We actually made a mistake in this area, once: we canceled some older credit card accounts, thinking that this would be helpful to our FICO score. It wasn't— because (a) it eliminated the good history behind those cards, and (b) it increased our debt-to-credit ratio. We didn't make *that* particular mistake again!

Mastering Real Estate Investment Strategy No. 64: Master the Lending Process

First things first: we would like to tell you that the process of getting a loan is fun, but frankly, it isn't. In fact, it is slow, tedious, and frustrating. But once again, the system is what it is. You won't be able to buy real estate until you understand how it works, and how to move through it as quickly as possible.

The first thing you need to understand is that, as we noted at the outset of the chapter, lending is heavily regulated. While lenders tend to be conservative by nature, having the government looking over your shoulder (making sure that your bank is making good loans) only adds to the pressure they're under and reinforces their conservative nature.

Once you understand and accept this, it will help you be patient. Patience will stand you in good stead when you are asked more questions than you thought was humanly possible, and when you are asked to sign documents that are thrust upon you at the last possible moment that you don't have time to read even if you wanted to. But guess what: a lot of the bureaucracy and paperwork associated with traditional banks actually *works in your favor* in the long run. In fact, the farther you get away from this kind of stuff—the farther down the lending food chain you find yourself, and the more unconventional the lender you embrace—the more cautious you need to be.

Step 1: Create a positive financial statement. The first step in any loan process is to complete the lender's loan application and financial statement. Loan applications are fairly short in today's lending world, but the complicated appearance of the financial statement still intimidates some people. Fortunately, the credit report you just obtained (right?) makes the financial statement easy to complete because most of your assets, liabilities, and lenders' names, addresses, and account numbers are already listed. It is a simple matter of transferring the data from one place to another and adding anything that's missing. While it would be wonderful if you could fill out a single, universal financial statement—something like the so-called common application that lots of colleges use today—you can't. Lenders all have their own financial statement forms (even though they are almost the same), and each will insist that you fill out its version. Don't fight the process, because you won't get anywhere.

When you complete the financial statement, do so with care, because you will be asked to sign it—and it is a federal offense to file a false one. No, you don't have to worry about getting every last credit card down to the last dime, but you are responsible for giving an accurate accounting of your assets and liabilities, so be complete. In addition, some lenders scrutinize your frankness in reporting as an indicator of your trustworthiness—and they'll have ways to double-check. For instance, your loan application will ask you easy questions, like, "How much are your monthly payments on your home?" Well, guess what? They are going to find this out, in precise detail, once they run your credit report. So why do they ask? Call it a lender's lie detector. They want to see if you'll fudge. Don't.

Step 2: The loan committee. Up until this point in the lending process, you have dealt principally with a loan officer. Now, your loan application will be processed by the loan committee, sometimes known as the "lending committee." The loan committee may strike you as being something like a secret society, because you can't see its members or talk to them. This is deliberate; they don't *want* to see you, because they don't want to risk having their judgment clouded by any personal knowledge of you. They are supposed to be unbiased and to make decisions based solely on the cold, hard facts contained in your loan application.

In fact, you'll never know exactly what went on behind those closed doors. If you get turned down, your loan officer will be sympathetic and will blame it all on the committee. If your loan is approved, the loan officer will take all the credit, explaining in detail (probably including some exaggeration) how hard he fought for you.

Let's assume that your loan has gotten past the loan committee and is now moving forward. Depending on the size of the loan and the size of the lender, your loan package may now be sent to "Underwriting" for pre- or postapproval. "Underwriting" translates roughly into "Department of Bean Counting." Its job is to dot every "I" and cross every "T" in the loan process. Well, as noted, some of these people are inherently fussy. But more important, since most loans are packaged up and sold to large institutions or funds, the packages have to be prepared to the ultimate buyer's specifications. Once the local lender sells the loan, it has more money to lend, and the process starts all over again.

Underwriting is usually where loans hit snags. Our advice, therefore, is to respond to Underwriting's requests for more information as quickly and as thoroughly as possible. Just picture someone sitting at a desk in some small room. On the desk are two rubber stamps. One says "APPROVED," and the other says "REJECTED." Give Underwriting as many reasons as you can to pick up the "APPROVED" stamp.

Step 3: The loan commitment. Particularly in the case of a commercial property, you are likely to get a loan commitment sent to you from the bank telling you how much it is willing to lend, the terms of the financing, the costs, and a list of all the documents you will have to supply to get your deal done. Frankly, this is the point in the process where we start running out of patience. We often ask ourselves if it is *really worth it.* Getting everything together seems so tedious and so time-consuming!

It's also when we have to remind ourselves (and when you should remind yourself) that this kind of short-term aggravation is a small price to pay for long-term gain. Hang in there!

If you are new to the real estate business, the loan commitment appears to be etched in stone. But it isn't. The banker would prefer that you not know this, but the loan commitment is simply an *offer*, which you can accept, reject, or make a counter to.

This is a *negotiation*, despite the hard-nosed sound of "commitment." Everything is negotiable—particularly if you are lucky enough to have secured two commitments.

Lenders don't really like you to shop deals around among multiple lenders. Frankly, when we have a working relationship with a lender that has proved successful in the past, we tend to stick with that lender. But shopping *does* result in competition, and competition results in savings. Your position is immensely stronger at the commitment stage if you can play one lender against another.

Lending has also changed in recent years because of the Internet and the creation of sites like Lendingtree.com. If you use one of these sites, you will get multiple offers on all kinds of loans from competing lenders. This has really made the process faster and cheaper for the consumer, who only a few years ago had very few choices. Be forewarned, however, that you will continue to get e-mails from lenders long after your closing. It's an aggravation, but (depending on the deal you get) it can be well worth it.

Step 4: Accepting the lender's offer. Once you accept the lender's offer, you move to the closing stage of your transaction. Between the lender, the attorneys, and the federal government, closings can be a bureaucratic nightmare. You will sign more papers than you think is possible, and (for some reason) you will get only a limited amount of time to review them. Sure, they say you get longer, and you'll even be asked to sign an affidavit that says you have had time to review everything.

Sign it. And rest assured that some day, when you least expect it, somebody's going to answer your angry question by saying, "Well, you signed it at closing." At that point, you can just smile, like the rest of us, and know that you've been had by the process.

Once again, though, these are little bumps in the road. You need to keep your eye on the big picture. Don't drive yourself crazy looking backwards. Keep looking forward.

THE LOAN CHECKLIST

☑ **GET YOUR CREDIT IN ORDER FIRST.** Take advantage of the Fair Credit Reporting Act's provisions, and get your free annual credit report from all three major credit reporting agencies. Scrutinize the reports for mistakes, and get those mistakes fixed! Get outdated entries removed. Annotate your record, if there were mitigating circumstances that explain some negative entries.

☑ **PUSH THAT FICO SCORE HIGHER.** Get your FICO score, and start working on ways to push it higher— and get the benefit of lower interest rates as a result. How? Establish your credit history, make timely payments, keep your debt-to-credit ratio down, don't make any sudden credit-related moves, and let your good history work for you.

☑ **UNDERSTAND AND WORK WITH YOUR LENDERS.** Lenders are a strange breed, and they play by strange rules. For better or worse, you have to play by those rules, not your own. Be patient. Create the strongest possible financial statement. Work with each of the key players in sequence: the loan officer, the loan committee, and Underwriting. Figure out whether a little healthy competition will work in your favor. (It sometimes does and sometimes doesn't.) In the commitment and closing phases, be prepared to sign a blizzard of papers—some of which may come back to haunt you some day. Don't lose any sleep over this. You're getting rich, and Underwriting is not.

CHAPTER 11

Landlord Magic

B eing a landlord is both an art and a science. It is an art because you have to deal with so many different people, personalities, and problems that you need the ability to go with the flow, think on your feet, and improvise. It is a science because if you are not absolutely systematic and organized, landlording is sure to drive you crazy—and you are likely to give up a lot of the profit potential that is inherent in every one of your properties.

We thought that rather than beat around the bush, we'd tell you our secret to landlording right off the bat. Are you ready? Here it is: *let someone else do it.*

OK, now we feel better. Yes, we are finally admitting that there's something we *don't* like about real estate, and that is the job of managing properties. At one time, we even operated a property management business, which actually made good money. No matter; to us, it isn't worth it.

Now, we are well aware that there are some landlord types out there who will read this and get a get chuckle about how much money we are giving up to someone else—"just to do property management," as they would put it. Well, more power to them. You can't do everything. We would much rather let someone else manage, and let us go out and find new deals.

So, based on this admission, you might think that this won't be a very interesting or useful chapter. We hope that's not the case. In fact, many of the things we don't like about management grew out of mistakes we made while trying to manage properties. So whether or not you were born to be a landlord, you can certainly learn from the mistakes made by people who were not.

Ranking the Properties

The first Landlording Truth for you to get your arms around is that *not all landlording is the same.* Single-family rental management (which we have done) is on one end of the real estate spectrum, and high-end commercial property management (and we have done that, too) is on the other. The latter is a lot easier, and a lot more profitable. At the same time, it also provides contacts and sometimes even turns up good leads for properties to buy. So if you like this kind of work, go for it.

Handling single-family rentals is another thing altogether. It is very tough work, and you sometimes have to deal with very emotional situations—such as having to evict people who, through no fault of their own, are going through a difficult period. (Your actions are making it *more* difficult.) You also have to deal with people who strike you as obnoxious, dangerous, or both.

We keep reminding ourselves that some people really *like* this work. Even today, we fondly remember a battle-ax of a woman who handled all of our residential rentals many years back. She could hold her own in any verbal battle, and she was *tough as nails* when it came to collecting rent. If you paid on time, you didn't have a problem. If you didn't, you were *gone.* No exceptions. She knew the legal system, and she understood landlord and tenant rights (as summarized in our state's Landlords and Tenants Act) better than any attorney in town. She could post a three-day eviction notice faster than anyone else we have ever known—and if you missed the day, you were out, because she knew all the judges from having dealt with them so often in their courtrooms. They knew she knew what she was doing, and so they ruled in her favor most of the time. She was truly amazing, and paying her 10 percent of the rents she collected was the best money we ever spent.

Mastering Real Estate Investment Strategy No. 65: Learn the Property Rule

The lesson of that particular story is that as a property manager, you absolutely *must know* the Landlords and Tenants Act (or similar statute) in your state. They are different in all states, and there are even some local city rules that you may have to follow in your area—and follow them you must! Yes, if you have bad tenants, they can "work" you, and you'll lose some money as a result, but if you unlawfully evict someone, you can expose yourself to additional liability and (in some cases) fines. So, read your Landlords and Tenants Act, and if you don't understand it completely, hire an attorney to explain it to you.

The next thing you have to do is *get a good lease* to use. Unfortunately, you can't just go out and buy a standard lease from your local stationery supply store. Standard-form leases are simply too pro-tenant. The good news is that we have included a sample of a great lease later in this chapter—a lease that we used for many years, and that we have shared with people all over the country with never a negative remark. The lease is very simple, and it has some great pro-landlord language that we'll go over with you.

The bad news is that our lease is included here *for educational purposes only*. You are *not* encouraged to simply copy it and use it. Why? Because if you do so, you might unwittingly create problems for yourself somewhere down the line, and we don't want that. So, take the lease to your attorney, and have him review it and give you his blessing, with whatever changes he suggests. *Then* feel free to use it. Fair enough?

Mastering Real Estate Investment Strategy No. 66: Get the Best Tenants

At the time we write this, getting tenants for residential property is not difficult, because there is strong demand. Occupancy for commercial properties is also high. This changes with the economy, however, in cycles of about seven years. If you're in the game long enough, sooner or later you'll experience both high demand and slack demand. You have to be prepared to deal with both.

The first step toward being a good landlord, and having good tenants, starts with buying the right property. There is an old saying that you "buy the neighbor, not the house." What goes on with your rental is often determined by the type of neighborhood your property is in. You can always improve the property, but you can't fix the neighborhood. It may sound harsh, but if you buy in a run-down neighborhood, you're likely to have run-down tenants.

Buy your properties in areas where people *want* to live, not where they *have* to live. The closer your rental is to shopping, churches, schools, and recreation, the easier it will be to find tenants. You want Middle America, and Middle America wants these amenities.

If you buy properties in "rental areas," they will not be as attractive to tenants, because, generally speaking, people really do want to live in the best part of town. If you can get residences in owner-occupied areas, you're going to have your pick of tenants, and they will stay longer.

You really don't want much from a tenant—just to *pay on time and take reasonable care of the property while you are here.* Pretty simple, huh? But to make things go a little more easily, there are some things you need to do:

1. *Get a rental application from the tenant.* You want to know as much as you can about this person while you are on good terms with her, and this is the easiest chance you will have. Find out where she works and how much she makes, and get references from past landlords. Call the references. If you don't call the references, you will regret it.

2. *Run a credit report on each tenant.* As a landlord, you can get authorization to run credit checks on people who want to rent from you. We have discussed how thorough-going credit reports have become in recent years. If you run a report, you will find out a lot about your prospective tenant, including his payment history and if he is creditworthy. If the tenant has a recent habit of paying late, there is a strong likelihood that this will continue while he is in your property. Understand that if you

accept this tenant and he pays you late, you may be late on your mortgage payment, which could then affect your credit. You will need a reserve as a minimum.

3. *Get a decent security deposit* (a sum of money put up by the tenant against possible damage she might cause to the property). "Decent" is up to one month's rent. The more you can get, the less trouble you will have. If the tenants can't make the deposit all at once, consider spreading it out over a couple of months for them. The market will dictate how hard-nosed you can be on this, but the bottom line is, *the more you can get, the better off you are.*

Mastering Real Estate Investment Strategy No. 67: Manage People, Not Property

A friend of ours once told us that he managed *people*, not property, and we thought that made a lot of sense.

Problems with properties are pretty easy to deal with. You occasionally run into a true disaster, but for the most part, fixing a property problem means calling the plumber, the electrician, or the HVAC guy; making sure he knows what he's doing; then making sure that he does what he says he's going to do; and finally making sure that you don't pay too much.

Problems with people are not so easy. The truth is that from the very beginning, you must *learn to control your tenants, or they will control you.* This includes being selective from the start. Like we said, if they have been late payers before, chances are they will be again. You need to establish controls quickly. State the rules and the consequences of breaking the rules. Then *enforce* the rules and impose the consequences.

Learn to Keep Good Records

As a landlord, you need to keep a lot of records. At the very least, these include

- Income and expense reports
- Receipts for repairs
- Correspondence with tenants
- Legal files for leases and eviction notices

Landlording is a paper-based business. You need the records to show you and your tenant what was paid and when you received it. The oldest trick in the book is for the tenant to say, "I sent you the check." Well, maybe she did, but it doesn't count unless you got it. Keep copies of all the rent checks you deposit. And on the other side of the ledger, file away all of your canceled checks. You will need the income and expense reports for tax time, and you will also have to keep maintenance and repair records in case you are audited.

Official correspondence with tenants should always go by certified mail, with a return receipt requested. You want proof that (1) you sent the notice and (2) the tenant got it. The worst thing for your position as landlord is to get into a disagreement about whether or not you sent a given notice. Without backup paperwork, you lose. So plan ahead. If any problem starts looking like it may lead to legal proceedings, start a separate file. Make sure everything is put in writing. If you have a conversation with the tenant in question, send a confirming memo about what was said and when you said it (certified mail, return receipt requested). If it's a close call, the party with the better paper trail usually prevails.

Setting the Rent

There are rules of thumb for everything in real estate. Historically, annual rents on a property were pegged to cover 1 percent of the purchase price, collectively. But given the rise in purchase prices over the past few years, you'd have a lot of vacancies if you tried to hit that lofty target. Likewise, setting rents based on your mortgage payment doesn't work very well, either. What you have to do is set the rate based on comparables in the area.

To determine comparable rents will require a little detective work, but not much. Set aside a day to investigate the local rental options. Call and visit other properties similar to yours, and see what they charge. Some people do this by posing as a tenant, but we believe it's better to always be straight up with people—telling them what you are doing and asking for their advice. You may find that the owner or property manager knows of some good tenants who are looking for a property like yours. You may even find someone who's ready to sell and who represents your next great deal.

Five Key Decisions

Once you have set your rental rate, there are other key questions you have to answer:

1. *How long a lease will you require?* The right answer is usually a 12-month lease. If you can anticipate a time of year that brings lots of potential renters to town (like the end of summer in a college town), you might want to time the end of the lease to correspond to that peak period. We'll discuss longer leases in a subsequent section.

2. *Will you rent to people with children?* It's tempting to exclude kids, who may make excess noise and tear the

place up. There are two problems with this: by excluding kids, you will screen out a large part of the rental population, and you may run afoul of local antidiscrimination statutes. Check with your lawyer.

3. *Are pets allowed?* Obviously, pets can be a problem. On the other hand, if you *do* accept pets, you can tap into the pool of pet owners who have been barred from renting elsewhere. If you accept pets, set up a separate pet agreement, with an associated security deposit. You can also charge a little more rent, but not much.

4. *How big a security deposit will you require?* As noted earlier, one month's rent is fairly standard. Some landlords can get away with asking for the first month's rent, the last month's rent, and a security deposit equivalent to a month's rent. That's a lot of money for a renter to come up with at once, and you may have to be flexible.

5. *What specials will you offer?* You want to rent the place quickly. (Your time is money, and an empty unit is lost money.) Will you offer tenants a discount if they sign an application today?

Mastering Real Estate Investment Strategy No. 68: Search for Great Tenants

Finding tenants may be easy. But finding *great* tenants is never easy. You have to work at it. Here are some tips:

- *Put a sign in the front yard.* Use one of those signs with a tube attached, in which you can insert a flyer with property information. Let the "lookers" read the information and prescreen themselves.

- *Post flyers on community bulletin boards.* Most grocery stores and drugstores maintain these as a community service. Use them.
- *Canvass your neighbors.* Ask if they know anyone who might be interested in renting your property.
- *Advertise prominently in community papers.* They are much cheaper than city papers, and they usually generate a good response.
- *Advertise selectively in city papers.* This is expensive, so you need to be concise. In the ad, include the phrase, "recorded message," with a phone number. Have that phone answered by an answering machine, which gives an upbeat (even glowing!) description of the property. State your price and terms, and how people can get in touch with you if they are interested.

What's the point of these strategies? They broaden the pool, helping you find the great tenants. They let you establish control of the process from the start. And they don't require you to sit around waiting for your phone to ring. When times get leaner and tenants get scarce, you may have to get more personally involved (discussed later in the chapter). For now, though, enjoy the upside of the cycle.

Showing Your Property

If you are the landlord or building manager, it's your job to show the property. And since most people can't see it except when they are off work, you're talking about working a lot of nights and weekends. If you follow the traditional approach of meeting the prospects at the property, you're going to spend a lot of time at the property waiting for the potential tenant to show up—which may not happen. Sometimes you get "stood up."

We favored a different approach. Have the prospective tenants come to you and pick up the key (but not at your home). Have them leave a credit card, check, or cash deposit (say, $20) for the key. In some cases, you might want to run a credit check on the tenant first, to minimize your risk.

An alternative is to buy a combination lockbox with a key inside, and mount it temporarily by the door of the property. Give prospective tenants the combination when they call, and when you rent the property, have it rekeyed.

A third alternative is to make one appointment to view the house with all the tenant prospects at the same time. To create some urgency, tell them that this is what you're doing. There is nothing more productive than a bidding war, and when prospective renters go to a property with the "competition," bidding wars may result.

The Rental Application

Getting a completed rental application is important because (1) it sets a professional tone for the transaction and (2) you gain valuable information about the tenant. Here's a form we have used:

RENTAL/PURCHASE APPLICATION

Property Applied For:_____ Move-in Date: _____

Monthly Rent:_____ On Time Disc:_____ Term:_____

Months Security Deposit: _____ + Nonrefundable Pet
     Deposit: _____

Tenant/Purchaser Name Last: _____ First: _____

SS#:_____ Date of Birth:_____/ _____/ _____

Nearest Relative Not Living with You:_____ Phone: _____

Emergency Contact Name:_____ Phone: _____

Current Residence

Current Residence Address: _____

Apartment #_____ City: _____ State/Zip: _____

Current Home Phone:_____

Landlord: _____ Phone: _____

How Long Have You Lived There? _____Monthly Pmt: _____

Address on Driver's License: _____

Why Moving: _____

Driver's License #/State: _____

Type of Car: _____ Year: _____ Tag #/State:_____

Employment

Occupation: _____ How Long? _____

Employer: _____

Address: _____

Employer Phone Number: _____ Contact Person: _____

Monthly Income: _____ Other Income: _____

Source: _____

Dentist: _____ Phone: _____

Doctor: _____ Phone: _____

If I/we are accepted, the following persons will be living with me/us:

Name	Relationship
1) _____	_____
2) _____	_____
3) _____	_____
4) _____	_____
5) _____	_____
6) _____	_____

Description of Pets: _____

Bank References

Checking _____ Account # _____ Balance: _____

Savings_____ Account # _____ Balance: _____

Credit Cards (VISA/MC/AMEX)

Name: _____ Account # _____Exp Date: _____

Name: _____ Account # _____Exp Date: _____

Do you own any real estate now? ( ) Yes ( ) No

If Yes, give address below _____

Have you ever filed for bankruptcy? ( ) Yes ( ) No

If Yes, discharge date _____

Have you ever been evicted from tenancy? ( ) Yes ( ) No

Please List Any Skills You May Have Relevant to Property Maintenance:

I hereby certify that the answers that I have given in this application are true to the best of my knowledge. I understand that false answers or statements made by me will be sufficient grounds for eviction/foreclosure and loss of all monies paid. Furthermore, if for any reason I become delinquent in my rent, I authorize you to use my MasterCard, Visa, or other credit card listed above or that I may obtain. I authorize you to examine any information located on my credit and criminal records.

Applicant Signature: _____ Date: _____

A couple of observations: first, *check those references.* It's amazing how often references don't check out. Make the call yourself, and see.

The application also contains a place to list all of the individuals who will occupy the property, and your lease should specifically list each person. There have been many occasions where tenants have tried to add family members later, or even sublet rooms. You have to control this situation, or your property can get worn out very quickly.

You will note there is a place for tenants to list their relevant skills. We have found this helpful when something needs to be repaired at the property or at one of your other properties. If you can, pay the tenant to do some of this work. He will probably do a better job than someone equally skilled who doesn't live there, and this can help build a stronger relationship between you and the tenant.

Finally, you will note that there is a place for the prospective tenant to sign and certify that the information provided is true. If it isn't signed, this is grounds for termination, and that gives you some strong leverage if you need to go to court.

Mastering Real Estate Investment Strategy No. 69: Have a Strong Lease

To protect yourself and your interests, you must have a strong lease. Should you ever have to evict the tenant, the lease will control your actions.

Some leases feature very small print and therefore are tricky to read. Don't be tricky. Use standard 8½" by 11" paper, and prepare it in an easily readable form. Make two copies, and have all the tenants sign or initial each page to indicate that they have read it. Then make enough copies to go around.

The lease that follows is the one we mentioned earlier. Again, *please have it reviewed by your attorney*, and ask her to adapt it to your state laws and local customs. We suggest that you scan it first, and then read the comments that follow it:

RESIDENTIAL LEASE AGREEMENT

THIS LEASE AGREEMENT is made and entered into this _____day of_____, 20_____, by and between _____ ("Landlord") having an office or mailing address residing at _____ and _____ ("Tenants") residing at _____.

1. Landlord leases to Tenant and Tenant leases from Landlord, upon the terms and conditions contained herein, the dwelling located at _____for the period commencing on the _____ day of _____, 20_____, and thereafter until the _____day of _____, 20 _____, at which time this Lease Agreement shall terminate.

2. Tenant shall pay as rent the sum of $_____ per month, due and payable monthly, in advance, no later than 5:00 p.m. on the first day of every month. Tenant further agrees to pay a late charge of $3.00 for each day rent is not received by the Landlord regardless of the cause, including dishonored checks, time being of the essence. An additional Service Charge of $20.00 will be paid to Landlord for all dishonored checks.

3. As an incentive to Tenant to make rent payments on time, and for being responsible for all minor maintenance of the premises, a discount in the amount of $_____ may be deducted from the above rental amount each month. Said discount will be forfeited if Tenant fails to perform as stated above.

4. Tenant agrees to use said dwelling as living quarters only for _____ adults and _____ children, namely: _____, and to pay $50.00 each month for each other person who shall occupy the premises in any capacity.

5. Tenant agrees to accept the property in its current condition and to return it in "moving-in clean" condition, or to pay a special cleaning charge of $75.00 upon vacating the premises.

6. As additional rent, Tenant agrees to pay a nonrefundable pet fee of $10.00 per month for each pet. All pets on the property not registered under this Lease shall be presumed to be strays and will be disposed of by the appropriate agency as prescribed by law. A Pet Agreement, if applicable, is attached hereto as Exhibit B, and incorporated herein by reference.

   PET NAMES AND DESCRIPTION: _____.

7. Tenant agrees not to assign this Lease, nor to sublet any portion of the property, nor to allow any other person to live therein other than as named in paragraph 4 above without first obtaining written permission from Landlord and paying the appropriate surcharge. Further, it is agreed that covenants contained in this Lease, once breached, cannot afterward be performed, and that unlawful detainer proceedings may be commenced at once, without notice to Tenant.

8. Should any provision of this Lease be found to be invalid or unenforceable, the remainder of the Lease shall not be affected thereby, and each term and provision herein shall be valid and enforceable to the fullest extent permitted by law.

9. All rights given to Landlord by this Lease shall be cumulative to any other laws that might exist or come into being. Any exercise or failure to exercise by Landlord of any right shall not act as a waiver of any other rights. No statement or promise of Landlord or his agent as to tenancy, repairs, alterations, or other terms and conditions shall be binding unless reduced to writing and signed by Landlord.

10. Tenant will be responsible for payment of all utilities, garbage, water and sewer charges, telephone, gas, association fees, or other bills incurred during the term of this Lease. Tenant specifically authorizes Landlord to deduct amounts of any unpaid bills from the security deposit upon termination of this Agreement.

11. No rights of storage are given by this Agreement. Landlord shall not be liable for any loss of Tenant's property by fire, theft, breakage, burglary, or otherwise, nor for any acciden-

tal damage to persons or property in or about the leased premises resulting from electrical failure, water, rain, windstorm, etc., which may cause issue or flow into or from any part of said premises or improvements, including pipes, gas lines, sprinklers, or electrical connections, whether caused by the negligence of Landlord, Landlord's employees, contractors, agents, or by any other cause whatsoever. Tenant hereby agrees to make no claim for any such damages or loss against Landlord. Tenant shall purchase renter's insurance on all personal property if such coverage is desired.

12. Any removal of Landlord's property without express written permission from the Landlord shall constitute abandonment and surrender of the premises and termination by the resident of this Agreement. Landlord may take immediate possession, exclude Tenant from property, and store all Tenant's possessions at Tenant's expense pending reimbursement in full for Landlord's loss and damages.

13. Landlord has the right of emergency access to the leased premises at any time and access during reasonable hours to inspect the property or to show property to a prospective tenant.

14. Tenant agrees to pay a Security Deposit of $_____ to secure Tenant's pledge of full compliance with the terms of this agreement. **NOTE: SECURITY DEPOSIT MAY NOT BE USED TO PAY RENT UNDER ANY CIRCUMSTANCES!** Any damages not previously reported as required in paragraph 25 will be repaired at Tenant's expense with funds other than Security Deposit.

15. Release of security deposit is subject to provisions of law and the following:

   A. The full term of the Agreement has been completed.

   B. No damage to the premises, buildings, grounds is evident.

   C. The entire dwelling. appliances, closets, and cupboards are clean and free from insects, the refrigerator is defrosted, all debris and rubbish have been removed from the property, carpets are vacuumed and shampooed and left clean and odorless.

D. All unpaid charges have been paid, including late charges, visitor charges, pet charges, delinquent rents, etc.

E. All keys have been returned.

F. A forwarding address for Tenant has been left with Landlord.

Within thirty (30) days after termination of occupancy, the Landlord will mail the balance of the deposit to the address provided by Tenant in the names of all signatories hereto; or Landlord will impose a claim on the deposit and so notify the Tenant.

16. The acceptance by Landlord of partial payments of rent due shall not, under any circumstances, constitute a waiver of Landlord, nor affect any notice or legal proceeding in unlawful detainer theretofore given or commenced under state law.

17. If Tenant leaves said premises unoccupied for 15 days while rent is due and unpaid, Landlord is granted the right hereunder to take immediate possession thereof and to exclude Tenant therefrom; removing all Tenant's property contained therein and placing it into storage at Tenant's expense.

18. Payment of rent may be made by check until the first check is returned unpaid. Regardless of cause, no additional payments may afterwards be made by check. Rent must then be made by cashier's check, money order, or certified check.

19. Rent may be mailed through the United States Postal Service at the tenant's risk. Any rents lost in the mail will be treated as if unpaid until received by Landlord.

20. Tenant agrees, without protest, to reimburse Landlord for all actual and reasonable expenses incurred by way of Tenant's violation of any term or provision of this lease, including, but not limited to $10.00 for each Notice to Pay, Notice to Quit, or other notice mailed or delivered by

Landlord to Tenant due to Tenant's nonpayment of rent, all court costs and attorney's fees, and all costs of collection. Both Landlord and Tenant waive trial by jury and agree to submit to the personal jurisdiction and venue of a court of subject matter jurisdiction located in _____ County, State of _____. In such event, no action shall be entertained by said court or any court of competent jurisdiction if filed more than one year subsequent to the date the cause(s) of action accrued.

21. Tenant agrees to accept said dwelling and all of the furnishings and appliances therein as being in good and satisfactory condition unless a written statement of any objections is delivered to Landlord within three (3) days after resident takes possession. Tenant agrees that failure to file such statement shall be conclusive proof that there were no defects in the property. Tenant agrees not to permit any damage to the premises during the period of this agreement to woodwork, floors, walls, furnishings, fixtures, appliances, windows, screens, doors, lawns, landscaping, fences, plumbing, electrical, air conditioning and heating, and mechanical systems. Tenant specifically agrees that he will be responsible for, and agrees to pay for, any damage done by rain, wind, or hail caused by leaving windows open; overflow of water or stoppage of waste pipes, breakage of glass, damage to screens, deterioration of lawns and landscaping whether caused by drought, abuse, or neglect. Tenant agrees not to park or store a motor home, recreational vehicle or trailer of any type on the premises.

22. Tenant's obligations are as follows:

    A. Take affirmative action to ensure that nothing is done which might place Landlord in violation of applicable building, housing, zoning, and health codes and regulations.

    B. Keep the dwelling clean and sanitary, removing garbage and trash as it accumulates, maintaining plumbing in good working order to prevent stoppages and leakage of plumbing fixtures, faucets, pipes, etc.

C. Operate all electrical, plumbing, sanitary, heating, ventilating, air conditioning, and other appliances in a reasonable, safe manner.

D. Assure that property belonging to Landlord is safeguarded against damage, destruction, loss, removal, or theft.

E. Conduct himself, his family, friends, guests, and visitors in a manner that will not disturb others.

F. Allow the Landlord or his agent access to the premises for the purpose of inspection, repairs, or to show the property to someone else at reasonable hours on request, and to specifically authorize unannounced access any time rent is late, or this Agreement is terminated, or for purposes of controlling pests, making maintenance estimates, serving legal notices, or responding to emergencies.

G. Comply with all provisions of this Agreement, particularly with respect to paying the rent on time and caring for the property.

Tenant warrants that he/she will meet the above conditions in every respect, and acknowledges that failure to perform the obligations herein stipulated will be considered grounds for termination of this Agreement and loss of all deposits.

23. No additional locks will be installed on any door without written permission from the Landlord. Landlord is to be provided duplicate keys for all locks so installed at Tenant's expense within 24 hours of installation of said locks.

24. Tenant agrees to install and maintain a telephone, and to furnish the Landlord the telephone number and/or any changes thereof within three (3) days of its installation.

25. In the event repairs are needed beyond the competence of the Tenant, Tenant is urged to contact the Landlord. Tenant is offered the discount as an incentive to make his own decisions on repairs to the property and to allow Landlord to rent the property without the need to employ professional management. Therefore, as much as possible, Tenant should refrain from contacting the Landlord or his agent

except for emergencies, or for expensive repairs. Such involvement by the Landlord or his agent will result in the loss of the Discount and/or deductible.

26. Tenant warrants that any work or repairs performed by him will be undertaken only if he is competent and qualified to perform it. Tenant will be totally responsible for all activities to assure that work is done in a safe manner that will meet all the applicable codes and statutes. Tenant further warrants that he will be accountable for any mishaps and/or accidents resulting from such work, and will hold the Landlord free from harm, litigation, or claims of any other person.

27. Tenant is responsible for all plumbing repairs, including faucets, leaks, stopped-up pipes, frozen pipes, water damage, and bathroom caulking.

28. Appliances or furniture in the unit at date of lease, per the attached Exhibit A, are loaned, not leased, to Tenant. Maintenance of appliances or furniture is the responsibility of Tenant who will keep them in good repair.

29. Tenant is responsible for all glass, screen, and storm door repairs.

30. No money is to be deducted by Tenant from rent payment **for any reason** without express **written** permission of Landlord.

31. Regardless of assignment of responsibility, Tenant agrees to be responsible for the first $50.00 of any repair or maintenance required on the major systems of the property for the term of the lease. This deductible applies per occurrence.

32. Tenant accepts entirely the responsibility for recharging air conditioner compressors and the cleaning of furnace or replacement of furnace filters.

33. All parties agree that termination of this Agreement prior to termination date will constitute breach of the tenancy and all Security Deposits and one full month's rent shall be forfeited in favor of Landlord as liquidated damages, at Landlord's option, following termination.

34. From time to time, owner may be represented by an agent who will carry identification.

35. In this Agreement the singular number where used will also include the plural, the masculine gender will also include the feminine, the term Landlord will include Owner or Lessor; and the term Tenant(s) will include Resident, Lessee, or Rentor.

36. Unless specifically disallowed by law, should litigation arise hereunder, service of process therefore may be obtained through certified mail, return receipt requested; the parties hereto waiving any and all rights they may have to object to the method by which service was perfected.

ACCEPTED THIS _____ DAY OF _____, 20____, at

_____[city and state].

Tenant 1: _____

Tenant 2: _____

Tenant 3: _____

LANDLORD OR AGENT: _____

DATED: _____

Special Information or Conditions: _____

_____

_____

_____

EXHIBIT A

The following appliances and/or furniture are on loan to Tenant for the period of Tenant's rental agreement or lease on the following basis:

Tenant agrees, by the signing of this agreement, that all appliances and/or furniture herein listed are accepted by Tenant, individually, as being in good working order or condition. Tenant agrees to maintain said appliances and/or furniture in good working order at his expense.

Appliances and/or Furniture

Item	Appliance #	Condition	Location	Furn.	Descrip.
1.					
2.					
3.					
4.					
5.					
6.					
7.					
8.					
9.					
10					

TENANT

Dated:

EXHIBIT B

Pet Agreement

Dated:_____ (Addendum to Lease Agreement)

This agreement is attached to and forms a part of the Lease Agreement dated _____, 20, ____ between _____ (Landlord) and _____, Tenant(s). Tenants desire to keep a pet named _____ and described as _____ in the dwelling they occupy under the rental agreement or lease referred to above, and because this agreement specifically prohibits keeping pets without the Landlord's permission, Tenants agree to the following terms and conditions in exchange for this permission:

1. Tenants agree to keep their pet under control at all times.

2. Tenants agree to keep their pet restrained, but not tethered, when it is outside their dwelling.

3. Tenants agree not to leave their pet unattended for any unreasonable periods.

4. Tenants agree to dispose of their pet's droppings properly and quickly.

5. Tenants agree not to leave food or water for their pet or any other animal outside their dwelling.

6. Tenants agree to keep pet from causing any annoyance or discomfort to others and will remedy immediately any complaints made through the Landlord or his agent.

7. Tenants agree to get rid of their pet's offspring within eight weeks of birth.

8. Tenants agree to pay immediately for any damage, loss, or expense caused by their pet, and in addition, they will add $_____ to their security/cleaning deposit, any of which may be used for cleaning, repairs, or delinquent rent when Tenants vacate.

9. Tenants agree that Landlord reserves the right to revoke permission to keep the pet should Tenants break this agreement.

10. Tenant agrees to pay an additional $_____ in rent per month per pet.

TENANT
TENANT

We have added the following comments to give you additional insight into our favorite lease form:

1. Clause 3 is one of our favorite clauses for a lease. It shifts the responsibility for minor repairs of the property to the tenant in exchange for a discount. Some people define "minor repairs," but usually we don't. We find that people just fix things themselves and don't call you to save the $50.

2. Clause 4 helps the tenant's memory if he was planning to bring in other tenants. You don't want the tenant to bring more people into the property because it will cause more wear and tear and possibly disturb the neighbors.

3. Clause 6 is a pet clause. Ten dollars per month is enough additional money for a small dog, but $25 is more in line for a larger dog. You won't make money, in either case—in fact, you will probably lose money on the added charge. The reason you are taking pets is that it helps you lease the property. By the way, in a tenant's eyes, *all* dogs are small, and *all* are fully housebroken.

4. Clause 11 is more of a disclosure clause than anything else. Most tenants don't know that they are supposed to have their own insurance, so we tell them up front. This helps protect you if and when finger-pointing time comes.

5. Clause 13 is required by most Landlord and Tenant Acts to give you access to your own property.

6. Clause 15 is a complete clause that outlines specifically what a tenant needs to do to get his deposit back. We believe in being very specific, so that people understand their obligations.

7. Clause 20 is a waiver of a trial by jury. Jury trials are costly, and juries tend to come down on the side of the tenant. (Nobody loves a landlord.) Also included is an attorney's fee provision, allowing you to collect if you prevail. This is very important to have in your lease, because your legal fees can cost more than actual damage. You don't want to win the battle but lose the war because of legal fees.

8. Clause 21 is one of those clauses you wish you didn't have to have. You would think that most people would know to close the windows when it rains. Just in case they don't, we advise them to do so, or it may cost them.

9. Clause 30 tells the tenant he can't just take a deduction off his rent check. This is the tenant's favorite threat. If

you have this language and he does it, he is now in default of his rent and can be evicted.

10. Clause 31 creates a deductible for repairs. Fifty dollars is borderline. You want it high enough so that the tenant doesn't call just on a whim, but not so high that she doesn't call you until major damage is done. Fifty dollars seems a good balance.

We hope you agree that while this lease is thorough, it isn't harsh. You do not want to scare your tenants, or they won't sign the lease. What you want is a lease that explains everything and that protects you if the tenants don't live up to their end of the bargain. We think this lease does that. Get your lawyer to agree or to change it so that she *can* agree.

Mastering Real Estate Investment Strategy No. 70: View Tenants as Future Buyers

Many landlords and tenants have an adversarial relationship. The smart landlord looks for opportunities to build *positive* relationships.

One of the best reasons is the chance of turning your tenant into an owner. There are many reasons why your tenants may not own property themselves. Finding out why offers you new opportunities. Consider offering your tenant an opportunity to buy your property at a future time (giving yourself a good profit, of course). It is easier for a tenant to qualify for financing on a property that he has been leasing for 12 months, and you can help him with seller financing.

Another option, if you have a real estate license, is to offer to represent the tenant as a buyer's broker when he buys someone else's property. You will earn a nice commission, and while you will lose a tenant, you will have some input on the moving date, which should help you pre-rent your property to someone else.

Finally, consider offering the tenant part of any equity appreciation in the property in exchange for her leasing the property for three to five years and taking care of any maintenance. You won't have any maintenance expenses during this period, and all you give up in return is some of your upside profit. If you do this, get an attorney to draft the equity participation clause in your lease so that there is no misunderstanding about what constitutes "profit," and who gets what percentage of it.

THE LANDLORDING CHECKLIST

☑ **UNDERSTAND THE CATEGORIES AND RESPONSIBILITIES OF LANDLORDING.** Renting apartments couldn't be more different from renting commercial units. Figure out what kind of property management suits your temperament and skill set. If nothing suits you, get someone else to do it. If you're going to do it yourself, you need to get intimately familiar with your state's landlords and tenants statute.

☑ **FIND GREAT TENANTS.** This is easier said than done, and a lot depends on the larger real estate cycle. Nevertheless, you can buy appropriate properties, broaden your pool of potential tenants, use a rental application that serves your purposes, check out prospective tenants' references carefully, show your property in smart ways, and so on. Ultimately, you want to wind up managing *people*, not buildings.

☑ **BUILD YOUR PAPER TRAIL.** Landlording is a paper-based trade. You need excellent records to protect your interests over the long run. Make copies of everything that you send out, and use certified mail and return receipts.

☑ **USE A LEASE THAT PROTECTS YOUR INTERESTS.** Standard leases favor the tenant. You want a lease that protects your interests. Start with our lease, and get your attorney to make it better for your needs.

☑ **BUILD GOOD RELATIONSHIPS.** No, your tenant isn't your friend, in most cases. But a professional relationship makes for a better tenancy, and (at the end of that tenancy) may create opportunities for both of you. Invest in building a strong relationship with your best tenants.

PART 3

Advanced Real Estate Strategies for Success

CHAPTER 12

How to Sell
Your Property

Whenever we buy or start a new business, we ask ourselves, *"What is our exit plan?"* What do we ultimately want to do with the business we are getting into? How can we sell all or part of it to make money?

You should always ask these same questions about the real estate you buy. What is your exit strategy? Do you intend to hold the property long term? Do you plan to fix it, rent it, and then sell it? If so, who is your target buyer?

Are you buying the property "wholesale," with the intention of selling it quickly? If so, to what group of buyers do you want to sell it, and how will you market it to them? Is there something unique about this property that you can use to create additional value? Is it more valuable in small pieces?

These are very important questions, yet surprisingly few people answer them before buying a property. We think this is a mistake.

We encourage you to ask yourself the tough questions early and to have a game plan (including what might be called an "end-game plan") for each property. True, all game plans are subject to change (and may even get scrapped entirely), but you're always better off starting the game with a well-thought-out plan and then adjusting it as necessary.

Are you going to keep this property forever? Probably not. So if you're going to unload this property at some point, you need to know how to sell it to produce the maximum return on your initial investment.

Most real estate books and seminars focus almost exclusively on how to *buy* property, rather than on how to sell it. And, yes, how you buy property is very important. But if you don't know how to sell your investments, you are likely to give up some of your hard-won profits unnecessarily. Conversely, if you maximize what you make on each deal, you'll have to find fewer good deals to make the same amount of money—and at some point in the investment cycle, it gets harder and harder to find good deals.

Common sense? Yes, but somehow, many people miss the point. When it comes time for these investors to harvest their earnings, they blow it. They get overanxious, sell at the wrong time, or wait until they become a "don't-wanter" of the property and let it go too cheaply. Before you say that this doesn't happen very often, think about all of the recommendations you have heard about "buying real estate wholesale." Well, in most cases, the reason you can buy wholesale is that someone has blown it at harvest time. And that someone could be *you*, one day, if you don't plan for your sale.

Advanced Real Estate Strategy No. 1: Price It Right

There is one overriding reason why something does or doesn't sell fast: *price*. We don't care what anyone says to the contrary. Show us a piece of real estate that isn't selling, and we'll show you an overpriced property. Drop the price, and the market will produce a buyer.

"But I don't *want* to lower the price," you say. Well, OK, we understand that you may not want to sell for less than that golden figure you have in mind, but that doesn't change the reality that price is the reason the property isn't selling. It may not be the only reason, but no matter what the other reasons are, there is a number that the price can be lowered to that will make every other reason you can point to go away. Price is the leveling factor for problems.

To put it the other way around, if you are a seller and you don't want to lower your price, then you are going to have to change some aspect of the property to make it more valuable. That isn't *nearly* as easy as adjusting the price—and if you have to invest money to fix the property, that's just lowering the price in disguise.

Advanced Real Estate Strategy No. 2: Use the Three Most Common Appraisal Methods

Setting the right price isn't as hard as it seems. You simply have to follow one or more of the three most common appraisal methods and use the result to price your property.

Property appraisals are based on three factors: *income, cost,* and *market*. Even if the property generates no income, you can still do an estimate based on comparables in the area. The cost approach is based on what it would cost you to build a similar structure on the property, plus land costs. The market or comparables approach is based on what similar properties in the area have sold for recently. For residential property, costs and comps are the most important; for income property, you blend all three to get the best answer.

If you know a builder, the cost of construction in the area is pretty easy to come by. Even if you don't, a visit to the local builders' association most likely will help you out. If you know a Realtor, he may run you some comps for free. But don't mislead him—for example, don't tell him that you are going to give him a listing if you don't intend to do that. Just be straight up with a friend in the business, and he will help you run some comps. Maybe you will work with him next time.

Once you know the approximate market price of your property, set a sale price that is close to the market price, but that gives you a little wiggle room to lower the price with buyers who feel that they must negotiate. For reasons we've never fully understood, people in our society like to haggle—even if they say they don't. If you won't "do something" for them on the price, either they think you're not serious, or they're offended by your "intransigent" attitude. So build in some wiggle room.

If you discover that you aren't getting offers within a reasonable time, lower your price. What is reasonable? A good way to determine time periods for sales is through your local Realtor. If most homes in your area sell through the Multiple Listing Service (MLS) in a certain number of days, yours should, too (if it is in the MLS), because it is getting exactly the same exposure as the others.

Advanced Real Estate Strategy No. 3: Find the Right Buyer

Right now we are in a seller's market, so finding buyers isn't all that difficult in most areas of the country. Some areas are better than others, of course, and a study of "time on the market" will help you see how fast things are moving, on average, in your area.

Eventually, economic circumstances will change (as they always do in the real estate business), and it will become a buyer's market, where finding good buyers is harder. When this will happen is anyone's guess. The point is, if you learn how to find buyers, you will always be able to accept the idea that the market changes and deal with what it gives you.

Here are four places to find your buyer:

1. The Internet
2. Newspaper ads
3. Open houses
4. Signs

1. *The Internet.* According to studies by the National Association of Realtors, about 70 percent of all home buyers search the Internet before they buy a property. No, they don't buy on the Web, but it is a big part of the search process, so your property will need to have a Web presence.

If you list the property with a Realtor or if you are one yourself, you can post your property on Realtor.com. You should also consider putting up a Web site just for the property—or for all of your properties, if you have an inventory.

As an investor, you want to make contact with those online shoppers, whether they buy your existing house or not. Like a Realtor who is in the business full time, you want to develop a list of potential buyers of investment property so that you can contact them next time. We know only a handful of investors who go to this much trouble in cyberspace today, but it's definitely the wave of the future. Imagine the type of database of buyers, sellers, and private lenders that you can build up in just a few years!

2. *Newspaper ads.* Newspaper advertising can be successful, but it is usually very expensive. If you use a newspaper, do it in conjunction with an open house that you hold at the property. The open house brings the buyers out to you so that you can meet them and so that both parties can see if the property is a good fit.

3. *Open houses.* Open houses can be successful with all types of real estate, and you should promote them using all of your media at once. Open houses bring you not only buyers for the current property, but buyers for other properties, as well. If you aren't going to try to work with these other prospects yourself, then try to work a deal with a Realtor. Let the Realtor pay to promote your open house, in return for which you give her all of the prospects that come to see your property. It's a great trade-off.

4. *Signs.* "For Sale" signs do work. As we mentioned in Chapter 11, we like the kind that has an information tube attached. Putting a rolled sheet of information in the tube gives property-related information 24 hours a day and helps buyers screen themselves for your property (in or out). The drawback to using this process is that it keeps you from speaking directly to the buyers and qualifying them for other property that you have. So use the tubes only if you aren't also prospecting for other properties.

Advanced Real Estate Strategy No. 4: Pass the Two-Minute Test

The key to improving the salability of anything is to know your buyer. For example, if you are selling a single-family home, a woman is likely to be involved in the process at some point in time. She may be the buyer, or she may be the spouse, mother, or friend of the buyer. This means that you want to make the home appealing to women, because they usually have the predominant voice in the purchase of the house. Call us old-fashioned, but for the most part, men walk through a house and worry about the money. Women walk through a house and worry about what they'll need to do to fix it up.

Here's the bottom line: failure to include the woman's viewpoint when you are planning the sale of a home or other property will very likely cost you money. The more appealing you can make the property to the woman, the more you will get for it.

Do you know how fast people decide whether to buy a house? Realtors say that the decision is normally made within the first two minutes of being inside the house. Almost as soon as they walk in the door, people know whether they want the property; after that, it is all negotiation of the terms.

Knowing how quickly that decision takes place (often before the prospective seller has gotten very far into the house), we encourage you to concentrate on two things: *look* and *smell*.

Let's back up two steps: to the yard. What do people see when they pull up? If the house has no "curb appeal," some potential buyers will never even get out of the car. Common sense tells you to get the grass cut and the shrubs trimmed. We aren't talking about spending lots of landscaping dollars, but we are talking about making the house have that "fresh look" that creates a good first impression.

This also includes a fresh coat of paint. Here's a place where you may not want to scrimp, depending on the age of your property. A professional house painter can turn a worn-out Victorian pile into a brand-new-looking showpiece, for what turns out to be a relatively low price. Now let's walk in the front door (in the footsteps of your prospective buyer). A bad smell in the house kills a sale about as fast as anything else. No, we aren't suggesting that you spray perfume around liberally, because that has a negative effect on some people, as well. But you should certainly get rid of any carpet that smells. Look out for mold or mildew—with that dead-giveaway dank odor that makes a lot of people sneeze the moment they walk into the property. People have gotten absolutely paranoid about mold, and, if they see it or smell it, your sale most likely will be lost.

Just because you like animals doesn't mean your buyer will. That favorite dog or cat could cost you a bundle if it or its smell is around when the home is being viewed. Why put yourself in the position of losing a lot of money? Take your animals out of the picture when your property is being shown. Ask a friend whether your house "smells like dog," or cat, or whatever—and if the answer is yes, try to take steps to solve that problem. One friend of ours had to replace a hardwood floor (and the subfloor below it) to get rid of a persistent dog smell.

On a happier note, we used to know a Realtor who liked to bake cookies. Every time she had an open house, she'd bake a batch of chocolate chip cookies. The cookies were great, but the smell was what she was really after. Everyone who walked into the house got warm fuzzies as a result. They didn't always buy, of course, but her houses *never* failed the "two-minute test."

Don't forget the kitchen. Don't forget the kitchen. Yes, we repeated that sentence on purpose. Remember, women tend to be the key decision makers, and you can bet that they will focus on the kitchen. The kitchen is a place where the woman of the family tends to spend a lot of her time (even if it's not her favorite room in the house), and so she wants it to be modern-looking and convenient. Depending on the price range of the house, you probably don't have to load it up with lots of expensive new appliances. On the other hand, don't show a kitchen with appliances that scream "old!" and "outdated!" You are better off spending a little money to put in some new and moderately priced kitchen equipment.

Make sure the house is *clean*. We have seen people inspect property wearing white gloves. Maybe *no one* could have met their standards, but the point is that you need to keep your property reasonably clean. This can be a problem if you have tenants still living in the property who aren't models of cleanliness. Sometimes it is better to just wait until the lease expires before you try to sell, because you're unable to get the property in the best condition. You won't like the negative cash flow the property has without the tenants, but it will cost you more to keep them there in the long run.

After the kitchen, bathrooms are the next big inspection point in a house, including income property. In the bathroom, clean is more than just a good idea; it's an absolute prerequisite. Are you going to market with broken toilet seats or with stains in the sink or tub? Very self-defeating of you! These items can generally be replaced for peanuts, relative to what's at stake in the proposed transaction.

Should You Use a Broker?

As with most good questions, there isn't a simple, unqualified answer to this one. We have talked to a number of investors who always insist on selling their property themselves. These investors are quick to point out the exact number of dollars they "saved." When we hear this kind of talk, we make a mental note to ourselves: *this person has absolutely no idea what he is talking about, so be wary about doing business with him in the future.*

Let's assume that you've sold a property yourself. Have you saved a commission? Obviously. But have you really saved money, or have you lost it somewhere else in the transaction? For example, was the price you set too low? Hopefully not, but that depends on your experience and your knowledge of the area. We recently bought a piece of property where the owner used a relative to list the property and was rebating the commission back to the seller to save the commission. Smart business, except that the owner priced the property between 10 and 15 percent below market from the beginning because the agent/relative was inexperienced.

Using a real estate agent opens the doors for contacts that you may not have. Anytime you introduce a professional into the equation, you have the opportunity to hear of some other deal that you might exchange into instead of doing a straight sale. You may get turned on to a group of investors in the marketplace whom you've never heard of and who might be interested in other property you have.

The bottom line is that *anytime you make hard and fast rules in real estate*—like never using Realtors or always using Realtors—*you are being unrealistic.* You're not acknowledging the fluidity of the real estate market, and you're not positioning yourself well within it.

Let the transaction dictate who should sell the property. If you're talking about a simple transaction, there is nothing wrong with trying to sell the property yourself, particularly in the seller's market we are now in. Even in this case, though, you should stay open to overtures from Realtors who contact you. Offer to pay them the traditional "selling" side of the commission if they bring you a buyer. That amount is normally 3 percent of the sales price, which you can reduce under certain circumstances. If you make an offer like this, protect the Realtor, and *never* go around him to deal directly with the buyer. Remember, you're trying to create a picture of yourself as a responsible member of the local real estate community. The only way to create that picture is to *act* that way!

A long time ago, we made the decision as an investor to open our own real estate brokerage firm. Some people don't agree with this course of action; they say that it hurts you in the long run, because you have to disclose more if you have a license than if you don't. That never bothers us, because we think you should disclose everything anyway.

On the plus side, being a real estate brokerage firm gives us instant access to Realtors' tools like the MLS (Multiple Listing Service). We gain knowledge about who the agents in the community are and who the real players are for every type of real estate. We keep these agents in our database, and when it comes time to sell something, they are the first ones we call. This gives them a little edge with any buyers they have, and it puts our product out to the right people at the right time. At the same time, these agents also get used to dealing with us and learn what we are looking to buy. This often gets us early information on listings before they hit the market.

Having a real estate license also gives us an immediate discount on the commission when we buy a property, and, over the years, most of the property we have bought has been listed. We acknowledge that this isn't true of all real estate investors, particularly those who invest heavily in the wholesale market, but it is true for the types of property we deal with. Additionally, having a license allows you to act as a broker in a transaction, even if that isn't the normal way you conduct your business. We have found this to be a profitable sideline to the general flow of investing. Why? Because when you have property to sell, you will get buyers to call you. If you take the time to screen the buyers, you'll discover that even if they don't buy your property, they may be interested in other property that you know about, and you can make a full real estate commission. At the very least, you can earn a referral fee from a top real estate broker you know. Our referral fees this year alone will probably be in six figures. We think getting a license more than pays for itself, and so we encourage you to at least look into the process.

Working with Real Estate Groups

In Chapter 4, we talked about building your master mind referral group. Now, when you're selling a property, is a good time to use that group.

Even before you put the property on the market, tell the members of your group that it is available and that they can have the first shot at it. If the members of your group know that you price real estate fairly, some are likely to be interested. And since many will be buying for reasons other than their relationship with you (for example, for a long-term hold), they won't mind the fact that you are going to make a little profit, as long as you are leaving something in the deal for them.

After you have offered the property to your inside group, you might want to go to the local real estate investors' group meetings and offer it there. Again, the reason you are doing this is to identify yourself as a player in the game, to see who's interested, and to learn what people may have to offer. Real estate, as we've emphasized in previous chapters, is a very *network-oriented* business. The more active you are, the more opportunities you find. The more opportunities you take advantage of, the more will be presented to you. That's simply the way it works.

Follow Up!

Think of all the times you've expressed interest in something, made a call, and gotten no response. Frustrating, right?

Please, *don't fall into that camp yourself.* Follow up. The buyer leads that finally help you sell a property are a precious commodity. Well, those didn't come from nowhere. Follow up with the sources of those leads, thank them, and determine how you can help them, now or in the future.

This is the essence of building a lasting and serious real estate business. Learn who the buyers are in the marketplace, what they are looking for, and if they are open to working with you in the future. Work with the people who know the buyers you *don't* know. If you can't do this follow-up yourself, then delegate it to someone who will. Follow up! Nothing is more important to making your real estate investing career a success.

THE SELLING CHECKLIST

☑ **FIGURE OUT YOUR EXIT STRATEGY.** The day you make your offer on the property, you should have some plan for how you're going to get your money back out of it. Too many people either don't think about this at all, or just assume that they're going to live forever, or "pass it on to the kids," or whatever. Don't be in this rudderless crowd. Develop your exit strategy, and then be prepared to be flexible.

☑ **PRICE IT RIGHT.** There's basically one reason why your property won't sell, and that is that you've priced it too high. Use one or more of the three basic appraisal methods to put a reasonable price on the property, and consider adding a small upward "bump" to make it easier for you to negotiate your price downward. Get a sense of how long it takes to sell comparable properties in your locality. If others are selling and yours isn't, lower your price.

☑ **FIND YOUR BUYER.** Getting to know the buying community will help you sell this property—and the next one, and the next one after that. Build a database of buyers using the Internet, newspaper ads, open houses, and signs with listing sheets attached.

☑ **PASS THE TWO-MINUTE TEST.** Put yourself in the shoes of your prospective buyer (which in the case of a residential property is very likely to be a woman). How does the property look as you come up the drive? How does it look and smell when you walk in the front door? If the first two minutes of experiencing your property aren't pleasant, you won't sell the place for a decent price. And don't forget the kitchen!

☑ **USE BROKERS SELECTIVELY.** If it's a simple transaction, if you have the time, and if you know the local market for properties like the one you're trying to sell, go ahead and take a shot at selling it yourself. Otherwise, get someone to sell it for you. Remember, you need to be in the deal stream. Letting a pro earn a good commission on your property creates a new ally for you.

☑ **WORK YOUR NETWORKS.** Selling your property gives you an excellent opportunity to work your networks—both your master mind group and local real estate groups. Give the people in those groups the first shot at your property. You have a chance to create an opportunity for them without giving up much yourself—and again, you may make a powerful ally for the long term.

CHAPTER 13

Buying Real Estate Wholesale

Everyone likes a bargain, and that includes us. But in real estate, as in other realms of bargain hunting, bargains are usually in the eye of the beholder. To one person, a run-down property with broken windows and a serious mold problem is a disaster. To another, it is an ugly duckling waiting to be turned into a swan.

As you get deeper and deeper into real estate investment, you'll hear the phrase "buying wholesale" more and more often. It's a phrase borrowed from the world of selling goods, where there's a retail level (the store) and a wholesale level (the company or distributor that sells to the store). In real estate, though, the term *wholesale* gets a little complicated.

In an earlier chapter, we talked about buying a property that had just doubled in price, and yet we were able to sell it in less than a year at double the price again. Did that mean that we "bought wholesale"? Or were we "retail" customers until the day we sold the property? At the end of the day, it doesn't matter much. You're "looking to buy wholesale," or (same thing) you're "looking for a bargain." Either way, you want to find properties that you can buy below retail and then sell at retail. The better you are at determining the difference between wholesale and retail, the better you will be at making money.

In this chapter, we are going to look at five ways to buy wholesale:

1. Buying direct from the owner
2. Buying foreclosures
3. Buying out of probate
4. Buying as a result of a divorce settlement
5. Buying out of a tax lien sale

It's unlikely that you will use all of five of these approaches regularly in your real estate investing business. More likely, you will settle on one or two that you will adopt as the niche in which you can make consistent profits. And although none of the methods we discuss in the following pages is "better" than the others, some of these strategies *do* work better at certain times, or in certain parts of the country. Some work better if you have an "inside track," which you may not have at first, but which you may be able to develop over time. For example, if you develop good relationships with well-connected attorneys, you will find opportunities in probate and foreclosures. These two areas of specialization alone can keep you plenty busy.

Advanced Real Estate Strategy No. 5: Buy Direct

When you are buying wholesale, most of the time you will be buying either direct from the owner or from the owner's representative, who is frequently an attorney. Obviously, then, this is different from building a relationship with a person (such as a real estate agent) with whom you plan to do multiple deals over time.

So buying direct requires a different skill set. When you deal directly with owners, you have to be able to establish a good rapport quickly and to build enough of a working relationship so that you can understand what the owner's problem is and what he needs to accomplish. The better you are at doing this, the more success you will have in the direct-from-the-owner wholesale business.

FSBO: For Sale by Owner

Buying direct means that you're buying from a property owner with no intermediary. In the business, these people are referred to as *FSBOs* (For Sale By Owner). In seller's markets, more properties are being sold by the owners themselves: they believe that it is pretty easy to sell real estate because (1) there are so many buyers, and (2) properties are selling fast. These owners feel comfortable with the transaction process themselves, and they want to save the agent's commission of an average of 6 to 7 percent. With the average home in the $200,000 range, that is a $14,000 savings to the owner (based on a 7 percent commission), and it's $70,000 on a $1 million property. So you can see why many people are motivated to sell their own properties.

Conversely, the number of FSBOs decreases in a buyer's market, because it is harder to sell the property. Once the number of listings increases and the average number of days a property sits on the market crosses the 90-day threshold, sellers become more concerned about unloading the property than about saving the commission, and they start looking for a Realtor to help them.

Are owners better off selling by themselves? Realtors would argue that the owners don't actually save anything, because they usually sell too low. We don't intend to get into the debate here, because (1) there are good arguments on both sides, and (2) it's not going to be resolved in any case. In addition, real estate commissions are becoming more negotiable, so the "right answer" depends on the facts and circumstances of the case itself. For our purposes in this chapter, FSBOs are a viable way for you to explore the wholesale marketplace.

Where Do You Find FSBOs?

You may recall that in an earlier chapter, we told you about the real estate investors who advertise with billboards proclaiming, "WE BUY UGLY HOUSES." This group deals primarily with owners who are selling direct, and they find owners through their unique advertising message.

So one interesting place to start your buy-direct program is with companies like this. Because of the volume they deal in, they can't buy everything they come across, and if you establish a good relationship with them, they may decide to either refer you to properties that they don't buy or "flip" you properties that they are willing to make a quick profit on, hopefully leaving something in the deal for you.

This may be particularly true of properties that fall into the "ugly" categories or that require substantial physical improvement before they can be put on the market for a good price. The group may be willing to take a short-term profit for finding the property, and let you spend the time, money, and effort to fix it up for the next level of profit. You will then sell the property "retail" to a user after you have fixed it up. (See how the terms *wholesale* and *retail* tend to slide around, depending on the circumstances?)

Your local real estate group or association is another source for finding properties that are being sold directly by an owner. Remember, these are investors just like you, and they want to make a profit. But their near-term profit may be your longer-term gain, if you eventually can get more for the property than you paid for it and put into it. The key to success, of course, lies in *understanding your real estate market.*

Additionally, investors often experience sudden changes in their circumstances. A good buy on a property that they planned to fix up can become a problem property for them overnight if the cash they need to fix it up is no longer available. Or maybe a better deal comes along that they don't want to miss out on, and they need to get their cash out of the property they already own. One really great thing about real estate is that good deals tend to bring you *more* good deals, and when that starts to happen, you just can't buy everything. So keep your eyes on the other guy's fortunes, good and bad. If he needs to make a quick reshuffle of the deck, this may create good opportunities for you.

The third broad category of direct sellers is the "pure" FSBOs. These are simply property owners (usually owners of single-family homes) who have decided to sell their property themselves to save on the commission. You can find these people advertising their property for sale in the newspapers or by spotting their signs when you drive the neighborhoods you work as an investor.

You see an ad, and you call the owner directly. You spot a sign, and you stop and talk to the owner. (Both the ads and the signs are likely to state that the home is "FSBO," because the seller knows that that has appeal to some buyers.) The more houses you see and the more owners you talk to, the more opportunities you will find.

How can there be so many opportunities? Because real estate is owned by people, and people's circumstances change every day. The price someone will accept for a property may be vastly different from one day to the next. Circumstances and prices are dramatically affected by divorce, sickness, death, foreclosure, and job transfers, to name just a few.

These examples may get you wondering whether you have to be some sort of vulture—a person who takes advantage of other people's misery—to buy direct at a profit. Yes, you're likely to encounter some sad situations, but you're also likely to come across some very positive ones. Lots of circumstances can persuade a seller to lower her price. A new job in another town, with the employer helping out with the costs of relocating, is just one example. Maybe the seller has found such a good deal on his next home that he simply can't wait to move out of his current home. The point is, there are *many* reasons why sellers sell, and they change all the time—even from day to day. Your job is to get out into the marketplace and *mingle.* See what is selling and why. Be open to all kinds of opportunities.

Another reason why sellers sometimes sell too low is that *they don't see what you see.* If you are in the real estate market all the time, you see neighborhoods changing. Real estate is your business, not theirs. You are reading about all of the changes and proposed changes to a neighborhood; they aren't, because they are involved in their own world. For example, a new development is announced today, and then nothing happens for two years or longer because it takes a long time to get an ambitious development off the ground. If you stay on top of these announcements, you will know what is going to happen in a way that others who are not keeping track of them do not, because doing so isn't of primary importance to them.

When neighborhood prices change, they may go up, but they may go up in steps, each of which may present an opportunity to you. For example, you may see upward movement upon the announcement of a new development and then nothing more until after construction begins. At that point, prices usually jump again, but then they fall back as the noise and dust associated with the construction begin to wear people down. This is another opportunity, because prices usually rise again the moment construction ends and the development comes on line. Finally, if the development is successful, you may see another movement in prices (and sometimes the biggest jump) once property in and around the development becomes scarce.

Again, the point is that there are many things (the evolution of a property, the stages in an owner's life) that affect the price that someone is willing to accept for a property at any point in time. Your job is to know the market, be in the deal stream, and be vigilant enough to spot opportunities.

Advanced Real Estate Strategy No. 6: Buy Foreclosures

Foreclosures occur when the owner's financial situation changes and she can no longer keep up her mortgage payments. Dealing in foreclosures is a specialty in itself. Those who understand the process do very well because, by definition, they are *always* buying wholesale. Rookie foreclosure participants spend a lot of time learning the ropes and learning how not to get burned.

We make this statement not to dissuade you from getting involved in the foreclosure process, but to make you understand that buying through foreclosure is a specialty and that you most likely will have to spend some time learning the process before you can get good at it. Fortunately, the process has improved somewhat, thanks to online databases that you can subscribe to that give you notice of foreclosures, complete with contact information.

The other big point to understand about foreclosures is that the number of available properties is directly dependent on the economy. The better the economy, the fewer the foreclosures, because people are doing better themselves. In weak economies, the foreclosure market heats up, and more properties become available.

There are four times when you can enter the foreclosure market:

1. Before the property goes into foreclosure
2. After the property enters the foreclosure process, but before the sale
3. At the foreclosure sale
4. After the lender takes the property at a foreclosure sale

In the first two instances, you will probably be dealing with an *owner* who is facing a problem. (Note that the foreclosure market blends into the "direct" market described earlier.) In the last two examples, you will be dealing with a *lender* who has a problem.

Let's look at the bank side of the equation first. Make no mistake about it: lenders who are about to own property through a foreclosure have a problem. Why? Because they aren't in the real estate business. Lenders are in the banking business, and the banking regulators don't like it when a lender forecloses. As a rule, foreclosure is seen by the regulators as evidence that the bank doesn't observe good lending practices, because, if it did, the property would never have gone into foreclosure. The regulators may even write the bank up for making lending mistakes—not a happy outcome for a bank!

The second reason that lenders don't like to take real estate in foreclosure is that they must carry the real estate "free and clear," which means that they have to tie up a lot of cash. This is money that they would otherwise be pledging at the Federal Reserve depository to borrow more money to lend out at a higher rate. This is the way banks *like* to make money, and it's how they make most of their money. They don't want to be in the real estate business, and they don't want to have real estate on their books.

The third reason banks don't like to take real estate is that most banks today are public companies. Real estate is considered a depreciating asset, which for us as investors is a good thing, because it effectively lowers our taxes. But for a public company, it's a bad thing, because the depreciation appears as an expense on its financial statements, which in turn reduces its profits for the year. Lower profits for a bank translate into a lower stock price, and a lower stock price will ultimately cause the senior managers to lose their high-paying jobs—a prospect that of course doesn't make them happy.

So, now that you're armed with this new insight into the world of real estate lending, you can understand why banks have a problem that you are helping them solve when you take property off their hands. And this is what foreclosure specialists do: they deal directly with a bank's "Real Estate Owned" department (commonly referred to in the industry as REO). Dealing directly with this department, and the person who manages it, can be a golden key to opportunities. If you can get one of these people into your master mind referral group, you are on your way to success.

The other side of the foreclosure process has you dealing directly with the owners themselves. This is a different type of specialty because you often are dealing with emotionally difficult situations. The owners know that they have a problem, and while they may recognize on some level that you are actually the answer to their prayers, they may not embrace you as an angel sent to solve their problem. In fact, they frequently will view you as a shark circling, in tandem with the lender, trying to take away their home (or other property). So be prepared to live with this sometimes jarring discrepancy: you're helping the owners out of a difficult situation, and they resent you for it.

The first thing you have to determine is whether the owner is being realistic about her circumstances. Foreclosure is not a good situation, because it stays on people's credit reports for 10 years and may keep them from getting loans of all types. If the owner isn't realistic about working with you to solve her problem, then you may be better off just talking with her, backing off, and possibly approaching her again at a later time.

Again, this is a difficult and emotional situation, and you may not want to get involved in it when the owner is under the greatest stress. Remember, though, that *reaching agreement with the owner at this time is best for both of you.* You can help her avoid the foreclosure on her record. She can help you get a property before a lot of extra costs are imposed upon it by the lender, through the foreclosure process.

Buying a property at a foreclosure auction is the final way to pick up a property in the foreclosure process. Auctions are exciting and fun, but you need to avoid getting caught up in the excitement of the moment and paying more than you should have. One good strategy is to see how active the auctions are in your area. In some areas, the lender is the only one bidding. In other areas, you'll have an active bid group, and this can lead to very different dynamics, including excitement and overheated bidding.

Keep in mind that foreclosure bidding usually includes rules that require you to "post" (set aside) all or a large part of the money needed to buy the property prior to bidding. Depending on the size of your bankroll, this could be a problem.

The simplest way to see if foreclosure buying is right for you is to go to some of the foreclosures in your area and just watch. You will quickly learn the process and the players, and you can make a much better decision after you see what happens. You may find that you don't like the process, but that you can develop a good relationship with someone who does. Contact that person, and you will probably find that he will be willing to flip some of his properties to you for a small, but quick, profit. No, you won't be buying at the very bottom, but you still will be buying "wholesale," and that is what you're looking to do.

Advanced Real Estate Strategy No. 7: Buy in Probate

When a person dies with a will, the property he owns goes through a process called *probate*, which means "proving the will." All of the individual's property is gathered together by the executor of the estate. The executor then has the responsibility of administering the estate by paying off any outstanding debts and taxes. If the estate includes considerable cash, this is relatively easy. If it doesn't, the executor must sell property (both real and personal) to pay off the outstanding liabilities.

Depending on the size of the estate, probate can take months (or even years), and the longer it takes, the more frustrated the executor is likely to become with the process, and the more likely it is that she will sell any real estate in the larger estate at a good price. There are some exceptions, such as executors who are being paid by the hour and therefore have no real motivation to do anything fast, but most executors eventually become eager to get out of that role.

Working in the probate process is a specialty that some people get very good at, and they are able to buy property at substantial discounts. These specialists work directly with probate attorneys on a regular basis, and they also watch for probate notices filed in the newspapers by the executors. They contact the executors listed in the notice and then begin the process of learning what the executor's plans are.

In summary, probate is an excellent source of leads on property that sometimes can be purchased at wholesale rates. It's a field in which patience, persistence, and hard work are frequently rewarded.

Advanced Real Estate Strategy No. 8: Buy Out of a Divorce Settlement

Maybe the subhead of this section makes you wonder if it's someone else's problem that tends to create your opportunity. The answer, in many cases, is "yes." But, as we pointed out earlier, you're actually presenting a solution to a problem that you didn't create. Maybe the person with the problem won't see it that way, and maybe he will decide to cast you in the role of the "bad guy." Well, so be it. You'll go away, and the problem will still be there. Eventually, some "bad guy" will have to solve it.

A divorce begins with the divorce filings. You can find these legal notices in the newspaper on a regular basis. Cross-check the names of the parties in the divorce case with lists of property owners (you can get lists of property owners at your local tax assessor's office), and you will quickly find out if there is property that may need to be sold in order to settle the divorce. Very often this is the case.

If there is, you will probably be working with the divorce attorneys, offering to buy the marital property in order to produce cash for an easier settlement. Once again, this is a specialty in which you prosper by becoming known to another group of specialists in your town (in this case, the divorce attorneys) as a problem solver.

Another way you can work the divorce field is directly through the individuals getting a divorce. In most cases, of course, this is a deeply distressing period in the life of one or both parties to the divorce. Tread lightly. Again, you may be seen as either a problem solver or a villain. If it looks like it's the latter, either back off a bit or get out of the discussion altogether.

Advanced Real Estate Strategy No. 9: Buy at Tax Lien Sales

In a subsequent chapter, we'll provide a thorough explanation of how to buy tax lien certificates for high income. If the certificates are not redeemed within the specified legal period (normally two years), the certificate holder can force an auction of the property.

There are three ways to get involved in the sale process. First, you can go to the auctions. These will be advertised, but regular visits to the tax assessor's office will keep you better informed.

Second, you can deal with whoever buys the property at the auction. People are always looking fo a quick profit in these cases.

Third, you can find out who the owner is before the sale and deal with her. In this case, you may loan her money to pay off the tax lien. The loan could be a straight loan, or you could structure an equity participation. The owner may also be interested in an outright purchase by you. As you can see, there are numerous possibilities. Again, remember that the seller has a problem and that you may have the solution. See if there's a way that the problem at hand can be turned into an opportunity.

THE WHOLESALE BUYER'S CHECKLIST

☑ **BUY DIRECT.** Figure out ways in which you can be first in line when an FSBO (for sale by owner) becomes available. FSBOs are more common in seller's markets and less common in buyer's markets. Sometimes FSBOs become available when the owner gets in financial trouble; other times, they represent a happy turn of events in the owner's life. In either case, you represent the solution to a problem that the owner is trying to solve.

☑ **BUY THROUGH FORECLOSURES.** Foreclosures happen when a property owner fails to make mortgage payments on his property, and the bank takes the property back. You can buy a property that's only threatened with foreclosure, or you can buy it at any time thereafter in the foreclosure process. Be aware that although you again represent a solution to a serious problem, the homeowner who's in financial difficulty may not see you that way.

☑ **BUY PROPERTIES IN PROBATE.** This means buying real estate from a deceased person's estate. In many cases, the executor of the estate needs to sell the property to generate cash to pay the estate's liabilities; in other cases, the executor is eager to finish up her role. Either situation can create opportunities for you.

☑ **BUY OUT OF A DIVORCE SETTLEMENT.** When a couple divorces, the primary residence often needs to be sold. As with probate cases, it's extremely helpful to get to know the local attorneys who specialize in these cases. Get a reading on the situation, and figure out whether there's a way that you can help solve the problem at hand and also "buy at wholesale."

☑ **BUY AT TAX LIEN SALES.** When a property owner doesn't pay his real estate taxes, that property may eventually be put up for sale so that the local government can recover the taxes owed. As with the foreclosure process, you may be able to get into the process at one of several junctures, and you may be able to work out a deal that enables you to "buy wholesale."

CHAPTER 14

Partners, Partnerships, Equity Sharing, and Syndications

There are many opportunities to partner in the real estate business, in part because the field is so diverse and because people have so many different resources to bring to the table.

The most common resource is *money*. There are lots of people who have a great deal of money that they want to invest in real estate, but do not want to make the time commitment. There are also a great number of people who don't have money, but who have the time and the talent to be successful in real estate. So for these two different groups of people, real estate offers an ideal opportunity to do business together. Once their first transaction is successful, they tend to continue on together, possibly with more investors inviting themselves to the table over time.

But partnerships have pitfalls as well. If you are interested in doing partnerships, you will need to be proactive in structuring the deals effectively. If the truth be told, most people don't know how to structure good deals, so they don't offer much in the way of ideas or suggestions. So for better or worse, you may find that it's often up to you to bring those ideas and suggestions to the table.

While partnerships do involve legal arrangements, these legal arrangements are relatively simple to set up after you've been through your first one. During that first partnering arrangement, in other words, you will work through structuring issues that will be repeated over and over in future ventures. If you take the time to do it right the first time, you will build your skill set and accelerate all of your subsequent deals.

We have been involved in many partnerships during our real estate careers. Some of the partnerships have been "one-offs"—a single venture with no follow-on. Others have lasted more than 20 years. For the two authors, this book project is a partnership of sorts, and we still do all of our current real estate deals together.

Will we always buy our real estate together? Probably not, because our goals are likely to diverge at some point in the future. For now, though, both our purchases and our exit plans for each property are in sync, and that is very important.

Many people have had bad experiences with business partnerships, just as many have had marital problems. Real estate partnerships are not usually long-term ventures, and sometimes you and your partner(s) may even enter into them with conflicting goals. Equity owners and lenders are an example of this type of relationship. The two may have a common goal of having a successful venture, but at times how those goals are managed can lead to conflict between the two.

For example, the lender may be eager to end his participation in a venture as long as he gets his money out, while the investor may want to stay in the deal longer because she sees a different type of opportunity with the property. If these goals reach a state of conflict that can't be resolved amicably, the result is likely to be a messy lawsuit.

This example also illustrates why we talk so much about real estate being a "people business" and why you have to play the role of problem solver far more often than that of buyer or seller or investor. If there's a problem, it usually isn't related to the property as much as it is driven by the people involved and by their individual circumstances.

Advanced Real Estate Strategy No. 10: Structure Your Ventures in Writing

Most partnership problems arise out of varying interpretations of what was agreed to. In many cases, when a problem occurs, it is the result of wishful thinking on the part of one of the partners, who is attempting after the fact to turn the deal into what he wanted it to be, rather than what it was. There is only one way to stop this and similar kinds of problems from occurring, and that is to *put everything in writing*—in simple language that everyone can understand.

In addition, it is often a good idea to use examples to illustrate meanings. If you say, for instance, "the partners are going to split net revenue," then show an example of how that is to be calculated. These examples are easier for everyone to understand, and they also make it easier for a court or arbitrator to see what was intended in the original agreement.

In the beginning of your partnership, you can make up examples so that everyone is able to visualize what phrases like "net revenue" mean and which specific items will be deducted from the gross before you have a net. Believe us: definitions without examples are bound to create misunderstandings. Eventually, this problem should diminish. The longer you are in a partnership, the more history you and your partners will have together, and the more examples you can cite to illustrate how things were done in the past. This should help everyone understand how future ventures will be handled.

Advanced Real Estate Strategy No. 11: Use Shareholder Agreements

Many times, you will structure your real estate ownership as a corporation or LLC (discussed in a later chapter) in order to provide protections to you that straight partnerships don't have.

Corporations are separate entities, intended in part to shield you from personal liability for things that can happen in the course of business. In a corporate structure, the people you would normally have been partners with (if you had used a partnership agreement) are now your fellow shareholders. You therefore need to pull together a shareholder agreement to define the same type of things that you would define in a partnership agreement.

An example would be a decision on how money is to be divided among the shareholders. This is particularly important if you are going to be a minority shareholder, because in the absence of such a document, the corporation is controlled by a majority vote—and you, as a minority shareholder, can effectively be frozen out of any decisions. True, there are some state laws that protect the interests of minority shareholders, but by and large these laws are not as clear or as helpful as you'd like them to be. So if you want far-reaching protection and if you want to minimize the risk of conflicts down the road, you need to get a shareholder agreement drawn up.

Elements of a Good Agreement

Both partnership and shareholder agreements have certain key elements that need to be defined and agreed to. These include the following:

1. Names of the parties
2. Ownership interests
3. Terms of the agreement
4. Required contribution
5. What happens if additional contributions are needed
6. What constitutes a default on the agreement and how that will be resolved
7. A buy-sell arrangement between the partners or shareholders
8. A statement as to responsibilities among the parties

These eight components are the fundamental building blocks of every good agreement. There will almost certainly be more, as you get into discussions among yourselves. At the very least, though, you want to have an open and frank discussion of all eight of these points and to *address them in the beginning*.

How do we know that this is important? Because in most cases where we did not follow this step-by-step process, problems developed. Should we have taken our own advice? Absolutely. Should you take our advice? Yes. Almost every time we've been sloppy in the deal-structuring phase, it has cost us untold amounts of time and money. Hopefully, you can profit from our mistakes—or at least not pay to relearn our lessons.

Figuring Out Who Gets What

This challenge may be the single biggest obstacle to putting partnership and shareholder agreements in writing. The parties don't know where to start. Maybe you're afraid to propose a certain arrangement because you think the other party will turn you down. Well, maybe she will. On the other hand, you never know unless you start talking about the options available and what everyone is willing to do. And as we always say, it is better to have tried and lost than not to have tried at all.

A good starting point with two partners is a 50/50 split, with increases or decreases in percentage based on special situations. Examples would be one party getting more of the profits in exchange for putting in more of the up-front cash, or one party putting in more work in exchange for a larger percentage of the deal.

If one partner is putting up all the cash and the other is doing all the work, then a good starting point is 50/50. Here again, however, you really shouldn't get hung up on whether this is the exact correct split or not. There have been times where we have given up more than we needed to on a particular transaction because we wanted to make sure that the deal got done. Why? Because giving up a six-figure profit several years down the road to make a symbolic point today is usually a dumb idea. In addition, the transaction on the table may be only the first in a long series of transactions to come. By making a concession, we moved this transaction along and kept the door open for more transactions (and righting the balance a bit) in the future.

If you are just getting started in the business, you may need to make concessions to make up for your relative inexperience—and to get the experience you need. Maybe this deal is a rare opportunity for you to work with someone who can help you learn the trade and make good contacts. (Again, this is all part of learning the ropes and building a track record.) On the other hand, it is reasonable for you to call your flexibility to the attention of the other party. Point out to him that you think a more correct split would be 50/50 but that you are willing to make a concession this time—your first time out together—and if you do another deal in the future, you will expect 50/50. If the other party is reasonable, he is likely to agree, and you will have set the tone for future deals. Success in real estate often boils down to how effectively you build relationships, which in part grows out of your approach to negotiations.

Advanced Real Estate Strategy No. 12: Expand Your Business with Equity-Sharing Partnerships

The concept of "equity sharing" was born in the mid-1980s, when real estate was harder to sell and lenders were tighter with their money than they are in the present economy. Simply put, equity sharing takes the different benefits of real estate ownership and spreads them out among the partners for maximum effectiveness. Even on small single-family rentals (not normally the venue for complex financing), there was joint venturing with investors who put up money. Sometimes the investors did nothing more than lend their financial statement to get a person qualified for a loan, in return for which they received a piece of the equity buildup over the years. It was a win/win situation, and many such deals were put together.

While these types of transactions are not as dominant today as they were two decades ago, you should consider the possibilities as you see investment opportunities. Don't be afraid to be creative. Don't be afraid to propose new ways to allocate the opportunities and obligations in a given deal. If you are just getting started and have only a small bankroll to play with, consider seeking out people who can help.

Let's look at an example. Say you are just getting started in the real estate business, and you need an investor. In most cases, as noted at the outset of this chapter, investors want great returns but no hassles. One possibility is to offer the investor a mortgage on the property. The mortgage would be junior to any other mortgage. If the investor doesn't need current income, you could ask for no payments, and his interest would accrue. The mortgage would be paid off when the property was sold, and you could agree on the date in the future that it would be put on the market. As an added feature, the mortgage could have an equity participation clause that would allow the investor to share in the appreciation of the property. If the interest rate on the mortgage was a market rate, then he might be happy with a bonus of 10 to 25 percent of the profits.

This transaction would give you a nothing-down deal, tax benefits from ownership, and most of the profit with no cash investment. If it involved a rental, you might have to handle the management, but it certainly would be fair for you to receive a management fee for that service.

See what you've done in this equity-sharing example? You've taken both the *benefits* and the *challenges* of real estate ownership and redistributed them among the participants in an interesting and mutually beneficial way.

The benefits are

- Income
- Tax deduction
- Equity buildup from mortgage reduction
- Appreciation
- Leverage

The problems in real estate are

- Negative cash flow
- Management responsibilities
- Maintenance cost and time
- Down payment requirements
- Financial qualifications

In each equity-sharing arrangement, you will be juggling benefits and problems. Generally speaking, the larger the problem that one of the parties solves, the bigger that party's relative participation in the benefits.

Following is a sample equity-sharing contract (one that we've used, over the years), which we've included so that you can see exactly how they are designed. Please note that this contract is *for purposes of illustration only*, and that you definitely need to work with your lawyer(s) to come up with a contract that is right for your specific needs. Also note that at the end of this lengthy document (toward the end of the chapter), we pick up our narrative again with an explanation of syndications.

EQUITY-SHARING AGREEMENT

THIS AGREEMENT, made and entered into this _____ day of _____, 20__, by and between

of _____ (hereinafter collectively referred to as the "Resident"); and

of _____ (hereinafter collectively referred to as the "Nonresident").

WHEREAS, Nonresident and Resident intend to acquire, as tenants in common, that certain real property (the "Property") as described in Exhibit A attached hereto and made a part hereof by this reference, and WHEREAS, Nonresident and Resident will each own an undivided interest in the Property in accordance with the information contained in Exhibit B; and

WHEREAS, the parties intend that upon acquisition of the Property, Resident will occupy the Property as Resident's principal residence; and

WHEREAS, the parties wish to enter into this Agreement in order to set forth their respective rights and obligations with respect to the Property.

NOW, THEREFORE, in consideration of the mutual covenants and agreements contained herein and other valuable consideration, the parties agree as follows:

1. **Term of Agreement.** The term of this agreement shall be for a period of _____ months unless otherwise agreed upon.

2. **Ownership.** Upon acquisition of the Property, Nonresident and Resident shall own undivided interests in the Property as tenants in common, the legal description for which is attached hereto as Exhibit B and made a part hereof by this reference. Notwithstanding the preceding sentence, the Appreciation in Value shall be allocated between the parties in accordance with the Appreciation Sharing Percentages specified in the Transaction Summary known as Exhibit B.

3. **Acquisition of the Property.**

(a) In order to purchase the Property in accordance with the terms of the agreement entered into with the seller of the Property, a copy of which agreement is attached hereto as Exhibit C, the parties intend to obtain a loan (the "Mortgage Loan") from a financial institution (the "Lender") in the amount and on the terms specified in Exhibit B; and the parties shall pay the balance of the purchase price and the closing costs, including the loan fees, in cash (the "Cash Closing Requirement"). *If personal liability is required by the Lender*, only the Resident shall have personal liability for prepayment of the Mortgage Loan unless otherwise agreed and Resident shall have no right of recoupment against Nonresident if Resident shall be required to pay any deficiency judgment to the Lender. The Cash Closing Requirement shall be furnished by the parties hereto and placed into the escrow on or before the date of purchase of the Property (the "Closing Date") in the respective amounts (or percentages) set forth in Exhibit B, and Resident shall be credited with such amount as Resident has previously paid toward such Requirement. The parties acknowledge that the Cash Closing Requirement may be furnished in percentages different from their ownership or sharing arrangement.

(b) It is expressly agreed that any deductions for federal income tax purposes generated by payment of closing costs for acquisition of the Property, including loan fees, shall be claimed by Resident and Nonresident in accordance with their respective Cost Sharing Percentages.

(c) The parties anticipate that they will obtain a commitment from the Lender on terms substantially as set forth in Exhibit B and agree to use their best efforts to that end. In the event that no such commitment is issued within the time period allowed therefore in the purchase agreement that is Exhibit C hereto (as such time period may be extended), then this agreement shall terminate.

4. **Restrictions.** Once the parties have acquired the Property, the prior written consent of both parties shall be required before any of the following actions may be taken with respect to the Property:

(a) Modification, amendment, alteration, or extension of the terms of any existing financing on the Property;

(b) Obtaining any new financing for the Property, or further encumbering the Property by grant of lien, easement, or otherwise;

(c) The sale, exchange, conveyance or other disposition of all or any portion of the Property, except in accordance with the terms hereof.

5. **Permitted Uses.** The Property shall be used only as Resident's "principal residence" (within the meaning of

Section 1034 of the Internal Revenue Code) unless otherwise mutually agreed in writing.

6. **Prohibited Uses.** Resident shall not do or permit anything to be done in or about the Property nor bring or keep anything therein which will materially adversely affect the insurability of the Property or any of its contents, or cause cancellation of any insurance policy covering the Property or any part thereof or any of its contents. Resident shall not commit or suffer to be committed any nuisance or waste in or upon the Property. Resident shall not use the Property or permit anything to be done in or about the Property that will in any way conflict with any law, statute, ordinance, or governmental rule or regulation now in force or that may be enacted or promulgated. Resident shall not use any portion of the Property for any commercial or business purpose whatsoever except with the prior written consent of Nonresident.

7. **Maintenance; Obligations as to Personal Property.**

(a) Resident shall, at Resident's sole cost, maintain the Property and every part thereof in good and sanitary condition and repair. Resident shall repair any and all damage to or in the Property occurring while the Property is held in concurrent ownership hereunder, whether or not such damage is covered by insurance.

(b) While the Property is held in concurrent ownership hereunder, Resident shall not, without the prior written consent of Nonresident, remove any of the following from the Property:

(i) any stove, dishwasher, disposal, refrigerator, washer, dryer, or other appliance;

(ii) any plumbing or lighting fixture; or

(iii) more generally, any item, the removal of which would leave a hole, or create any other condition requiring repair (cosmetic or otherwise), in any floor, ceiling, or wall of the Property (except that removal of picture hooks and the like for securing wall decorations shall be permitted without Nonresident's consent).

Provided, however, that removal of an item specified in (i) above shall be permitted without Nonresident's consent if (1) the item removed was not on the Property at the time of the purchase of the Property by Resident and Nonresident, and Resident has purchased such item with his own funds, or (2) such item was purchased from the seller of the Property to Resident and Nonresident as personal property for which Resident paid additional consideration over and above the purchase price of the Property.

Notwithstanding anything to the contrary which may be contained in this subparagraph (b), Resident shall replace any item specified in (i) or (ii) above with an adequate substitute of good quality in the event any such item ceases to function properly and such failure to function is not repairable.

8. Insurance.

(a) At all times while the Property is held in concurrent ownership hereunder, there shall be maintained at the sole cost of the Resident, comprehensive public liability insurance covering the Property, insuring against the risks of bodily injury, personal injury liability, and property damage on or about the Property with policy limits of not less than $300,000 per occurrence, and $500,000 in the aggregate as to bodily or personal injury and $50,000 as to property damage, coverage to be in comprehensive general liability form.

(b) At all times while the Property is held in concurrent ownership hereunder, there shall be maintained, at the sole cost of Resident, fire insurance (with those extended coverage endorsements which are prudent for the area in which the Property is located) upon all buildings and improvements located on the Property to not less than the fair insurable value thereof from time to time, as measured by the replacement value. Such insurance policy shall contain a provision (satisfactory to Nonresident) by which its coverage is automatically increased on an annual basis to cover increases in the value of the

Property. The right and authority to adjust and settle any loss with the insurer shall be exercisable only by the parties hereto acting jointly. Subject to the requirements of the Lender, the insurance proceeds received in the event of a casualty shall be used to pay for the restoration and reconstruction of the Property, to be commenced as soon as possible after receipt of the proceeds from insurance, and Resident shall use all due diligence to repair or reconstruct the Property within a reasonable period of time. Nothing in this Paragraph 8 shall be construed to grant Nonresident any interest in insurance maintained by Resident on personal property owned by the latter.

(c) In addition to Resident's responsibility for the prompt payment of premiums, Resident shall be responsible for ensuring that the terms of the insurance policies required hereunder are otherwise complied with. Each such policy shall name Nonresident as an insured party and provide that it cannot be canceled without 30 days written notice to both Resident and Nonresident. Promptly upon acquisition of the Property, Resident shall obtain and furnish to Nonresident certificate(s) stating that the policies required to be obtained under this Paragraph 8 are in full force and effect.

9. **Payment of Taxes, Betterment Assessments, and Mortgage Loan Installments.** Subject to the provisions of this Paragraph 9, Resident and Nonresident shall have responsibility for the Mortgage Loan installments, real property taxes and betterment assessments and the like to their respective Cost Sharing Percentages. Resident shall, from Resident's funds, make timely payments of amounts due from time to time on the Mortgage Loan installments (except to the extent required of Nonresident as provided below), real property taxes and betterment assessments and the like, if any, for the Property. Nonresident shall be obligated to pay to the Lender from Nonresident's funds such amount per month (or such percentage of the total monthly debt service requirement), if any, as is set forth in the Transaction Summary (Exhibit B) during the time period specified

therein, such payment to be applied against principal and interest due on the Mortgage Loan in the same percentages as the total payment for such month is applied. In the event that the amount of the Mortgage Loan installments (or the apportionment between principal and interest of such installments) should change due to a change in interest rate, such change shall not affect (i) the obligation of Nonresident as to the furnishing of funds (and the obligation of Resident shall be increased or decreased as the case may be) and (ii) the Cost Sharing Percentages. In the event that the Property is sold or the Nonresident's interest therein is acquired by the Resident pursuant to the terms of this Agreement prior to the end of the period during which the Nonresident is obligated to make the payments specified in the third sentence of this Paragraph, then such obligation shall immediately terminate and no credit in this regard shall arise in favor of the Resident. Any deductions for federal income tax purposes arising from payment of the interest component of the Mortgage Loan installments, real property taxes, and any other items that may be deductible for such purposes shall be claimed by the parties on the basis of their respective Cost Sharing Percentages. If any delinquency or late charge should be incurred by reason of a late payment to the Lender, the party whose failure to make timely payment caused such charge to be incurred shall be required to pay the same in full. Funds for the payment of the items specified in the first sentence of this Paragraph 9 shall be furnished by the parties in the percentages or amounts specified in this Paragraph 9 and in the Transaction Summary. The parties acknowledge that such funds may be provided in percentages different from the Cost Sharing Percentages.

10. **Personal Property Taxes.** Resident shall pay from Resident's funds, prior to delinquency, all taxes assessed during the time the Property is held in concurrent ownership hereunder against all personal property in the possession of Resident, or installed in, upon, or about the Property. Any deductions for federal and/or state income tax

purposes attributable to such payments shall belong exclusively to Resident.

11. **Utilities.** Resident shall pay for all water, gas, heat, light, power, telephone service, and all other services and utilities supplied to the Property during the time the Property is held in concurrent ownership hereunder.

12. **Alterations.** Resident shall not make or suffer to be made any alterations, additions, or improvements to or of the Property or any part thereof that would materially detract from the value of the Property.

13. **Liens.** Resident shall keep the Property free from any liens arising out of (i) any work performed or materials furnished with respect to the Property or (ii) any obligations incurred by Resident. Resident shall give notice to Nonresident prior to the commencement of any work that could give rise to a mechanic's lien, if the value of such work, together with the materials to be furnished, is likely to exceed $500.

14. **Entry by Nonresident.** While the Property is held in concurrent ownership hereunder, Nonresident may enter the Property only in the following cases:

(a) In case of emergency;

(b) To cure defaults by Resident of any of his obligations hereunder with respect to the maintenance of the Property;

(c) When Resident has abandoned the Property;

(d) Pursuant to court order; or

(e) On a periodic basis not more often than annually.

Except in cases of emergency or when Resident has abandoned or surrendered the Property, or if it is impracticable to do so, Nonresident shall give Resident reasonable notice of Nonresident's intent to enter and *shall* enter only during normal business hours. Twenty-four (24) hours shall be presumed to be reasonable notice in the absence of evidence to the contrary, except that an inspection made pursuant to

(e) shall require at least seven (7) days prior written notice. Nonresident may engage an agent for purposes of this Paragraph 14 provided that Nonresident notifies Resident of such engagement in writing.

Notwithstanding anything contained herein, if circumstances should occur such as to give Nonresident the right to sell the Property pursuant to this Agreement, then, effective upon such occurrence, Nonresident shall be authorized to enter the Property for purposes related to such sale and shall be entitled generally to equal possession of the Property with the Resident.

15. **Eminent Domain.** If all or any substantial part of the Property shall be taken or appropriated by any public or quasi-public authority under the power of eminent domain (a "Taking"), either party shall have the right to terminate this Agreement upon thirty (30) days prior written notice to the other party. In the event the Agreement is not terminated as provided above upon a Taking, Resident shall repair and restore the Property, at Resident's sole expense, to substantially the same condition as existed prior to such Taking, taking into account the reduced area of the Property occasioned by such Taking. All cash proceeds resulting from an award upon such Taking shall be distributed to the parties as if they were proceeds of a sale of the Property as stated herein.

16. **Default.** Resident shall be deemed in default hereunder upon failure of Resident to make any payments hereunder required promptly when due or upon the abandonment and vacation of the above-described Property for a period in excess of twenty (20) consecutive days, unless notice is given to Nonresident in advance thereof. Resident shall also be deemed to be in default upon the failure to perform any provisions of this Agreement of his part to be performed as herein set forth.

(a) If Resident shall default hereunder, then Nonresident may regain possession of the premises and Resident agrees that, in the event of default on his part, his right to possession of the premises shall terminate and all interest he may have in the Property shall be forfeited. Resident agrees to immediately vacate the premises and surrender the possession thereof to Nonresident. Further, if Resident shall default hereunder, Nonresident may proceed to invoke any and all legal remedies. In the event of any dispute between the parties that shall result in litigation, nevertheless, Resident shall pay all costs, charges, and expenses in connection with the property and its maintenance, all as herein set forth, during any period of litigation.

(b) In the event of default of any money payments hereunder required to be made in connection with the Property by Resident, Nonresident shall have the right to pay the same in order to protect the property and his investment and Resident shall be obligated to pay to Nonresident the sum equivalent to the maximum legal rate of interest permitted under state law thereupon.

(c) If Nonresident shall fail to make any payments required of him hereunder to be made promptly when due, he shall be in default and Resident may cure such default at Nonresident's cost. Any sums paid by Resident otherwise hereunder required to be paid by Nonresident and if not paid shall bear interest at a sum equivalent to the maximum legal rate of interest permitted under state law thereupon.

(d) The Parties further agree that if Resident shall default, then the entire value of Nonresident's investment, as hereinabove set forth, shall become immediately due and payable at Nonresident's option, and Nonresident may proceed for the collection thereof.

17. **Remedies.** In the event of a default under this Agreement or the Lease Agreement, the non-defaulting party shall have the option to utilize either of the following alternative remedies listed in Paragraphs 17.01 and 17.02 below, in addition to any other remedies available at law or equity:

17.01 **Quit Claim Deeds.** Concurrently with the execution of this Agreement, Resident shall execute a Quit Claim Deed in favor of Nonresident and Nonresident shall execute a Quit Claim Deed in favor of Resident, each such Quit Claim Deed conveying the respective interest of each party in and to the Subject Property. Such Quit Claim Deed shall be held in escrow by _____

_____ ,

as Escrow Agent. In the event of any default as defined here by either party hereunder, and if this remedy is utilized, the nondefaulting party shall give written notice of default to the defaulting party, particularly specifying the alleged default and demanding performance of the same. In the event such default is not remedied within 60 days from the date of mailing of such notice of default, the nondefaulting party shall give written notice of such failure to Escrow Agent. Upon receipt of said notification, Escrow Agent shall give written notice to the defaulting party of its intent to release and record the Quit Claim Deed vesting title to the Subject Property wholly in the name of the nondefaulting party unless such default is remedied in full within ten (10) days from the date of Escrow Agent's notification. Upon the failure of the defaulting party to remedy such default within the prescribed ten (10) day period, Escrow Agent shall release and record the Quit Claim Deed and this Agreement shall be deemed to be terminated; furthermore, in the event such defaulting party is the party in possession of the Subject Property, such defaulting party shall be deemed to be tenant-at-will, subject to the nondefaulting party obtaining possession of the premises in the manner provided by the laws of Unlawful Detainer in the State of _____ in effect at the date of such default.

17.02 **Legal Action.** In addition to the remedy described in paragraph 17.01, the nondefaulting party shall, as an alternative remedy, be entitled to bring suit and recover judgment for all delinquent payments and installments and all of the nondefaulting party's costs and attorney's fees. The use of the remedy on one or more occasions shall not prevent the nondefaulting party, at its option, from resorting to this or any other available remedy allowable at law or equity in the cause of a subsequent default.

17.03 Liquidated Damages. If the remedy described in paragraph 17.01 above is utilized and a forfeiture of the interest of the defaulting party is effected, the parties hereto expressly acknowledge and agree, as evidenced by their initials signed by this paragraph, that any and all amounts previously paid under this Agreement and/or the Lease Agreement by the defaulting party shall be retained by the nondefaulting party as agreed upon liquidated damages, in view of the fact that it is and will be extremely difficult and impractical to fix an exact amount of damages for any default hereunder.

Resident's Initials_____

Nonresident's Initials_____

18. Option to Purchase. The parties may agree at any time during the initial term of this Agreement or extension thereafter that Resident may purchase the interest of Nonresident in the Property at a purchase price and terms agreeable to the parties or that Nonresident may purchase the interest of Resident upon such price and terms as the parties may agree. If no purchase and sale shall take place between the parties upon the expiration of the initial term of this Agreement, Nonresident may obtain an independent appraisal of the Property to establish its value. The appraisal shall be conducted by either an FHA, VA, or MAI certified appraiser or one mutually agreed upon by both parties. Resident shall then have the first option to purchase Nonresident's interest in the Property at the appraised value thus determined and shall be granted thirty (30) days following the completion of the appraisal in which to do so. The value of Nonresident's interest shall be his ownership interest less the same pro rata portion of the mortgage, plus an initial investment. If Resident shall not elect to purchase Nonresident's interest in the Property, then Nonresident shall have the option to purchase Resident's interest in the Property for a period of thirty (30) days thereafter, based upon the appraised value thus determined. In such event, the purchase price for the Resident's interest shall be the equity value of his ownership interest determined by the appraisal. If neither party shall elect to purchase the interest of the other, as herein set forth, the parties may agree to list the Property for sale to a third party upon price and terms that the parties hereto may agree, and if the parties shall fail to agree upon such price, then, at the option of Nonresident, the Property shall be sold at the appraised value as hereinabove set forth and the net proceeds of such sale shall be distributed as follows: Nonresident shall first receive a sum equal to the initial investment as herein defined in Exhibit B, including any and all costs and advances made by him as herein set forth, and the remainder of the net proceeds of the sale shall be divided equally between the parties hereto in accordance with their ownership percentage after all costs of sale have been deducted. In the sale of the interest of either party hereto to the other, the selling party shall be charged with no costs or expenses other than the share of such party of the appraisal expenses and documentary stamps. If either of the parties shall be dissatisfied with the valuation of the property established by the appraiser as first above set forth, then said party may appoint an additional appraiser under the same qualifications and the sale price will be the average of the two appraisals; provided, however, that the election of the dissatisfied party for the use of another appraiser as herein set forth shall be made, in writing, to the other party hereto, within ten (10) days of the receipt of the appraisal by the first appraiser as first hereinabove set forth, failing which such dissatisfied party shall forfeit such right of election and the determination of the first appraiser first made as hereinabove set first set forth shall be binding upon the parties.

19. Distribution of Cash from Refinancing or Insurance. The net proceeds of a refinancing of the Property (other than in connection with Resident's or Nonresident's purchase of each other's interest), or the receipt of any casualty insurance proceeds or condemnation award with respect to the Property to the extent not used to reconstruct the residence on the Property or required to be paid to the Lender, shall be applied and distributed to the parties just as if it were Gross Sale Proceeds.

20. Relationship between Nonresident and Resident Not Partnership. The parties acknowledge to one another that it is their intention to hold the Property as tenants in common, that they have elected not to become partners, and that neither this Agreement nor any provisions of this Agreement shall be interpreted to impose a partnership relationship in either law or equity on the parties or either one of them. Accordingly, neither party shall have any liability for the debts or obligations of the other party.

21. Notices. Any notice or other communication required or desired to be served, given, or delivered hereunder shall be in writing and shall be deemed to have been duly served, given, or delivered upon personal delivery or upon deposit (within the continental United States) in the United States mail, registered or certified, with proper postage or other charges prepaid and addressed to the party to be notified as follows:

To Nonresident: at the address shown on the Transaction Schedule

To Resident: at the street address of the Property

22. Assignment; Successors and Assigns. Resident shall not during Resident's lifetime assign, transfer, sell, mortgage, pledge, hypothecate, or encumber this Agreement or any interest therein, including Resident's interest as tenant in common in the Property, except that a transfer of Resident's interest to Resident's then spouse shall be permitted. Nonresident shall have the right to assign this Agreement including Nonresident's interest as tenant in common in the

Property at any time after the termination of Nonresident's obligation to furnish funds hereunder; and prior to such time, such assignment shall be effective only if Nonresident agrees in writing with Resident to remain liable for such obligations. Subject to the foregoing restrictions, this Agreement shall inure to the benefit of and bind the heirs, executors, administrators, successors, and assigns of the respective parties hereto.

23. **Waiver of Claims.** Nonresident shall not be liable to Resident for, and Resident hereby waives *and releases* any claims, *demands, and liabilities of or against* Nonresident in respect of any injury or damage to any person or property in or about the Property by or from any cause whatsoever *other than the negligent or willful conduct of Nonresident or Nonresident's agents.*

24. **Indemnification.** Each party shall indemnify the other party for all damages and expenses for which the parties may become liable as a result of any act committed by such party in contravention of the provisions of this Agreement. In addition, Resident shall indemnify and hold Nonresident harmless from, and defend Nonresident against, any and all claims of liability for any injury or damage that shall have been caused by the act of Nonresident or Nonresident's agents.

25. **Entire Agreement.** This Agreement contains the entire agreement of the parties with respect to the matters covered herein, and no other agreement, statement, or promise made by any party that is not contained herein shall be binding or valid. This Agreement may be modified or amended only by a written instrument duly executed by both parties hereto.

26. **Arbitration.** All disputes, claims, and controversies relating to the interpretation, construction, performance, or breach of this Agreement shall be settled by arbitration with a single arbitrator, to take place in the location identified in the Transaction Schedule, pursuant to the Commercial Rules of the American Arbitration Association. Any party request-

ing arbitration under this Agreement shall make a demand on the other party by registered or certified mail with a copy to the Regional Office of the American Arbitration Association identified in the Transaction Schedule. Judgment upon the award rendered by the arbitrator may be entered in any court having jurisdiction thereof.

27. **Attorneys' Fees.** In the event any party brings legal action, including arbitration proceedings, to enforce any of the provisions of this Agreement, the party that does not prevail in such legal action agrees to pay the costs and reasonable attorneys' fees of the prevailing party in such legal action. *This Paragraph 27 shall not be effective if the Property is located in a state that does not authorize such payment.*

28. **Waiver of Right of Partition.** Nonresident hereby waives, for the term of the Mortgage Loan (but in no event for a period of more than 30 years), Nonresident's right to cause a partition of the Property in all circumstances except in the case of sale or unless otherwise agreed.

29. **Severability.** The provisions of this Agreement are intended to be severable. If any term or provision of this Agreement is illegal or invalid for any reason whatsoever, such illegality or invalidity shall not affect the validity of the remainder of this Agreement.

30. **Miscellaneous.** This Agreement is governed by the laws of the State identified in the Transaction Summary, and any question arising hereunder shall be construed or determined according to such law. Headings at the beginning of each numbered paragraph of this Agreement are solely for the convenience of the parties and are not a part of this Agreement. The waiver of Nonresident of the breach by Resident of any term, covenant, or condition herein contained shall not be deemed to be a waiver of any subsequent breach of the same or any other term, covenant, or condition herein contained. Time is of the essence of this Agreement.

31. **Homestead Exemption.** *The parties acknowledge that Resident intends to make the Property Resident's permanent*

Residence; and the parties agree that Resident *and members of Resident's immediate family are* exclusively entitled to claim the homestead exemption from judgments and *from* real property taxation, if *and to the extent* available under the laws of the State specified in the Transaction Schedule. Nonresident *acknowledges that the homestead status of the Property may be affected by actions taken by Nonresident and agrees to use best efforts to prevent liens from attaching to Nonresident's interest therein.*

32. Failure to Acquire Property. Notwithstanding any other provisions hereof, this Agreement shall terminate and all deposits made pursuant to this Agreement shall be returned if the Closing Date does not occur within 180 days of the date hereof or any extension mutually agreed upon.

IN WITNESS WHEREOF, this Agreement is entered into on the date first above written.

NONRESIDENT

DATED:_____, 20_____   By:_____

DATED:_____, 20_____   By:_____

RESIDENT

For Florida Transactions Only

The undersigned spouse of the above-identified Resident hereby joins in the above Agreement.

SPOUSE OF NONRESIDENT

FOR ILLUSTRATIVE PURPOSES ONLY

STATE OF _____)

: ss

COUNTY OF _____)

BEFORE ME, the undersigned authority, duly authorized to administer oaths and take acknowledgements, personally appeared:

to me known to be the person(s) described in and who executed the foregoing Equity Sharing Agreement as Resident, and _he_ acknowledged to me that _he_ executed the same for the purposes therein set forth as _____ free act and deed.

WITNESSETH, my official hand and seal this _____ day of _____, 20__.

My Commission Expires:

    NOTARY PUBLIC

    State of _____ at Large

STATE OF _____)

                    : ss

COUNTY OF _____)

BEFORE ME, the undersigned authority, duly authorized to administer oaths and take acknowledgements, personally appeared:

_____

to me known to be the person(s) described in and who executed the foregoing Equity Sharing Agreement as Resident, and _he_ acknowledged to me that _he_ executed the same for the purposes therein set forth as _____ free act and deed.

WITNESSETH, my official hand and seal this _____ day of _____, 20__.

My Commission Expires:

    NOTARY PUBLIC

    State of _____at Large

      FOR ILLUSTRATIVE PURPOSES ONLY

EXHIBIT B

Transaction Summary

Ownership Sharing Percentages:

    Resident: _____

    Nonresident: _____

Appreciation Sharing Percentages:

    Resident: _____

    Nonresident: _____

Cost Sharing Percentages:

    Resident: _____

    Nonresident: _____

Mortgage Terms:

    Amount of Loan: _____

    Interest Rate: _____

    Monthly Debt Service:

    Term: _____   Closing Costs: _____

    Lease Amount: _____

    Cash Closing Requirement:

    Resident _____ including $ _____ previously furnished

    Nonresident _____ including initial investment of $_____

Amount of Additional Security:

    Resident: _____

    Nonresident: _____

    Monthly payment required of Nonresident: _____

    Time period during which above payment is required to be made: _____

    Address of Nonresident: _____

    Location of Arbitration: _____

Regional Office of American Arbitration
Association to be notified: _____
State: _____

FOR ILLUSTRATIVE PURPOSES ONLY

INITIAL PAYMENT RECEIPT

[DATE]

THIS RECEIPT in the amount of _____
_____ Dollars ($_____) for
payment made by

in connection with that certain Equity Sharing Agreement,
dated _____, 20__, by and between said parties and

This payment is nonrefundable and is in addition to all other
payments called for in said Agreement.

Attest:_____

Attest:_____

Syndicating Real Estate

Putting a group of mostly passive investors together in a larger transaction, with one person taking responsibility for running the operation, is known as *syndicating*. There are big syndications like REITs (real estate investment trusts), but there are also small ones.

It's possible to make a great deal of money in syndications if you're the person who puts them together. Basically, you are leveraging your time and any money you may put in with money from both investors (who will be putting up the bulk of the money) and the bank you finance with. In the more successful syndications we've structured, and seen others structure, the syndicator puts up some of the investment and then invites other investors to put up the balance. All investors as a group (including the syndicator, if he puts in money) receive a preferred return on their investment (about 8 percent in today's market) before the syndicator makes anything except a management fee. The management fee is customarily 10 percent of the income.

After the investors get their money back plus the preferred return, all of the other income or profit is split 50/50 between the investors and the syndicator. Obviously, this can be very profitable for the syndicator if he does a good job, because he will get 50 percent of all of the equity buildup and appreciation. On large projects, this can be substantial. Naturally, there are also risks, because (it almost goes without saying) rich investors tend to be unhappy if the deal doesn't work out as planned. In such cases, conflicts can arise.

Syndications can also carry potential added risks. A great number of local syndications (as opposed to national REITs) are structured as limited partnerships or LLCs. While this is a very effective legal structure, it is also considered a form of security—in other words, something that is pledged to guarantee the repayment of a loan. The security classification means that you must comply with state and federal security laws requiring you to either register the security publicly or seek to structure it as an exempt offering, which most people do.

Because of these kinds of legal hoops, we encourage you to work with a real estate or securities lawyer who understands the ins and outs of the syndication process. Don't get put off by the initial confusion that you're likely to experience. Like equity-sharing arrangements and some of the other creative strategies we have discussed in this book, syndications seem more complicated than they really are. Once you work through the first one, you will quickly get comfortable with the process.

The other disadvantage of syndications, as suggested earlier, is the added hassle of dealing with multiple investors, who can be demanding. If your project works out great, your headaches are likely to be small. But things *don't* always proceed as planned, and you must be mentally prepared for the added challenge.

THE PARTNERSHIP AND EQUITY-SHARING CHECKLIST

☑ **STRUCTURE YOUR VENTURES IN WRITING.** No matter which partnership structure you choose, make sure to get it down in writing. Learn the elements of a good partnership agreement. Tackle the tough issues, such as the buy-sell arrangement, in advance, while everyone is still feeling kindly toward one another. Figure out who gets what, keeping in mind that long-term benefits may argue for short-term concessions.

☑ **LOOK FOR EQUITY-SHARING ARRANGEMENTS.** Use equity sharing to redistribute the benefits and challenges of real estate ownership. Like the other strategies outlined in this chapter, equity sharing is an opportunity for you to be creative—for your own benefit, but also for the benefit of your partners. Think "outside the box," as they say—and then check with your lawyer!

☑ **CONSIDER SYNDICATIONS.** Most people think "huge venture" when they think of syndications, but syndications actually come in all shapes and sizes. Syndicating a property is a good way for you to leverage other people's money to your advantage—and for them to get the benefit of hard, hands-on work by someone as diligent as you. Participation by a savvy lawyer and accountant is an absolute necessity, since syndications often overlap with securities and securities-related regulations.

CHAPTER 15

Save on Taxes by Investing in Real Estate

There are two great and legitimate tax shelters left in this country: small businesses and real estate. If you follow through with the things we show you in this book, you will be able, through investing in real estate, to avail yourself of most of the tax shelters provided by each of them.

Advanced Real Estate Strategy No. 13: Reduce Your Taxable Income

What is a tax shelter? It's any legitimate way of doing business that saves you money on your taxes. Let's underscore that word *legitimate*. Over the years, there have been scores of tax-sheltering techniques that have been dubious at best and unlawful at worst. We don't intend to advocate anything like that in this book. When we speak of tax shelters, we are speaking only of legitimate, IRS-recognized and Congress-sanctioned ways to structure transactions to minimize your tax obligations and save you money.

Remember, there's nothing wrong with minimizing the amount of money that you hand over to the government in taxes. In fact, the government has passed these laws in part out of recognition that the buying and selling of real estate (and the operation of small businesses) helps make our economy strong.

Your Home as a Tax Shelter

While most people think of their home as "shelter," they don't necessarily think of it as a *tax* shelter. But it's true: a home is a tax shelter because there are tax advantages to owning a home, conferred upon you because the government favors a nation of owners, rather than renters. Buying real estate, moreover, helps keep money circulating and the economy moving. Builders build to meet demand. Building supplies get manufactured and sold. Carpenters hammer, and plumbers plumb. The economy stays strong and vibrant.

One of the first tax benefits of your home is that you can refinance it any time after you have build up some equity. The money you take out from the refinancing is tax-deferred, at that point. (This is true of other real estate, as well.) So your real estate holdings can serve as a giant piggy bank. Unlike an IRA or 401(k) retirement plan, which has penalties for taking money out of it, your home can be looked at as a bank that you can use.

Some readers may take issue with us for suggesting that you use your home equity in this fashion, because they think you should never take money out of your home. They operate on the theory that you will spend your equity, and it won't be there for emergencies. (In other words, they don't trust you with your own money.) OK, we understand their potential concern. But if you let money sit in your house "bank," not working for you, then you won't build up other things for the future. You could argue, in fact, that someday you might actually lose your house and the equity you have in it *because* you were too conservative. On this issue, as on others we've discussed in recent chapters, there is no single right answer. Your specific circumstances have to determine *your* right answer.

Having presented both sides of the argument, we can tell you that we have used, and we'll *continue* to use, our house and all of our real estate as a bank that we can borrow from and pay back. What we don't do, and what you shouldn't do, is put built-up equity into things that don't have the potential to grow in value. We *don't* think, for example, that you should use your built-up equity to buy that hot new car you want mainly for the purpose of gratifying your ego. If, on the other hand, you were buying a new car because you needed it for work to help you make money, that would be fair game. The basic rule is, *avoid using your equity to buy a depreciating asset.* Over the years, we have used our "home bank" for college expenses, for starting new businesses, for buying more real estate, and (one time) to pay a tax bill we owed, but didn't have the money to pay at that particular moment.

Advanced Real Estate Strategy No. 14: Use Your Home's Capital Gain Exclusion

One of the best gifts Congress doled out in the past decade is that you can sell a principal residence that you have lived in for two of the past five years and take out the gain without tax. The amount excluded is up to $500,000 if you are married and filing jointly, or $250,000 if you are single.

The new law, passed in 1997, doesn't require you to buy another house, as the old one did. This is a gift, pure and simple. It allows you to build up equity and then "capture" it without having to pay tax on it. You don't have to wait until you are 70 or any other specific age. All taxpayers can get this "free money" in the form of a generous tax break.

To qualify, as noted, you have to have lived in the house for two of the last five years. "Living in the house" means using the property as your home. It does allow for vacations and short-term absences, but you must really have intended that house to have been your home during those years.

Even if there were no other reason to buy a home (and of course there are many), we would encourage you to buy a home to get this gift of tax-free money. Even at the relatively low capital gains tax rate of 15 percent, it can save you more than *$75,000* in tax liability.

Advanced Real Estate Strategy No. 15: Take Advantage of Business-Use Deductions

Even as recently as a few years back, the IRS took a dim view of people who took deductions for the business use of their home. It *allowed* this, yes, but it didn't *like* it, and it sometimes gave people a hard time about it in audits. That has all changed with the IRS's recent attempts to present a friendlier face to the taxpaying public. You do need to keep good records of your home's use as a business office, but this isn't difficult, and you aren't likely to get hassled if you can show that your home office is legitimate.

You can take deductions for your home if you meet two main criteria. First, you must conduct business in the space you are claiming as an office. Second, the business space you are claiming must be used exclusively for that purpose. This last requirement just means that if you are calling something your "office," don't also use it as a bedroom, because in the government's eyes, that isn't an office. This is only common sense, but people seem to have trouble with it.

Once you have space that qualifies, you can also deduct a portion of your other expenses equal to the amount of your home that is used for business. For example, if you have a 2,000-square-foot house and 25 percent of it is used for business, as just described, then you can also deduct 25 percent of the payments you make on your utilities, phone, yard care, painting, and maintenance. Do the numbers, and you will see that this starts to mount up to a tidy deduction. You start to benefit from these deductions as soon as you get started—and since your real estate operations will eventually require you to have an office, why not start today?

By the way, just to dispel a persistent legend: it used to be that if you had a home office, part of the gain on the sale of your house would have to be treated as the sale of business property and would therefore be a taxable event. (In other words, it couldn't be part of your $500,000 couple's exclusion.) This is no longer true. When you sell your home and take the exclusion, you no longer have to allocate part of the sale to the sale of a business office.

Advanced Real Estate Strategy No. 16: Take Vacation-Home Deductions

If you have a vacation home, you can deduct mortgage interest and property taxes on that property as itemized deductions. This makes most of your payments deductible. Unfortunately, there *are* limitations on the amounts you get to take. The second home cannot be a rental, or it is considered a rental property (which is not bad, per se; it's just a different class of deductions). Taken together, your acquisition debt on your vacation home and your principal residence can't total more than $1 million, or you begin to have phased-out deductions. Additionally, your total income cannot exceed $139,000 for a married couple filing jointly.

If you make your vacation home a rental, as noted, you get different kinds of deductions. You can depreciate the property as income property, and you can deduct the mortgage interest, property taxes, utilities, repairs, and even travel expenses to inspect the property. All of these expenses are used to offset any income you get from the rental. If there is extra loss over and above what you made on the property, you can deduct that up to "limitations for passive activity," if that rule applies. Before you start renting a property, meet with an accountant who can set you up with a record-keeping system and explain the rules for your particular circumstances.

Selling your vacation home gets a little tricky, because it isn't your home and it isn't a rental. If it had been your home in recent years, you could have qualified for the capital gain exemption we just discussed. If it had been a rental, you could have elected to defer the gain through the use of a tax-free exchange, which we will discuss in a moment. Since it fits neither situation, however, you will have to pay the capital gains tax. (Hey, the good news here is that you had a gain to pay tax on. You can begrudge the government its share, but don't fail to celebrate your own much larger share.) To avoid the tax, consider either converting the vacation home to a rental property prior to sale (so that you can qualify for a tax-free exchange) or moving into the property for two years, thereby qualifying it as your home.

Advanced Real Estate Strategy No. 17: Defer Taxes Whenever Possible

Paying tax on the profits you make from the sale of real estate is expensive, and it keeps you from having more money working for you. Rates range from the investor's relatively low capital gains tax rate all the way up to "dealer treatment," which requires you to pay ordinary income tax rates even on your property sale. Obviously, under these circumstances, you want to remain classified as an investor. And to encourage you to keep putting the money back into real estate, the IRS allows you (as an investor) to defer the tax by using a "like-kind exchange" into another property. The authorization for this comes in Section 1031 of the federal tax code; hence the name "1031 exchange."

To get the benefits of a tax-free exchange, you'll have to go through some hoops. We'll discuss them here, but when the time comes for you to actually *do* an exchange, make sure to use either a professional accountant to structure the exchange or an exchange accommodator, who can help you with escrow arrangements.

The three main requirements for a tax-deferred exchange are as follows:

1. You must either make the exchange at the same time or meet the escrow requirement for a deferred or "Starker" exchange. For a delayed exchange, you must prepare a list of three properties you think you will exchange into. The list must be filed within 45 days of your sale, and you must close on the new property within 180 days of the sale of your first property. During the period between the sale of your property and the exchange, you cannot take possession of the cash proceeds. They must go into an escrow account handled by the Exchange Accommodator.

2. The property exchanged must be of "like kind." This isn't as complicated as people try to make it out to be. It doesn't mean that you have to exchange an apartment house for an apartment house. You could exchange an apartment house for vacant land. All that "like kind" means is that you have to exchange an investment property for an investment property—nothing more complicated than that.

3. The two properties exchanged must both be held for productive use in a trade or business or for investment. Again, this is not difficult, since we are talking about investment property.

Your home used to be totally excluded from exchange benefits, but now you can use the capital gain exclusion to qualify your home. If you exchange an income property for a home that you live in and you live there for five years, you can use your $500,000 capital gain exclusion. If your gain is more than $500,000, you will have to pay tax on that amount, but at least you will have deferred it for that length of time.

Advanced Real Estate Strategy No. 18: Maximize Rental Property Deductions

When most people think of the tax advantages associated with owning real estate, they normally think of rental property. When you buy a property for rental, whether it is a small home or a large apartment complex, you get to depreciate the property from a tax standpoint.

This tax advantage arises from the theory that a building is a wasting asset, and, sooner or later, it won't be worth anything because it will be worn out. To give you some benefit each year for this depreciation, the IRS allows you to take a deduction for the depreciation and use it to shelter income that comes from the property—or, in many instances, income from other sources. As you might expect, there are rules and limitations governing these deductions, so you must check with your tax adviser to see how they apply to you personally.

Meanwhile, here's an overview of how this tax savings works. You must first divide the cost of the property between land and building. As a rule of thumb, 80 percent is allocated to the building, and 20 percent to the land. Only the building is considered a wasting asset that is subject to depreciation. So you want to try to make the allocation as favorable as possible—i.e., more building value and less land value. Next, the IRS has established tables for the life of assets. In the case of a single-family house, you would get to depreciate it over a period of 27.5 years. If you use "straight-line" (or year-by-year equal) depreciation, this means that you can take the same amount each year as a deduction against your rental income.

In addition to depreciation, you get more deductions on rental property. You can deduct the interest you pay on your loan, all expenses of operation, and travel to inspect the property. This provision can become important if you own property in Hawaii, for example, and you have to put up with annual trips (preferably during rotten weather at home) to inspect the property. You can get a deduction and a tan on the same trip, with the government's blessing.

Advanced Real Estate Strategy No. 19: Use All Available Write-Offs

You can deduct your "ordinary and necessary" local transportation expenses if they result from your efforts to collect rental income or to manage, conserve, or maintain your rental property. This includes your personal car, pickup truck, or SUV.

You can deduct your expenses using one of two methods: actual expenses, or at the standard mileage rate. For 2005, the standard mileage rate is 40.5 cents per mile. (See IRS publication 463.)

Advanced Real Estate Strategy No. 20: Use the Section 179 Expense Write-Off

As your real estate operation evolves into a going concern, you can qualify for some special write-offs. Section 179 of the tax code allows you to write off up to $105,000 of long-term assets in the year you acquire them. This gives you some quick deductions, even though you may have financed the purchase. It's interesting: by financing the purchase, you didn't lay out cash, but you started making payments. So, according to the government's logic, you get to deduct 100 percent of the value of the property, giving you instant cash flow. Sounds good to *us*.

Until Congress closed the SUV loophole this past year, your sport utility vehicle qualified for full 179 expense write-offs, helping to save you cash for your down payment on an SUV of over 6,000 pounds used in your business. You can still write off $25,000 on an SUV, and, if your vehicle is a pickup truck weighing over 6,000 pounds, you can deduct up to the full $105,000 179 expense in 2005.

Advanced Real Estate Strategy No. 21: Deduct Expenses Used to Produce Income

You can deduct investment expenses as miscellaneous itemized deductions on Schedule A of your 1040 tax form. The expenses must be either directly related to the production of income or related to an income-producing property.

Examples include

Attorney's fees
Accounting fees
Clerical help
Office expense
Investment counsel or advice
Safe deposit box
Local transportation expense
Travel expense outside local area, if related

Advanced Real Estate Strategy No. 22: Access Free IRS Publications to Learn about Deductions

The IRS does a great job of supplying tax information regarding your deductions. Just remember: the information you get from the IRS on any possible deduction will be the most conservative information you can find.

Start online at IRS.gov (the IRS Web site), which is excellent. You can either read topical publications online or order them. The IRS will also send you the publications if you call 1-800-TAX FORM (1-800-829-3676).

Free publications we think you will benefit from ordering from the IRS are

Publication Number	Name
463	Travel & Entertainment
535	Business Expenses
946	How to Depreciate

THE TAX-SAVING CHECKLIST

☑ **SAVE MONEY THROUGH TAX SHELTERS.** The government wants, and needs, a healthy real estate sector. Therefore, it's willing to extend tax benefits to investors like you. Use your home as a tax shelter. (If you do nothing else, buy and hold, and build up $500,000 in equity—which you and your spouse can take tax free when you sell.) Use your built-up equity as a sort of "piggy bank" when you see an opportunity to buy assets that are likely to appreciate. Locate your small business in your home (carefully following the IRS rules) and take more deductions. Vacation homes are trickier, but they still offer opportunities for tax breaks.

☑ **DEFER TAXES WHENEVER POSSIBLE.** Keep your money working for you, rather than for the government. Use 1031 exchanges to defer taxes by using a like-kind exchange with a similar commercial property.

☑ **MAXIMIZE RENTAL PROPERTY DEDUCTIONS.** The power of depreciation can be enormous. Depreciate your rental property to realize big tax savings year after year. Deduct all the expenses associated with the property—including that annual visit to the property, which is (preferably) located in an area you don't mind visiting.

☑ **USE ALL AVAILABLE ADDITIONAL WRITE-OFFS.** This may sound obvious, but not everybody does it. *Take all the deductions to which you're entitled.* Write off legitimate car expenses. When you acquire significant assets in your business, write those off under the provisions of Section 179 of the IRS tax code. Go to the source (the IRS) for good information up front, and ask your attorney or accountant to interpret things for you.

CHAPTER 16

Using Option Strategies

Many of you will love this chapter because, just as options can create opportunities in the stock market, real estate options can create tremendous opportunities.

Many people consider stock options to be aggressive. We aren't going to debate that here, but we urge you to at least not consider real estate options in the same light. Simply put, an option in real estate is a right to buy a particular property in the future for a stated price and on stated terms. Real estate options reduce your risk because all you risk is the small amount of money needed to secure that option, which, of course, is far less than putting up all the money needed to buy the property.

While many of you will love this chapter, there will no doubt be a subset of readers who are skeptical, and will remain skeptical, that options can be pulled off. All we can say to those people is, *keep an open mind.* Based on our own experience, this can be a highly profitable and not particularly management-intensive way to be involved in the real estate business.

Advanced Real Estate Strategy No. 23: Use Real Estate Options

As noted, an option in real estate is a right to buy property in the future for a stated price and on stated terms. When you are given an option, you pay something of value, and, in return, you control that right as long as the option remains open (that is, until the stated expiration date). This means that you can exercise your option, sell the option to someone else and profit from that transaction, or let the option expire. Best of all, during the option period, you don't have to worry about the kinds of problems (management issues, making mortgage payments) that you would have if you were the owner.

This *doesn't* mean that you won't be working. Not at all. Of course, in some situations, you may get lucky and flip the property for a quick profit. But, in other cases, in fact, you may find yourself very much involved in correcting problems with the property, or participating in the process of getting it rezoned, or supervising the preparation of architectural plans for changes to the property. Even in these more hands-on situations, however, you'll be free to do what you do best in the world of real estate, and all without actually owning the property.

In this chapter, we will discuss four types of options that we have been involved in over the years. We will show you how you can use them in your real estate arsenal, and we'll lay out both the advantages and the disadvantages of each. The four types are (1) the buyer's contract option, (2) the pure option, (3) the lease option, and (4) the divided lease option.

1. *The buyer's contract option.* We have used this option most often in our own ventures. It isn't technically called an option, mainly because some sellers resist giving an option on their property. They are afraid you are trying to get something from them "on the cheap," and they resist that. This is an understandable mistake on their part, but it's still a mistake. Why? Because in reality, the *pure option*, which we discuss in a moment, would actually give them more money in most cases than the buyer's contract option, but the latter is easier to get because it is structured without the word *option*. A pure option is usually accompanied by an option payment that is nonrefundable, and the buyer's contract option is normally structured with a payment that is refundable. (Now you know why we prefer the buyer's contract option when we are buying!)

The buyer's contract option is based on a real estate purchase contract. It is a "buyer's" contract because the terms in the contract are structured in ways that benefit the buyer. (See Chapter 7, "How to Write Money-Making Contracts.") Deposits, as noted, are refundable. The specified time periods in the contract are long and therefore favor the buyer. The more time the buyer can get in the contract to perform things like zoning changes, the longer the time he will have the property under contract, and the better the chance he will have of selling his position to someone else.

Don't infer that this is necessarily a bad thing for the seller. If the seller has structured her side of the contract to get what she wants and needs, then she has received the benefit of a bargain that she has already decided was a *good* bargain for her. A buyer's contract option, moreover, is most often used in the case of substantial developments, where parties tend to be represented by their lawyers and other advisers. For the most part, both the buyer and the seller know what they're getting into.

Recently, we were looking at a 40-acre tract of land to develop for upscale residential homes. The property was located on a lake—for us, one of the best possible selling points of a property—and in an area with a rapidly growing population. So this property had great potential value for what we wanted to do, but it also had one problem: a pair of nesting eagles.

Now, we love eagles, and we weren't about to get involved with a development that was going to either (1) cause a problem for the eagles or (2) attract the attention of the federal government. On the other hand: the seller wanted to sell, and according to the U.S. Constitution, his property rights were also protected, and he therefore had the right to get the maximum amount he could out of his property. Obviously, we all faced a dilemma.

The solution came from a very successful real estate broker, who believes in looking at a problem as simply an opportunity to be creative. He proposed that we enter into an agreement to buy the property at the price we would pay if there were no eagle problem. In return, the seller—knowing that he had a buyer for his property if he could solve the eagle problem—would hire a consultant to study the eagles' habitat, movements, and nesting periods, to make sure that development of the property would not hurt the eagles.

So we entered into a formal contract to buy the property, giving us a long period of time within which to perform various feasibility studies (and, incidentally, giving the seller time to solve *his* problem). We put very little money down, and all of it was refundable if the seller could not deliver the developable piece according to our specifications. The seller was pleased because he had a contract that gave him his money if he could achieve a goal he thought was attainable. We were pleased because we had a property under contract that gave us the right to close in the future, at our option price, if we were satisfied with what the seller came up with.

So to summarize: under this contract structure, we could secure an option on the property for a substantial period of time with little money of our own in the deal, all of which would be refundable if the property did not meet our specifications. We would now be free to either do the necessary planning, marketing, and packaging of the property to sell it to someone else (before the eagle problem was solved) or, if we preferred, to close on the property ourselves, whichever was to our advantage.

Do transactions work out like this all the time? No, they don't. (In fact, this particular one fell through.) But this is our favorite way to structure deals like this, because they have large upside potential and require very little up-front cash. In most cases, these transactions (if they are carefully structured up front) turn out to be win/win deals for everyone. And there is another fringe benefit that grows out of participating in deals that require unique solutions: you eventually get a reputation for being a problem solver. The result is that you start getting more and more interesting deals presented to you, many of which have inherent challenges that require time to resolve. If you are looking for option possibilities, these kinds of challenges always work in your favor.

2. *The pure option.* This involves the use of an actual option contract, as opposed to a contract to purchase. It gives you the right to buy the property for a certain price and on certain terms within a stated time period. Generally the option contract requires an option payment that is released to the person granting the option. Normally, the payment takes the form of cash, but we have seen other assets used for this purposes, like securities, promissory notes, or even personal property like boats.

Boats? Yes, strange as it may seem. Sometimes the offer of something the seller can't readily go out and get for himself is an added enticement. A classic car or boat might be more attractive to the seller than cash, because he might not normally go out and buy the car himself. The option arrangement gives him the opportunity to get something he has always wanted and maybe still wind up with the property. This can be a difficult proposition to turn down. In the case of women who are sellers (or who are in control as the wife of the seller), vacation trips are sometimes the right lever. Imagine going home to your wife one day and saying, "Hey, honey, some guy is offering us a trip around the world on a private yacht if we give him an option for a year to buy our 2,000 acres for the price we want . . . and we may not even have to sell it"!

When cash is involved, there is no absolute fixed amount that you should offer for the option. But to give you a ballpark estimate, a number somewhere between 1 and 3 percent of the proposed purchase price usually works for people. If you can keep the amount in the 1 percent range or lower, you will probably have many more winning options. As with most real estate ventures, however, you may decide that paying more to get a deal you know you can really make a lot of money on is well worth it.

It is interesting to note that in times when listings on property have been hard to get because properties were selling so fast, some Realtors have offered this range (1 to 3 percent) to get listings on properties that appeared have a high potential for profitable resale. Since they would receive anywhere from 6 percent (on a home) to 10 percent (on vacant land) as a commission, they were willing to gamble 1 percent or more to get the listing. They also knew that a good listing would attract buyers for other properties that they could make more commissions on, so one good listing could become very profitable, indeed.

And just to sweeten the deal even further: typically, they could also get that 1 percent paid by the buyer of the property, since the fee paid would show up as a credit on the settlement sheet if the property was sold. Which Realtor would you choose to list your property? Someone who was offering to pay you, or someone who just said that he could sell your property? Interestingly enough, the reality of this kind of deal is that the listing agreement becomes a form of option, just with a cap on the upside of the sale equal to the amount of the listing commission. The real estate agent has tied up the property, and, if it sells to anyone, he makes up to the capped amount. See how it works? And can you see why, if you *structure* an option well, it isn't necessarily hard to get, because everybody in the deal can benefit?

3. *The lease option.* Probably the option technique that is talked about most in real estate seminars, the lease option, is the easiest to get and fits into the normal kinds of conversations that go on with the buying and renting of single-family homes. Here's how it works: you find a seller who wants to lease her property, and you offer to be the tenant for a longer term than is common (three years is often used in lease options), but you request the right to buy the property at the end of the term for a price you negotiate today.

Lease option agreements are interesting to landlords in part because you are offering to take on the management headaches of operating this property—headaches that so many people (including us) can't stand. The degree to which the landlord can't stand it largely determines the option price you can negotiate. Property management has turned off these owners, and they have become what are known in the business as "don't-wanters." Frequently, these are people who should never have been in real estate in the first place. They either got caught up in the excitement of doing a deal, or listened to a get-rich-quick presentation that made everything look easier than it is. But that's not really your concern. When you find a don't-wanter, you will find a good deal—and there are a *lot* of don't-wanters out there.

The advantage of the lease option is that you usually don't have to pay anything additional for the option, and the purchase price that you nail down is often little more than the current market value. So your upside is the potential appreciation on the property over the next three years. With some areas of the country experiencing double-digit appreciation every year, that upside could be significant. Additionally, in three years, you are likely to qualify for good financing, because you have built up equity in the property. The big downside of this arrangement is that unless you are going to occupy the property yourself, you now have the management headaches that the owner was trying to get rid of. In that case, you'd better like property management—or you may turn into a don't-wanter yourself over the next three years.

Lease option arrangements are also good for first-time buyers who can't qualify to purchase a property. Maybe they haven't established good credit yet, or maybe they've had a credit problem in the past, and sufficient time hasn't passed for them to be considered a good risk on the lenders' computers that calculate these things. The solution for these buyers is to lease the property for at least a year—and if they can get a longer lease option, so much the better. If they can demonstrate that they have made regular lease payments on the property on time during the past 12 months, it is fairly easy for them to get qualified to purchase the house based on their rent payment history on the property. Also, depending on the length of the option, they have one to three years of equity buildup over their option price (assuming, of course, that property values have gone up).

4. *The divided lease option.* Although similar to the lease option, for a divided lease option you draft two separate documents instead of having the option to purchase included in the lease contract. One document is the lease, and the other is the option itself. While this practice is not as common as structuring the transaction in one document, there are some advantages to doing it this way.

The divided lease option creates two separate contracts that are not necessarily related to each other. Under the regular lease option, if you default on the lease in any way, the option is void. With two separate contracts, a default would not affect both contracts unless the seller insisted on tying the two together.

By using two separate agreements, in addition, you could assign the rights under each to different parties. For example, you could find a tenant to enter into a sublease arrangement and cover you under the lease, and then you could sell the option to someone else. Depending on how you structure your lease in the beginning, you might still be responsible for the lease, should your sublease tenant not keep up the payments; but that just means that you have to step back in and find a new tenant for the remaining term.

The final reason the divided lease option is sometimes preferred is that the traditional lease option is specifically named as a transaction that violates the "due on sale" provision of most residential mortgages or deeds of trust. While we don't know of any case where this has actually occurred, it is in the federal banking regulations [Section 591.2 (b) of Title 12, "Banks and Banking," in the Code of Federal Regulations, if you're interested] and could be used if the lender felt that his loan was threatened. Check with your lawyer.

The lease option is the most common of the forms of option structure we just discussed. It is also our least favorite and the least profitable. The primary reason is economics, and the secondary reason is management responsibility.

The buyer's contract option and the pure option have the largest potential profit, and you don't have to manage the properties. While property management may not strike you as a big deal, it strikes *us* that way because it is time-consuming, and time is money. You can either spend your time managing the properties and making small profits for that time spent, or you can be out putting together more pure options.

Amazingly, this is a very difficult concept to teach to new "students" of real estate, the stock market, or business in general, but it is also one of the most profound. You have only so much time to spend making money. That is the one element you have no control over. What you *can* control is how you spend that time. The more you spend the fixed quantity of time you have on more productive and profitable deals, the more money you will make—and, frankly, the more fun you will have. This is our "law of time management," and you should remind yourself of it every day. It is one of the reasons we like having a business partner: one of you usually remembers it even when the other doesn't.

Advanced Real Estate Strategy No. 24: Realize the Risks in Using Options

Every transaction in real estate has an associated risk. When you compare the risks and rewards, you get what's called the *risk/reward ratio*. We consider the risk/reward ratio for options to be very good, but there *are* risks, and you should know about them. So let's start with the bad stuff (the "cons") first.

1. *The property you have an option on can be destroyed.* If it is vacant land, this isn't usually a big problem, but there are sinkholes and storms that damage property. If the property is improved, you have to keep an eye on things, just as you do if you are the owner, because hopefully your option will have real value to it before it expires. Because you do have an insurable interest, you can get insurance to cover risks like fire. This additional cost is a factor you have to weigh just the way you do all other expenses, and you assume that cost only if it provides an economic benefit to you.

2. *The property you have an option on can be foreclosed on.* If this happens, it complicates your life, but it doesn't necessarily put you out of business and may even put you in a better position. Your option position can ultimately be wiped out in foreclosure, but there are all sorts of things you can do to make the lender's life difficult, such as filing a suit to protect your interest and slow down the lender's foreclosure. Lenders are by their very nature conservative, and what they want is their money. If you help them out (just as you would in any other foreclosure situation you got involved in), you may actually be able to negotiate a better price than you had before the foreclosure.

3. *The property can be placed under the jurisdiction of a bankruptcy court.* If the seller files for bankruptcy during your option period, all of his assets will go into the protection of the bankruptcy court. This doesn't mean that your option won't be honored, but it does mean that the court now controls what happens, and courts sometimes issue some strange decisions. It means at a minimum that you

will have to get involved in the process, which means hiring an attorney and adding expense. If you're dealing with a multimillion-dollar piece of property, it might be worth it. If the property is a single-family home, you might be better off just walking away from your option and not wasting time.

4. *The property can be taken by the government.* There are various governmental actions that could arise, such as condemnation (usually for road rights-of-way) or government seizure (if your seller was a bad guy and got involved in some shady deals the government didn't like, or if he didn't pay his taxes). The chance of these events actually happening is vanishingly small, and it can often be determined ahead of time by a title search for any governmental filing on the property or the owner before you get your option in the first place. This is why title searches are *always* a good idea, any time you get an option.

Advanced Real Estate Strategy No. 25: Learn the Advantages in Using Options

Now we are going to give you the good news: the benefits of options.

1. *Control of property without owning it.* You don't have to own something to make money on it; you just have to control the benefit of property appreciation, and that is what you do with an option.

2. *Reduced transaction cost.* The option has few costs other than the drafting of the option agreement and the price of the option itself. You don't have closing costs or any of

the other expenses normally associated with closing on a property until you decide to close on the property—and in many cases, you will either sell the option or walk away from it.

3. *No management headaches.* We have already disclosed our personal dislike for property management, but for those of you who have never had the pleasure, options avoid the problems of dealing with tenants, collecting payments, filing evictions, cleaning up the property before and after tenants, finding tenants, and spending money to get new tenants. You get the idea.

4. *No debt service.* With an option, you don't normally deal with debt service. While some options can be structured where you *do* make payments (instead of a one-time option fee), this isn't the norm, and it is up to you how you structure the transaction.

5. *No qualifying for a loan.* Since you don't get a loan, you don't have to qualify for one. This makes options a good route for people who have credit problems or otherwise have difficulty getting a loan. You also don't have to list the property debt as a liability, so your net worth isn't reduced. In fact, if you can show that your option has increased in value, you can list that value as an asset.

6. *No loan-associated costs.* There are no points to be paid on an option, or interest payments, or inspection fees, or any of those other buyer line items.

7. *No liability.* As the holder of an option, you don't have the possibility of getting sued if something happens on the property. If someone slips and falls on the property or gets hurt in any fashion, the owner will probably get sued, but your option interest won't.

8. *No negative cash flow.* Since there is no debt, you don't have any payments to make.

9. *No debt liability.* If something goes wrong with your finances, your job, or anything else, your liability is just your option price. You can walk away and be totally free and clear.

10. *No property repairs.* While you don't want things to go wrong with the property while you have an option on it, at least you don't have to worry about them if they do; the seller does.

11. *No carrying charges like insurance and taxes.* All of these ongoing costs belong to the owner of the property, and that isn't you . . . yet.

We think that the pros of options far outweigh the cons. And while options are a specialty, most real estate investors eventually get involved with one or more of the option examples we have discussed.

THE OPTIONS CHECKLIST

☑ **BECOME FAMILIAR WITH THE FOUR TYPES OF OPTIONS.** Each of the four basic types of options— the buyer's contract option, the pure option, the lease option, and the divided lease option—has special characteristics. Each may be more or less appropriate to your specific circumstances (which, of course, will change from opportunity to opportunity). Use one of these four varieties of options to solve a knotty problem, and not only will you make money, but you'll get a reputation as a problem solver—and you'll get more deals as a result.

☑ **PICK THE "RIGHT" OPTION.** Of course, the seller will have a lot to say about this. But to the extent that you can structure an option deal that (1) puts you in a position to capture future appreciation, (2) doesn't demand a lot of your cash, and (3) doesn't commit a lot of your time to property management, you'll have a winner.

☑ **LEARN AND WEIGH THE PROS AND CONS OF OPTIONS.** Yes, options have risks. But in our experience, the benefits of options *far outweigh* the risks. Run the calculations yourself. Once you're convinced, go find those option opportunities for yourself—and believe us, they're out there!

CHAPTER 17

Buy Real Estate Tax Liens for High Income

Tax lien certificates are among the best investments in America. If you weigh the pros and cons of purchasing tax lien certificates against those of traditional forms of investments, you'll quickly see that this is true.

The problem with tax lien certificates as an investment vehicle is they aren't well known—and by the way, most certificate investors think that's just great. Why the secrecy? One reason may be that no commissions are paid on the sale of the certificates; consequently, you don't have a large group of local brokers promoting their sale. Instead, promotion of the certificates is left to local county governments, which have never been known for their sophisticated marketing skills. The upshot is that a great investment is being purchased only by the few investors who have taken the time to learn about it.

A few years back, we took a camera crew to film a live tax lien auction in Orange County, Florida. We were producing a tax lien video, and we had got permission from the tax assessor's office to do the filming. When we came into the auction with the cameras, we were actually *booed* by the other investors attending. They knew that we were going to expose their secret profit arena to more people, and they didn't like it. Some were so mad, it was almost funny.

In a nutshell, tax lien certificates are notes against unpaid property taxes, auctioned to third parties at tax certificate sales. The proceeds of the sale are loaned to the delinquent property owner, who uses them to pay the overdue property taxes. The county receives its taxes, the property owner gets temporary relief from paying taxes when he does not have the money to pay, and a third-party investor receives an above-average return on her investment. No wonder tax lien certificates are so successful; they truly create a win/win situation for all concerned.

Tax lien certificate sales are conducted in something like 30 states across the country. The form the sale takes varies, as do the type of interest and the rate of return. Florida is one of the most favorable states for tax lien certificate sales, from an investor's point of view. But many states are just as good, and a few are even better.

Advanced Real Estate Strategy No. 26: Use Tax Lien Investing

The first and most obvious advantage to investing in tax lien certificates is the return offered. In Florida, the rate of return begins at 18 percent, and, because of the early payoff of certain certificates, there are ways in which an investor can make substantially more than that. When you compare this with a typical risk/reward ratio, the return for investing in tax lien certificates is extremely high.

Tax lien interest rates were bid down lower this year because interest returns on other investments were much lower, as well. The way this works is that investors bid the amount of interest they are willing to accept, and the low bidder wins. Each year, the rate is determined by the bidders on each property, and bidding starts at 18 percent.

The reaction of most investors upon hearing about this 18 percent annual return is, "If it looks too good to be true, then it probably *is* too good to be true!" While this statement is accurate in almost all other circumstances, you'll find that the risk involved in investing in tax lien certificates is *extremely low* compared to that of other forms of investment that promise high returns. In tax lien certificate investing, not only is the rate of return guaranteed by the local government, but an investor also receives security in the form of a lien against real estate. This security has priority over *all other liens*, with the exception of some federal tax liens. This means that your tax lien certificate must be paid off ahead of even a first mortgage on the property. Compare that to the risk a typical lender is willing to accept when it loans money on real estate, and you will find that tax lien certificates are actually *safer.*

Most lenders would feel that if they had an 80 percent loan-to-value ratio on a piece of residential real estate, they would have a relatively safe investment. Why? Because if they actually had to foreclose on the property, they would be protected by an equity cushion of at least 20 percent. But in the case of a tax lien sale, since the purchaser of the tax certificate is paid off ahead of even a first mortgage holder, the tax lien holder has the greater security *by far.*

Tax lien certificates provide a number of advantages to the investor, including low cash requirements, upside potential, ease of investing, and lack of management headaches. Let's look at these one at a time.

1. *Small investments.* One of the traditional obstacles to investing in specialized situations is that you tend to need a lot of money to get into the game. That is not the case with tax lien certificates, many of which are sold for less than $100, more of which are sold for less than $1,000, and an equal or greater number of which are sold for between $1,000 and $5,000.

Buying small certificates is easier than buying larger certificates, because the competition for larger certificates is growing. Certificates with values in the hundreds of thousands of dollars tend to be the object of heated bidding at auction, with investors willing to accept a rate lower than 18 percent. These are the kinds of certificates that banks and other large institutions go after because they can borrow the money from the Federal Reserve at 3 to 4 percent, bid the rate on a tax lien certificate down to as low as 6 to 7 percent, and still maintain an extremely safe spread on their investment. A nice return for a low risk on 100 percent borrowed money!

2. *Upside potential.* It's rare to find a good income investment that also offers upside growth potential. Tax lien certificates have this potential, because you can ultimately force a sale of the property, creating an opportunity to buy it at auction. At auction, based on the amount you have paid on the tax lien certificate, either your lien will be paid off with your stated amount of interest, or you may receive the property itself. Although you might doubt that people would let their property go for the price of a tax lien, it *happens,* and during weak economic periods or recessions, it happens more frequently.

3. *Ease of investing.* Investments with a good chance of high returns are frequently complicated. But in the case of tax lien cer-

tificates, the investment is made simple by the local counties that conduct the auction. Remember, it is in their interest to have as many people participate in the sale as possible, to ensure that the certificates will be sold. Consequently, the counties are very helpful with information about how to purchase tax lien certificates, and they make the process quite simple. You just call the tax assessor's office of the county that you want to buy in and ask it to tell you the procedures for participating in the auction. Normally, auctions are held once a year. We have met people who, in their retirement years, do nothing but travel the auction circuit.

4. *No management headaches.* One of the biggest problems with traditional forms of investment is the management headaches that arise once the investment is made. This is particularly true of real estate purchases; not only does the investor need money, but she has to be willing to accept the responsibility of ongoing management of the property. Investors in stocks or mutual funds must either commit themselves to doing research or blindly accept the whims of the overall market.

A tax lien certificate, on the other hand, is a payment of money with the collection process handled by the local county authorities. The only management required is keeping track of the number of certificates you have and the length of time you hold them. Only if you actually buy properties at auction will you be accepting the additional management responsibilities that go along with real estate—and that's not what we're talking about here.

We certainly don't want to overlook the disadvantages of tax lien certificates. These can be considered in two categories: reduced liquidity and risk. Again, let's look at them one at a time:

1. *Reduced liquidity.* This is perhaps the biggest disadvantage of tax lien certificates. Unlike stocks, bonds, or money market funds,

an investor cannot simply cash in his tax lien certificates when con-venient. He must either wait until the owner of the property elects to pay off the certificate or, after the minimum waiting period of two years, go through the process of asking the county to sell the property at auction. In either event, liquidity is controlled by fac-tors other than the investor's immediate financial needs.

The liquidity disadvantage can be minimized by staggering the purchase dates of your tax lien certificates, so that you will always have certificates available to cash out. This approach is similar to one used by investors when they stagger the maturity dates of their CDs. Some counties also have investor lists available, should a tax lien purchaser need to liquidate. Some investors on these lists may ask for an additional discount, hoping for a higher yield, but others may be satisfied with your 18 percent interest.

2. *Risk.* There are potential risks, and, although these risks are minimal, you should know what they are. You may worry, for instance, about problems that may arise if the owner of the prop-erty on which you own a tax lien certificate goes into bankruptcy. If the court should determine that whatever assets the debtor has must go to other creditors rather than to pay off your tax lien certificate, the argument goes, you would lose your investment. But while a judge theoretically could take such a position, it would be most unusual. As noted earlier, a tax lien certificate holder is a *secured creditor*, and in the bankruptcy process, secured creditors' liens are paid first out of the proceeds from the sale of the property they secure. The real risk is the normal risk of tax lien investing, and that is whether there is adequate secu-rity in the real estate itself to pay your certificate.

Of course, in the event of a bankruptcy filing, you face the likeli-hood of protracted delays. The process can take as long as a year or two, during which time your investment cannot be liquidated. The chance of any individual not recouping her original investment plus some interest is slim; however, the bankruptcy judge is free to lower your interest rate if he feels it is in the best interest of other creditors.

The second risk in purchasing tax lien certificates is the risk of environmental hazards—in other words, the chance that you'll end up purchasing a certificate on real estate with hazardous waste problems. This is a bogeyman conjured up by large tax lien certificate investors to scare off potential competition (like you, for example). Although hazardous waste is a risk, you can easily minimize that by limiting your tax lien investments to residential real estate. In addition, Congress has passed various laws protecting holders of liens on property where hazardous wastes are found. These actions were taken on behalf of banks, but they should also protect tax lien certificate holders. (At the present time, however, this application of the law has not been tested.)

The third risk, alluded to a few paragraphs back, is that the security may be less than what was expected. An example of this is when a tax lien certificate is purchased on property with a mobile home on it. Let's imagine that after a couple of years, the owner of the property removes the mobile home, leaving the tax lien certificate holder with a vacant plat of land worth less than the certificate. Again, an investor could eliminate this possibility by purchasing certificates based in areas that don't have mobile homes.

Advanced Real Estate Strategy No. 27: Create a Database of Auction Dates and Procedures

In most counties, tax lien sales must be conducted by June 1 of each year. Counties hold sales at different times, and you should call the tax assessors' offices to find out the date and location of auctions scheduled in your area. The time and place of tax lien certificate auctions will be announced in the local newspaper, but obviously it is better to know in advance so that you can plan accordingly.

The first thing you should remember is you are going to an auction, although a somewhat unusual auction. That means that it will be easy to get caught up in the excitement of the bidding process. People have been known to bid down the price of a tax lien certificate to a return less than they were willing to accept before they attended the auction. The way to head off this outcome is to have a plan of attack. Decide how much you want to invest in tax lien certificates before you go. Think about neighborhoods you would prefer to bid on. Know what you want going into the auction to ensure that you buy certificates only on properties with adequate security.

Advanced Real Estate Strategy No. 28: Create a Specific Tax Auction Plan

The auction process for tax lien certificates is simple. As with most things you are unfamiliar with, however, you'll probably need to go through the process at least once before you become comfortable with it. Be prepared with a specific plan of action so tht you avoid getting caught up in the auction excitement.

When you arrive at the auction, the first thing you need to do is check in and put up a deposit. The amount of the deposit is predetermined. Call the office ahead of time to find out what it is. In most cases, the official will accept a personal check, but cash or a certified check is sometimes required, so it always pays to find out in advance. Remember, there is usually only one auction per year in each county, and you don't want to be shut out of it because you aren't prepared.

Each person who puts down a deposit receives a bidding number. This number is on a card, which you will hold up during the auction in order to place your bid. If you want two numbers so that you have a better chance of having your number called as the winning bid (discussed later), you can put down two deposits. But since only one number is allowed per person, you will have to bring someone else along to help you during the auction. This is frequently done by large institutions such as banks, which bring several people to the auction so that they can get a larger number of certificates.

At the beginning of the auction, the auctioneer sits at the front of the room and calls out a number from the prepublished list of available tax certificates. Anyone interested in purchasing that tax lien certificate raises his card, and the auctioneer calls out one of the card numbers. On most certificates, everyone in the room raises his card, indicating his willingness to buy the certificate. The auctioneer randomly selects a bidder, who is awarded that particular certificate.

Once a number is called, other people in the room have the option of bidding a lower interest rate. For instance, when the opening number is called, the person who holds that number will earn 18 percent interest on his tax lien certificate unless someone bids the certificate down. If another person is willing to accept a lower rate—17 percent, for example—she will call out that amount. Now others may join the bidding, and the price (the interest rate to be paid) may be driven down. If the original investor (the one whose number was called initially) would like to participate, he must bid along with the others for the lowest interest rate. This happens very quickly, and you must remain alert, or you can be left out.

Once you are awarded a successful bid, you must settle with the staff and arrange for payment of the entire balance. In most cases, the tax collector's office will bill you for the balance within the next few days, and you will then have 48 hours to pay that amount or forfeit your original deposit.

During the auction, one way to minimize the risk on your investment is to base your bid on the assessed value of the property. If the assessed value of the property is low compared to other values in the neighborhood, you may consider this to be a potential problem and elect not to bid on that property. Often the assessed value by the property appraiser can give you an idea as to the real value of the property you are bidding on. A bad piece of property, such as a small strip of land that is not usable because of its size, will have a lower assessed value than other property in the area. You can mentally eliminate this kind of property from your purchase list.

Another way of potentially reducing your risk is to get to know the tax assessor's staff on an individual basis. The staff will be able to tell you whether any of the properties going up at auction are less desirable than others or have unusual restrictions on them. In many counties, the staff actually goes through the list of properties ahead of time and withdraws from the auction those that are not suitable for building. Speaking with the staff before the auction will enable you to determine whether this is a policy of the county in which you have decided to buy tax certificates.

Getting to know the staff also helps you learn of additional certificates that may become available after the auction. Sometimes people bid on properties and then, for some reason, don't follow through with their bid. These become "no-sale certificates." No-sale certificates can be purchased directly from the county, after the auction, by contacting the local tax collector's office.

Some counties also provide a list of individuals who need to sell certificates because their circumstances have changed. Although they do not provide a formal marketplace, as a courtesy to both buyers and sellers they will frequently make different parties' interests known. Some investors buy certificates in this after-market and ask for an additional discount above the 18 percent interest. Since the certificates aren't sold at auction, you also have more opportunity to check out the underlying value of the property you desire.

Advanced Real Estate Strategy No. 29: Redeem Your Certificates

Once you own a certificate, it can be redeemed in one of a number of ways. The most common is for the property owner to pay the county the taxes owed plus interest, whereupon the county sends you a check in the mail. Many certificates don't even last a full year as an investment. The property owners have simply neglected to pay their taxes, and once they realize that a certificate has been sold, they pay off their debt. In this case, you receive a minimum stated interest of 5 percent of the face value of the certificate. From a calculation standpoint, since you immediately received 5 percent of the full face value of your purchase price, even after only one day's investment, the true rate of return in this case is astronomical.

Tax certificates are good for seven years. During that time, the property owner can pay you off at any time, as long as she pays you the full amount plus interest. After two years, though, you may ask the county to sell the property. After the sale, you will either have your tax certificate paid off or receive a tax deed. If you elect not to ask the county to sell the property, you may hold the certificate for up to seven years. If anyone owns a certificate for longer than seven years, however, it becomes worthless!

If after two years you elect to have the property sold by the county at a tax sale, you must notify the county that you would like to have your tax certificate redeemed. It will send you an application, and then you must pay all other taxes owed on the property, including any additional certificates sold on that property (plus interest and penalties) after yours was purchased. You will also be required to pay for a title search of the property to show any other liens and encumbrances, because the holders of these must also be notified that a tax sale is about to take place.

Once the tax collector's office accepts your application, it delivers it to the circuit court and requests that a tax sale be scheduled. A tax sale cannot occur sooner than 30 days following its acceptance by the circuit court. The sale is advertised by the circuit court during the four consecutive weeks prior to its scheduled date. Each of the parties who showed up in the title search as having a potential interest in the property must also be notified that the sale is about to occur.

The opening bid against the property is the amount you paid with your original application for the tax sale. If there are no other bidders, you will be the automatic winner of the property and will receive a tax deed. If someone else makes a higher bid than your application amount, then the only way you can win the property is by bidding a higher price for the property. This is the protection that other lien holders, such as mortgage holders, have against having the property taken away from them and foreclosed. At the end of the sale, the winning bidder at the tax action will receive a tax deed conveying full ownership of the property to that individual. In most cases, there are very few bidders at these auctions.

You now have a good introductory understanding of tax lien certificates and why they're such a great investment. Although we have referred several times to our home state of Florida, other states also present their own unique advantages. Michigan, for example, pays as much as 50 percent on its certificates. Other states conduct outright property sales instead of paying interest on certificates. And, yes, as noted, there are other states that are *not* as good as these, but that is what shopping is all about.

THE TAX LIEN CERTIFICATE CHECKLIST

☑ **LEARN THE ADVANTAGES OF BUYING TAX LIEN CER-TIFICATES.** These include relatively low risk and high return, low cash requirements, upside potential, ease of investing, and lack of management headaches. All in all, a good package!

☑ **UNDERSTAND THE RISKS.** Actually, there's not much to write about here. The money you tie up in tax lien certificates is relatively illiquid (although there are ways around this). Most of the risks associated with tax lien certificates are either mainly theoretical or essentially inconveniences. They are far outweighed by the benefits listed earlier.

☑ **LEARN HOW THE SYSTEM WORKS SO THAT YOU CAN GET GOOD AT IT.** The tax lien auction is like any other aspect of business. When you get good at it, you stand a better chance of making good money. Study the process, go prepared, don't get caught up in "auction fever," and know how to follow up *after* an auction. And finally, learn how to redeem your certificates or (if necessary) force a tax sale. This is the route whereby you might actually wind up owning the property on which you held a certificate.

CHAPTER 18

Making Money in Mortgages

Historically, one of the best ways to make money is to find someone who's successful at something and copy what that person does.

If that's true, a logical place to look for success is *where all the money is*, and where better than a bank? If money lending is profitable (and it is), then it should follow that an investor who goes into this business will also do well. The investor's task is the same as the bank's: to consider lending possibilities and weigh the various risk factors each opportunity offers compared to a profitable return.

Traditionally, lenders have viewed home loans as being among the most conservative types of loans. In the past, this was due in large part to the fact that homes appreciated rapidly. A lender's loan-to-value ratio, after all, constantly improves as the value of the home increases. Yet even when the mid-1980s ushered in a nationwide change in real estate values and appreciation was no longer automatic, home mortgages continued to be valued as a conservative investment. The lender simply changed its loan-to-value ratio to reflect the new reality. Today, when appreciation is once again running high, your risk of any lending is reduced.

Advanced Real Estate Strategy No. 30: Buy Discount Mortgages

Banks and savings and loan associations are what are known as *primary lenders.* If you need money, you normally go to an institution in one of these groups. If you are dealing in real estate, the institution will ask for a mortgage on the property as collateral.

There are times, however, when *individuals* also make loans secured by real estate. The most common example arises when someone is selling a house. Let's say a buyer is interested in your property but doesn't have quite enough money for a down payment. In order to facilitate the sale, you agree to loan him the small additional amount he needs. Being a prudent person, you ask for a mortgage on the property to secure the loan. This mortgage is recorded and "takes a second position" to the first mortgage, which is held by the bank.

This kind of transaction goes on every day. The buyer is happy, the bank is happy, and (for the most part) you (as the seller) are happy. We say "for the most part" because that's not always true. Yes, you sold your house, but it's possible that you would rather have received all cash than loan the buyer money. After all, your kids are in college, you are buying a new house, the new house is going to need carpets and drapes and furniture—you get the idea. You really didn't want to be a lender, but you wound up as one.

Across town, another person just opened her bank statement and saw that her CD is coming due and that she can renew it for a whopping 2½ percent. "There has *got* to be a better way," she says to herself in frustration. And there is.

If our CD investor only knew about your predicament, she could solve both your problems. She could take her money out of her CD and give it to you in exchange for the mortgage you took as security. Just like that, the investor would increase her return three to four times without substantially increasing her risk. She would be happy, and you would be overjoyed.

Sounds like a win/win situation, right? But in reality, our investor would have overpaid for the mortgage she bought. Why? Because of an imbalance in motivation. While our theoretical investor would like a higher return, you *really want* cash. Because of the inequality in motivation, the mortgage investor can actually increase her return and still have a win/win situation. She can offer to buy your "seller's" mortgage at a discount, instead of the full amount you are owed. Every dollar of discount she gets off the purchase price increases her yield, because the original buyer (i.e., the borrower) will pay the full amount agreed to when the loan was initiated.

The challenge in this transaction is to find the balance point. What is the lowest price the investor can pay for the mortgage that still "works" for the seller? If they can agree on that price, a transaction will occur. This is the world of discount mortgage investing. It happens every day, all over America, and it produces yields to investors as high as 25 to 30 percent. By way of comparison, normal transactions yield 11 to 15 percent.

Still interested? Good. We're going to put some numbers behind our illustration to give them more meaning and to help you see how a mortgage is actually discounted. The number one reason why people don't invest in discount mortgages is that they have to use a little math. It's not particularly *complicated* math, and they're even allowed to use a calculator. Nevertheless, it's still math, and that turns some people off. But bear with us as we lay out our example:

$180,000	Sale price
$135,000	Loan—first mortgage (75 percent loan-to-value, or LTV)
$45,000	Down payment required
$35,000	Amount buyer has for down payment
$10,000	Amount buyer needs from seller as second mortgage

Terms for the second mortgage: a $10,000, seven-year loan at 8 percent interest, fully amortized, with payments of $155.86 per month.

Now let's replay that in prose form, and extend it a little bit. In our illustration, the seller sold her property for $180,000. After the buyer got his bank financing, he was short $10,000. The seller agreed to loan him that amount and "take back" a second mortgage, to be paid off over seven years.

On the other side of town, our CD investor learns about this transaction from a Realtor friend who sold the property and knew that the seller would have preferred cash. She likes the sound of 8 percent much better than the 2½ percent the CD gives her, but she also knows that there is some additional risk. She likes the property as security, and she decides that she would be happy if she could get 14 percent interest on her money.

In order to solve this problem, we must use a financial calculator that you can pick up at any office supply store. A financial calculator is designed so that you can easily lay out the formula for our discount mortgage. The terms stay the same: monthly payments of $155.86 for seven years. The interest rate changes from 8 percent to 14 percent. Press the answer key for the amount, and the calculator gives you $8,316.96. This is the amount the investor would pay for the $10,000 mortgage to get a 14 percent yield on her money for the next seven years.

Will the seller accept the $8,316.96 now, or will he decide to wait and collect the full $10,000 at $155.86 a month? Naturally, it depends on his circumstances and motivation. If he doesn't need the money, he may wait. If he needs the $8,000 for a tax deficiency due on his house next week, what do you think he'll do?

Or perhaps the seller presents a counteroffer: "I won't take $8,316, but I *will* take $9,000." Our investor changes the number in her calculator, recalculating the new interest rate, and gets 11.37 percent. Much better than a CD, she says to herself. Will she take it? Would you?

What we have just gone through is a simple but common transaction for buying discount mortgages. As you might guess, there is more. How much you learn about this kind of investing depends on the amount of time you are willing to spend. For example, you will learn that you can buy *parts* of a mortgage, rather than the whole amount. You might buy the first 12 payments, or the last 12, or just the balloon payment.

The variations are almost limitless. Each technique you learn is designed to help you create a transaction in which, mathematically, you increase your yield to the level you seek. As we mentioned earlier, 25 to 30 percent yields are not out of the question.

Why would you do this? Why would you want to spend time learning something new? Let me show you. Let's assume you have a $50,000 portfolio and 20 years until retirement. If you earn 3 percent CD rates, you will have a nest egg of $91,037 at retirement. If, instead, you invest in discount mortgages and make 20 percent on your money, your nest egg would grow to *$2,641,376* over the same time period. A big difference, right?

Your first decision is whether to be an active or passive investor in a mortgage investment program. If you are active, you will need to learn some basic lending laws and work with an attorney or title company. This approach is a little time-consuming in the beginning because of the learning curve involved. It isn't difficult; it's just that the information isn't readily available to you.

If you decide that you aren't going to be active yourself, then you will deal with a broker who finds mortgages and flips them to you. The broker takes a negotiated spread for his efforts. In most cases, the broker is dealing for himself, and he will try to sell (lay off) the mortgage to you for a price that will yield him the greatest return. You can also hire brokers for a set rate to find a mortgage, also at a negotiated price. Although mortgage brokers are licensed in some states, this isn't required in most.

Advanced Real Estate Strategy No. 31: Find a Mortgage Broker Who Specializes in Discount Mortgages

Referrals are the best way to find a broker. The next best route is to take out the Yellow Pages and call every mortgage broker listed in your area. Ask the broker whether she deals in discount mortgages and what kind of yield you can expect to make. From these conversations, narrow your selection to three or four, and ask for client references. Confirm that the individual you have selected is licensed, and (if your state regulates mortgage brokers) call the regulators and see if any complaints have been filed against her.

If your state does not regulate mortgage brokers, call the Better Business Bureau and your local chamber of commerce. Neither of these organizations will necessarily provide you with conclusive information, but it is worth calling them to see if the broker has a complaint file.

Buying discount mortgages is another real estate specialty that you can learn to do either a little or full time. A friend of ours heads up the American Cash Flow Institute, where people are taught this opportunity as a career.

Maybe discount mortgage investing will be a career for you, or perhaps you will buy just one mortgage a year in your IRA and increase your yield and diversification. In either event, discount mortgage buying is another tool in your overall investment arsenal.

THE MAKING-MONEY-IN-MORTGAGES CHECKLIST

☑ **BUY AT A DISCOUNT TO INCREASE YOUR YIELD.** If you find the right seller—by which we mean a *motivated* seller—you should be able to take a good situation and make it even better. Do the math, and be prepared to dicker. (You have lots of room in your "spread" to give a little ground, if necessary.)

☑ **LEARN THE WHYS AND HOWS.** There is an almost infinite number of ways to make money as an individual mortgage lender. The more ways you master, the more flexibility you'll acquire, and the more opportunities will be open to you.

☑ **MAKE ALLIES.** You can decide to be a passive partici-pant in the mortgage market. To do this, you will need to find a mortgage broker who is willing to do business with you on mutually acceptable terms. Do your homework, and find the most qualified (and cooperative) person to work with.

CHAPTER 19

Twenty-Eight Creative Real Estate Strategies

This is one of our favorite chapters because in it we give you specific illustrations of how to use creative ideas to make money in real estate.

Anyone can buy a piece of real estate, but structuring a transaction so that you can make money—seeing the distinctive use that no one else sees, finding that "diamond in the rough"—is what brings excitement to the business of being a real estate investor.

In the next few pages, we are going to explore ideas that have been used to generate money-making opportunities in a variety of real estate markets. It isn't enough just to learn what to do in a seller's market such as we have today because, at some point, the tide will turn, and you will have to adapt to a buyer's market.

In addition, interest rates won't always be as low as they are now. We want you to be able to prosper no matter what the rate or the market. The point is, you have to learn to be flexible and to change along with the economy—because it will change.

The newer you are as an investor, the less receptive you may be to some of the ideas presented in this chapter, because they require some "outside the box" thinking. Well, if you come to a strategy that you don't feel fits *you*, don't let that keep you from appreciating and using the others. Just cross out the one you don't like, and move on. Someday you may come back and see that idea in a different context—one that works for you.

Advanced Real Estate Strategy No. 32: Use an Imaginary Down Payment

A property is being offered in the marketplace for what appears to be fair market value with 10 percent down. The loan is assumable at a reasonable interest rate. The only problem is, you don't have $6,000 to put down, and the seller won't agree to take back a second mortgage for $6,000.

House listed	$60,000
First mortgage	54,000
Down payment	$ 6,000

This example is typical of creative real estate. You can forget the property because you don't have any money for a down payment—or you can begin your career as a real estate investor.

Here are your real options with this property:

Option 1: You offer to buy the property for $62,000. You will assume the first mortgage and have the seller take back a second mortgage for $8,000. You are paying him more than he was asking because you want him to take back a second mortgage.

Option 2: If the seller is still unwilling to take a second mortgage on the property, see if you can get a hard-money lender.

Option 3: If you can't get a hard-money lender, get a partner.

Option 4: If you can't find a partner, increase the amount of the second mortgage to be generated on the property from $6,000 to $8,600. (You will have to put a clause in the contract guaranteeing $6,000 cash to the seller.) Offer the $8,600 second mortgage in the investor marketplace for $6,000 cash, which will go to the seller. (The discount of $8,600 to $6,000 is a $2,600 discount, representing a 30 percent markdown to the note buyer.)

Option 5: Ask the real estate broker to loan you the commission (normally 7 percent) and pay interest.

One problem, but five solutions. This is the essence of creative real estate. You must learn to think of different solutions and use different people in the transaction to solve a problem. This includes learning to use the real estate broker. The key to getting participation from brokers and others is to get them involved in looking for a solution, and networking on your behalf as well. For instance, the real estate broker might be reluctant, but what if you promised to list this property with her in the future when you sell? You could even add that to the contract. Now she makes *two* commissions.

The results of this concept are: (1) the investor gets a no-money-down purchase, (2) the seller gets his cash, (3) the note holder gets a good discount, and (4) the broker makes another sale.

Advanced Real Estate Strategy No. 33: Discount the Down Payment

Sometimes an entire transaction may rest on whether or not the contract shows the sale price that the seller has fixed in his mind. It may not make sense (from a market perspective, the price may actually be a little high), but for whatever reasons, the seller is holding firm. One solution that will allow you to buy the property at a lower price, and at the same time give the seller the price that he is asking, is to give the seller discounted paper for part or all of the down payment. *Discounted paper* is simply a mortgage on another property that you buy at a discount, similar to the way it was discounted in our first transaction.

Searching your newspaper, investor groups, and the general real estate marketplace, you will be able to find existing second mortgages offered at discounts by people who want cash now. You can buy the discounted mortgage and then use the note at its full face value as a down payment on the property. The seller won't know, and probably won't care, that that the note was bought at a discount. He will just focus on the fact that he will be getting the full price for his property through the full payments on the discounted mortgage.

To make the transaction go smoothly, you can also

1. Offer your personal guarantee that the note will be paid.
2. Double-secure the note payment with the property you are buying as well.

Remember, we are learning to be flexible and to look at problems in different ways.

Advanced Real Estate Strategy No. 34: Offer Monthly Down Payments

There are many cases today where people have large monthly spendable incomes but have not been able to acquire the necessary down payment to purchase the home that they desire. Frequently, this is true of young professionals, like doctors and lawyers, whose incomes have escalated rapidly in their first few years in their profession. If this is *you*, don't let it keep you from buying investment property. Instead of offering a single lump sum down payment, offer the payment over a period of months. Offer whatever is reasonable and whatever the seller will accept.

If the seller (or lender) is not willing to close on the property until the full down payment has been made, offer the monthly payments as a form of option money that applies to the full down payment. This option will be more attractive when new financing is being placed on the property, since the seller will be getting most of her cash immediately from the financed amount.

On investment property, this technique offers great flexibility, in that it defers the down payment over several months and also provides an opportunity to put the property back on the market immediately and possibly make a quick profit. For the young professional interested in buying the property for his own home, the program acts as a forced savings plan by allowing him to buy a piece of property immediately and begin building up equity, even though he has not yet saved up the down payment.

Advanced Real Estate Strategy No. 35: Subordinate Mortgages

Subordinating a mortgage means lowering its position as security on a property. A first mortgage can be lowered to a second, or a second to a third, and so on. Subordination is frequently done in land development, where prior lenders subordinate to a new construction loan.

Subordination of loans can also be used to create 100 percent financing opportunities. For example, let's say that you have searched the marketplace and you have found a seller who is willing to accept 20 percent down with an 80 percent purchase-money first mortgage (seller financed) on the property. If you need a nothing-down deal, you could offer the seller a contract to take back a second mortgage on the property with a higher interest rate than he was asking. In return, he would agree to subordinate his loan to a first mortgage that you would get for 20 percent of the value of the property. You use that money for the down payment made at closing. There are many combinations of offers that can be structured in this type of transaction, including more cash for the seller by increasing the new first mortgage.

Advanced Real Estate Strategy No. 36: Barter Your Services

Barter is the oldest form of financing in the history of mankind, and it is often used in real estate transactions when (unlike today) interest rates are high and money isn't as readily available. During these harder times, investors can offer their services in exchange for real estate equity. A doctor, for example, could trade medical services, an attorney could trade legal services, and an accountant could arrange to do taxes for a period of time in exchange for equity. There is virtually an unlimited range of possibilities, from real estate agents who offer their services on the next sale for free in exchange for equity now, to carpenters who agree to do work on other property owned by a seller free in exchange for equity on the present one. The possibilities for using this formula are limited only by your imagination.

For those of you who dismiss this idea as unrealistic, we want to tell you what our neighbor did just last year. He was building a new home, and the architect doing the plans offered his professional services in exchange for the house that was on the property. Our neighbor was delighted because he was going to have to pay for the architectural plans anyway, and he would also have to pay to tear down the house. The architect moved the house to a vacant lot 11 blocks away and created a tremendous value for himself. Everyone won from this bartered transaction because they had an open mind for creative real estate strategies.

Advanced Real Estate Strategy No. 37: Give Equity for Options on Other Property

We talked in Chapter 16 about using options as a way to control property with little money tied up. You can also use other real estate, instead of cash, as part or all of your option money.

We have seen vacant lots, time-shares, and mortgages all used as option money. Depending on how it is presented, a creative form of option money can actually be more attractive than cash. For instance, using a lot in Hawaii may mean to the seller that he and his wife now have the motivation they need to go to Hawaii to see the lot they own (the trip is now deductible). Getting the Hawaiian lot is worth letting this local property be tied up for a little while. In their minds, the sellers are getting something they want just for giving up a little time.

What if you threw in a couple of plane tickets for an extra six months on the option? See what we mean? It gets interesting. We knew a very successful real estate investor who bought large tracts of cheap land in Hawaii during the mid-1980s and broke up the land into higher-priced lots that he used as options just as we described. He was pleased with himself because he created a lot of quick equity by subdividing acres of vacant land. Considering what any land in Hawaii is now worth, both parties to this transaction got a good deal.

Advanced Real Estate Strategy No. 38: Use Personal Property to Buy Real Estate

If you attend an exchange meeting in your area, you'll soon learn that everything has value and that beauty is truly in the eye of the beholder.

It is not necessary to exchange real estate for real estate. In many cases, cars, boats, airplanes, and a wide variety of other items are successfully offered in exchange for property.

Not too long ago, our Sunday paper carried an ad from an individual who was offering a yacht as a down payment on real estate. Be creative! Offer anything valuable that you have that you no longer want for part equity in a piece of property. If the seller accepts, you've gotten rid of something that you don't want, and you've reduced the total amount of cash or equity needed for the transaction.

Advanced Real Estate Strategy No. 39: Use the Brokerage Fee as a Down Payment

Throughout this book, we have talked about various methods of raising money to buy a property. We have talked about using the seller's equity and having the seller herself carry back financing. The reserves, closing costs, and prepaid items are another source of potential financing at closing. An additional source is the real estate commission.

Although many real estate agents shudder at the thought of having to give away any of their money at settlement, brokers are often too uncompromising in their belief that they should receive cash only, while everyone else should be willing to take paper. Now, this is not to say that brokers should accept paper for their fees as the norm, but brokers should consider accepting paper if that is what it takes to get a contract through.

In real estate today, we are talking about brokerage fees that range from 5 percent to 10 percent on most transactions. In many cases, the broker's fee may be as much as the down payment called for in the contract, or at least a large portion of it. So using the brokerage fee creatively can facilitate sales that wouldn't happen otherwise.

In accepting a note instead of cash for a brokerage fee, a broker should be aware of certain liabilities that could result. First, the broker should know that unless the note is properly structured so that receipt of the fee is in some way contingent, the broker will have to pay income tax on his entire fee in the year of sale, not when the fee is collected. Depending on the broker's tax bracket, this in itself could be a considerable burden.

Recently, in a real estate development we were doing, the broker was selling lots we had developed to builders. To entice the builders, the broker offered to give them the real estate commission he was earning and let them use it as a down payment on the lot so that they could have a nothing-down deal. What he asked for in return was an exclusive listing on the homes they built. Since the homes would have a value five times that of the lot, the broker was trading a commission on the lot now for a higher commission on the house and lot a year later. It was very creative, and it was very profitable for both him and the builders we worked with. We were happy, too, because we sold out fast.

If a broker does accept a note as his commission in a transaction, the note should be secured by either a first or a second mortgage on the property. It should be written at an adequate interest rate and for a short term. The broker might suggest that the note be for a higher price than the standard commission, so that he can sell the note at a discount in the open marketplace. Increasing the value of the note gets the transaction done and allows the broker to get his same commission.

We have personally loaned the brokerage in transactions where we have acted as brokers, and we have also rolled the commission into the transaction and become equity partners. There are lots of options, assuming that you keep an open mind.

Advanced Real Estate Strategy No. 40: Create Home Partners

Over the past few years, we have been blessed with low-interest-rate loans. This has allowed a lot of people to enter the real estate market who have never done so before.

The next economic move is for rates to rise, as they have already begun to do. As rates increase, more and more buyers will no longer meet financing ratios and will find themselves shut out of the market.

One solution used in the past in high-interest-rate environments has been to match the prospective homeowner with an investment client. The home occupant and the investor will split the down payment (using any percentage split that works for the parties) and all closing costs in conjunction with the purchase of the property, and take title together. The home occupant then rents the house from herself and the investor, thus obtaining all the advantages of actually buying the home herself.

The agreement between the investor and the home occupant should run for a period of approximately five years, to give the investor an opportunity to achieve maximum profit potential from appreciation on his investment. At the end of the five-year period, the home occupant has the option of buying out the investor's interest for the current appraised value or placing the home on the open market.

The results of the plan are beneficial to both parties. The home occupant can now purchase the home she wants because she is able to qualify using the additional financial statement of the investor. The investor benefits because he has purchased a management-free investment that he can be confident the tenant will take good care of.

Advanced Real Estate Strategy No. 41: Time-Share Small Properties

Time-shares have gone from being a cottage industry to including big-time resort participants like Disney, Four Seasons, and Ritz Carlton. Smaller investors can also use the idea to their advantage, as long as they have a good lawyer at their side. For example, you could buy a beach house or ski chalet and then sell those weeks of time when you aren't planning to use the property anyway. (Check the local zoning.) By breaking the property up into smaller blocks, you can get more for the property than you paid, probably winding up with "free time" for your trouble.

The variations on this formula are as endless as the number of different ownership arrangements. The two most popular arrangements at present are fee ownership and license rights. As fee owners, the time-share holders actually get a deed and title to the property. With a license right, the purchaser simply gets a right to use the property for a stated number of years; on the termination date, the property returns to the developer of the project.

This strategy can also be used as a way to raise down payment money.

Advanced Real Estate Strategy No. 42: Create a Horizontal Condominium Complex

This technique can be used in almost any city in the country, and it applies to residential as well as commercial properties.

The key to the plan is to look for a property that has either (1) more than one building on it or (2) more than one use allowed in the zoning. One example we have seen was a church that could be rehabbed as an office and that had two residential homes on the property. Another was a beach retreat that had four cottages on the property.

Here are a couple of profit-making possibilities in these situations:

1. Secure an option on the entire church property with the right to market the property. Advertise the residences for sale with a simultaneous closing for each parcel. Use the cash from the residential sales (which are easily financed and could bring a higher price once they were broken away from the larger church property) as the down payment on the church. Result: no-money-down financing and a lower cost basis in the church.

2. The beach cottages were ideal for dividing up and selling separately at a higher price. Sometimes you can't break

the property up into smaller parcels because zoning won't allow it. In that case, each of the four owners could own the total piece, with individual license rights or leases to the individual cottages, much the way town homes are structured.

Sure, there are many problems that might go along with these transactions, not the least of which would be structuring the financing. We aren't saying that creative real estate is easy, but we are trying to open your eyes to possibilities and profits that others don't always see.

Advanced Real Estate Strategy No. 43: Devise a Subdivided Sale

When dealing with raw land, you are often faced with sellers who are unwilling to break up the property. These sellers may be highly motivated but at the same time are unwilling to subdivide because of a fear of being stuck with leftovers, or simply because they don't want to have to worry about multiple sales. The subdivided sale technique solves this problem.

Facts:

1. A seller has 100 acres priced at $200,000, or $2,000 per acre.
2. The seller wants to convey the entire parcel.
3. Twenty of the 100 acres are prime for development, with excellent road frontage and some commercial application.

Solution: Negotiate with the owner for an option to purchase the parcel for $200,000 within six months. Notice that if the option is exercised, the seller will get exactly what she wants; she is just giving you some extra time to perform.

Next, promote the valuable 20 acres at a substantially higher price per acre, and sell this portion of the property subject to being able to find a buyer for the remaining 80 acres.

Example: 20 acres purchased for $6,000 per acre equals $120,000.

$$
\begin{array}{ll}
\$200,000 & \text{total price} \\
-120,000 & \text{for the 20 acres} \\
\hline
\$80,000 &
\end{array}
$$

The remaining acreage can now be sold for only $1,000 per acre. Since you are looking for a profit on your venture, you could add $500 per acre to the remaining acreage as your profit and still be under market. Your profit would now look like this:

$$
\begin{array}{ll}
\$500 & \text{per acre} \\
\times\,80 & \text{acres} \\
\hline
\$40,000 & \text{profit}
\end{array}
$$

Notice the results of this transaction. Your original seller has received his full $200,000 asking price. Your two buyers are happy, and you are $40,000 richer for six months of work.

One word of caution if you have a real estate license: some states may allow a Realtor to take a profit equal only to his "customary" commission. Otherwise, it would be deemed an "overage." The best advice is to first check with your local board, or else consult your attorney.

Advanced Real Estate Strategy No. 44: Make Money with Phantom Ownership

Control is the name of the game. You don't have to own property to make money with it; you just have to control the benefits from it.

There are probably hundreds of properties in your area that rent at prices below current market rates. Frequently (particularly with smaller properties) the reason for such low rents is the fear that raising the rent will also increase the vacancy problems. The owner knows that she is at least happy with the rent she is getting now, and she's willing to accept smaller profits rather than have to worry about vacancy problems. This situation creates opportunity for those of you who enjoy working with tenants.

Consider offering the owner a long-term net lease on the entire property (multifamily or single family). Resist the owner's attempt to have an escalator clause (increases in rent). You will point out that you are taking the vacancy risk from the ownership and creating a management-free property for her. Once the agreement is completed, you now have effective ownership of the property. If you were right about the rents being low, you can raise them. If you are a great property manager, you can increase the rents each year and pocket the profit as you do so.

A good idea is to combine this strategy with an option to buy the property in the future. As you are successful in raising the rent, you are creating built-up equity when you buy the property. Your tenants will also be good potential buyers after you exercise your option.

If you can't get an option, then try to get a participation in the increased value you brought to the property by increasing the rents. If you are unable to get an equity participation, then get an agreement that you will get the listing on the property any time the owner sells it.

Advanced Real Estate Strategy No. 45: Profit from Rejected Offers

Never turn down a sale just because the terms are not acceptable. The terms may be perfectly acceptable to someone else.

> **Example:** An investor has a $90,000 strip center store that he wants to sell. He is primarily interested in getting as much cash as possible, and then leveraging the cash into a larger property.
>
> A buyer is interested in the store, but has little cash. She finally makes an offer of $5,000 down and asks the seller to take back a mortgage at 9 percent interest.
>
> This offer is totally unacceptable to the seller, since he wants cash to reinvest in other property. Under normal circumstances, the seller would either turn down the offer or counter with one that might be out of the buyer's reach. Instead, the offer could be accepted subject to being able to find an acceptable exchange.
>
> It is quite possible that there is someone who owns a larger piece of property that the seller would be interested in and who would exchange it for a nice, management-free income for part of the sale and the balance in cash from new financing.

By keeping the transaction open, the seller is able to get both the full asking price and the benefit of exchanging, thereby postponing the payment of any capital gains tax. In addition, because he has been offered a property for exchange with a sales contract attached, he has opened the door for many other potential exchange offers. A "cash out" (a property with a sales contract on it) is looked upon very favorably in investor groups, even if it's not all cash.

Advanced Real Estate Strategy No. 46: Offer Subsidized Interest Payments

Every time interest rates go up, buyers disappear from the marketplace, either because they can't qualify or because they don't feel they can afford the higher payments. Rather than sitting with a built-up inventory of unsold homes, some creative builders have offered to subsidize the interest that their purchasers must pay on mortgages. You should remember this as an individual investor, as well.

Example: Present rates for new loans are 11⅛ percent. You offer a rate of 8 percent, with a sales price of $65,000.

Using a $65,000 sales price and assuming a 5 percent down payment, the monthly payment on an 11⅛ percent, 30-year mortgage would be $594.65. An 8 percent, 30-year mortgage would cost $453.25 a month. To entice the buyer, you sign a contract to pay the $141.40 difference for 60 months or until the house is resold, whichever comes first. Since homes on average are sold every five to seven years, this is a good number of years to use for both parties.

This arrangement offers benefits to both parties. More buyers are able to qualify because of the lower monthly payments, and all buyers prefer the low interest rates. You profit by attracting more buyers to your property and selling homes when others aren't.

Advanced Real Estate Strategy No. 47: Raise Capital with a Discount/Sale/Buyback

Trapped: That's the feeling we all get when we're locked into a piece of real estate and, all around us, good bargains are slipping

ADVANCED REAL ESTATE STRATEGIES FOR SUCCESS

through our fingers. This can frequently happen in a buyer's market, where sellers aren't being offered what they want. The property we have may well be a good, solid investment, but because of the economic conditions, there is a scarcity of buyers for this kind of property. This problem often occurs with vacant land.

For the true investor who wants to continue her investment program, the discount/sale/buyback can provide the needed relief.

> **Example:** An investor owns an apartment site worth $1.5 million free and clear. This is a hard value, provided through a recent appraisal. The problem is, no one is building new apartments because of a present oversupply in the area. The investor knows that this economic condition is temporary, but because of his large equity position, too much of his money is now tied up in an unproductive investment. Although he might normally be able to borrow on his equity, money is presently tight, and even if banks would loan the money, they would require high interest rates, short terms, and high monthly payments.
>
> By advertising the property at a substantial discount, the seller finds a buyer who is willing to purchase the property on the following terms: $750,000 cash (50 percent of the appraised value). The buyer gives the seller an option to buy back the property anytime during the next five years at a 15 percent increase each year. The result is that the seller has effectively been able to borrow $750,000 at 15 percent with no payments. While 15 percent is a high interest rate, remember that this is a buyer's market. You can take the cash and leverage it into a larger property,

building your estate over the next five years. Remember, too, that since it is a buyer's market in this example, the cash you have will allow you to get some really good buys.

The purchaser in this transaction also receives a great return on his investment. He has a safe, management-free investment yielding a 15 percent return. In addition, he has the ongoing drama of waiting to see if the seller will be able to exercise the option or if, instead, he will gain an even more substantial profit from his investment if the option is not exercised.

Don't get caught up with the interest rate in this example. We are showing an extreme; you would naturally offer no more than you had to in order to attract attention and get your cash.

Advanced Real Estate Strategy No. 48: Refinance Your Life

It is a fact of our economic times that many people are getting into debt way over their heads. Often, because of the high monthly payments required to satisfy short-term debts, people are unable to take on the higher mortgage payments for a larger home. But by applying a little creative magic, they can get their dream home by "refinancing their life."

Example: The Joneses have an $80,000 home with a $50,000 mortgage and an equity of $30,000. They have a combined income of $55,000, and they would like to buy a new home outside the city with additional space for $100,000. Their monthly debt situation is as follows:

Mortgage payment	$500
Car payment (2)	$350
Charge cards	$100
Credit union	$150
Personal loans	$200
Total monthly debt	$1,300

At first glance, the Joneses do not feel that they can afford a higher mortgage payment with their current outstanding debts. What they have forgotten, however, is that their payments are high because their debts are short-term loans. The balances of these loans are

Cars	$6,000
Charge cards	$900
Credit union	$2,000
Personal loans	$3,000
Total debts	$11,900

Solution: If the Joneses sell their present home, they will net approximately $24,000 in cash. If they use part of this amount to pay off their current short-term debts of $11,000, they will have $12,100 remaining, with which they can then buy their $100,000 home by putting 10 percent down and financing the balance over 30 years at 6 percent. The Joneses' total monthly payments now come to $539.06 Prior to "refinancing their life," they had $1,300 in monthly payments. Thus, by converting their short-term debts to long-term debt, they have a net increase in spendable income of $760.40 a month, as well as having a larger home.

Advanced Real Estate Strategy No. 49: Use a Step Mortgage

This strategy was very popular a few years back, when it was also called a graduated-payment mortgage. Instead of a normal amortized mortgage with a higher monthly payment, the seller agrees to take a lower monthly payment of her purchase-money mortgage in the early years of the loan, and thus assures the buyer of cash flow on the property.

Depending on how low the buyer needs to push the payment down to generate cash flow, the payment may not be enough to cover the entire amount of interest due on the loan. In that case, the difference between the interest actually paid and that which is due each month will be added to the mortgage, actually increasing the amount of the mortgage. Such financing effectively assures the buyer of an adequate cash flow in the early years, while allowing him the opportunity to refinance the property later when the circumstances better fit his position.

This example was used for an income property, but it could also be used for a residual loan to help the buyer with payments in the early years.

Advanced Real Estate Strategy No. 50: Structure Notes to Match Seasonal Income

Contrary to the prevailing wisdom out there, monthly payments on mortgages do *not* have to be constant, nor do they have to be fixed in amount. In fact, this traditional approach to financing sometimes puts an unneeded burden on some buyers of property.

In the case of seasonal property, such as a ski resort, all of the income may be generated during a four- or five-month period.

Depending on when the settlement took place, the buyer of such a property might be burdened by having to make high amortized payments during the summer months, when there is no income. If she budgeted correctly, of course, she should be okay—but we all know the joys of budgeting!

The solution to this problem is simple. If the seller is anxious and motivated to sell, he should agree to receive payments on his purchase-money mortgage and note that coincide with the period during which the property is producing its highest income. For example, the seller may receive double payments during the five or six months of the ski season and no payments at all during the summer months, when there is no income being produced from the property. The variations on this type of payment plan are unlimited, and can be used whenever they help bring about a sale.

Advanced Real Estate Strategy No. 51: Eliminate Negative Cash Flow

If you've ever known anyone who was "land poor" (or if you've experienced the feeling yourself), you'll appreciate this happy solution.

A landowner has 1,000 acres of land with a good location and an ideal appreciation potential. His problem, though, is that he can't afford to carry his monthly payments (including taxes and upkeep) on the property. Yet, he wants to hold onto the property because he feels that most of the profit on it will come in the next couple of years, as the area continues to build up.

Our landowner's solution is to sell a one-half interest in the future profits of the property for one dollar, plus the investor's agreement to assume the mortgage payments and carrying charges until the property is sold. Proceeds from the final sale will go first to repay both the investor's money and the landowner's equity at its appraised value today. The remaining profits will then be split 50/50. The investor gets a good deal with no down payment, and the landowner gives up only half of his future profit.

There are many ways to take this idea of equity sharing and structure transactions that are helpful and profitable to all parties.

Advanced Real Estate Strategy No. 52: Use Balloon Mortgages

It is a central fact in all real estate investing that the more financing you have on the property, the less chance there is for any cash flow. This is particularly true when the seller is taking back a large second mortgage. Even though the seller may be willing to accept a 20- or 30-year amortization on the second mortgage, the combined constant interest rate on the first and second mortgages makes cash flow almost an impossibility.

One solution is for the buyer to make no payments on the second mortgage and have the entire mortgage balloon in five to seven years. This means that the entire amount of the second mortgage will be due and payable with interest on the due date. The disadvantage to the seller is that she is not receiving constant payments. However, if she currently has no need for the monthly payments, there is no resulting disadvantage at all. It would be no different from buying a CD for the same period of time.

The use of this strategy will result in some nice cash flow for the buyer, and also an easier sale. It is important, however, to remember that there is a debt on the property, and that at some point, the money will have to be paid. Although the due date may seem a long way off, the buyer may find himself in a bad situation if he has spent the additional cash flow rather than properly reinvesting it.

Advanced Real Estate Strategy No. 53: Amortize Your Balloon

There has seldom been an investor who truly expected that she would ever have to pay off a balloon note. When such a mortgage is set up, the five- or seven-year balloon seems so distant that it really doesn't matter. As the due date approaches, however, fear begins to develop in the investor's mind, and a scramble for new financing starts. Sometimes the unprepared investor is forced to sell her property, and, if this occurs during a period of poor market conditions, it may mean a loss rather than the profit she had expected.

In order to eliminate this potential problem, an option should be established that either allows the borrower to convert the balloon payment to an amortized mortgage or provides for an extension of the balloon payment in return for a penalty payment. The buyer should always attempt to have such a clause inserted whenever she is dealing with a balloon mortgage. One-year extensions are fairly easy to negotiate up front, because the seller still sees an end to the deal, and another year is usually no big deal. The penalty payment can actually be enticing. In negotiating these extensions, the noteholder should negotiate a penalty large enough that the buyer doesn't elect the extension too easily. You want her to try to refinance.

As the buyer, of course, you want this penalty to be as low as possible.

Advanced Real Estate Strategy No. 54: Use Longer Amortization

No matter what the interest rate or amount of a loan, the monthly payments can be decreased substantially by increasing the length of the amortization period. This is true in all cases, up to about a 30-year amortized mortgage. After 30 years, the payments do not decrease enough to outweigh (1) the increased length of time for payments on the mortgage and (2) the additional amount you would be paying in interest over the period.

> **Example:** A seller agrees to take back a $20,000 second mortgage at 10 percent interest amortized over 5 years. The payments on such a mortgage are $424.97 per month. However, if the same mortgage were amortized over 20 years, the payments would be $193.01. If it were amortized over a 30-year period, the payments would be $175.52. By increasing the length of the mortgage, we have substantially decreased the monthly amount required to pay off the loan. This lower monthly payment will naturally result in a higher cash flow for the buyer.

Since most sellers are not willing to wait 30 years for their payments, the normal procedure is to write the loan for 5 years and compute the monthly payments during that period using a 30-year amortization. At the end of the 5-year period, there will be a balloon payment, as the remaining balance will be due.

One of the times when this technique is not used as often as it should be is when a buyer is purchasing a property that already has a first mortgage on it. There may be a much greater benefit for the buyer if he negotiates with the existing lender to refinance the same loan for a longer period of time. Naturally, the lender will want some concessions, such as a higher interest rate. A buyer should consider this procedure whenever he is purchasing property on which a loan has existed for more than five years. After five years, the constant rate on the mortgage is high enough to generate a cash-flow benefit if the length of amortization can be extended.

Advanced Real Estate Strategy No. 55: Use Interest-Only Payments

The interest-only method of financing is one of the strategies most frequently used by investors to reduce payments and increase cash flow. Rather than a straight amortized loan, the buyer pays interest only, with the entire principal due at some future date.

The only problem with this strategy is that the early payments of any mortgage are mostly interest, and so the difference in the payment size isn't big. In order to increase the usefulness of this particular strategy, it should be combined with negotiating annual or semiannual payments instead of monthly interest-only payments. This solution relieves you (as the buyer) of the burden of a monthly payment and also allows you to build up equity and to save any money that might be produced from the property. During this period, it is likely that the rental income can be increased, and the property can be refinanced on more attractive terms.

Advanced Real Estate Strategy No. 56: Increase Flexibility with Multiple Mortgages

Most traditional seller financing stops at first and second mortgages. Rarely does anyone even consider the use of a third or fourth mortgage.

Depending on the amount of equity in the property, these junior mortgages can be used to achieve a variety of different results. For example, by breaking up the notes and having the seller carry back a second, a third, or sometimes even a fourth mortgage, the mortgages can later be sold to different investors at different rates if the seller needs money. Splitting the mortgages allows them to be used for different purposes. The second, for instance, might be discounted for cash, while the third is used as down payment on another property at full face value.

Another time that it might be beneficial for a seller to carry back a second or third mortgage is when a buyer cannot make a large down payment but expects to receive a raise in salary or a bonus at the end of the year. In such a case, the buyer might be able to make payments on the first and second mortgages while allowing interest to accumulate on the third mortgage, postponing payment until she receives her raise and/or bonus.

Financing can be tailored to the needs of both parties, utilizing such creative concepts as notes with no payments for extended periods of time, periodic balloon payments, or payments that increase in steps—all of which can be used with seller carry-backs.

Advanced Real Estate Strategy No. 57: Definance a Property

Occasionally, a seller can get locked into mortgage terms that may have been good for her at one time, but that are not attractive to a new purchaser. Selling the property thus becomes difficult, unless there's a cash buyer on hand. The solution here is to "definance," or remove the mortgage from the property.

Definancing involves offering the mortgage holder another security as a substitute for the property the seller is attempting to sell. Although the mortgage holder may be reluctant, you will have to show that the mortgage will be just as secure against another property as it is now. If, for instance, the buyer offers to move the mortgage so that it is safeguarded by his own home, the lender may be able to see the position as being at least as secure as before, since a person would typically rather lose an investment than his home.

Moving the mortgage to his home has numerous advantages for the buyer, especially if he doesn't want to sell his home. Another mortgage on the home shouldn't have any negative effect. It also will allow him to "crank" the equity out of his home, even if he doesn't have enough in it to borrow against from a commercial lender.

Transferring a mortgage to the home (or any other property that the buyer might own) frees the investment property to be sold at any time and allows the equity to be pulled out of the property, rather than paying part of it to the previous owner. This leaves the investor with considerably more flexibility in how he can offer his investment property for sale in the future.

Because this formula has such a wide range of possibilities and can be used in such a variety of situations, it is important to point out some potential inducements that may be offered to the seller:

1. Offer an increased interest rate to the seller or mortgage holder after he has made the move.
2. Pay off part of the mortgage, giving the seller a cash advance for making the transfer.
3. As a variation of no. 2, give the seller an increase in the monthly payments rather than the cash.
4. Improve the lender's position by placing his mortgage on property more valuable than that on which he currently holds a mortgage.
5. Improve the seller's position by increasing her priority from a third mortgage to a second, or from a second mortgage to a first.

Because of the flexibility that moving mortgages gives to a buyer, this strategy should have a star by it. Shifting the borrowing to a property that you are *not* selling (the home, in this example) frees up an asset that you can sell for cash. Being able to offer the property with various terms allows you greater flexibility in selling it without the old debt, and thus gives you the potential for higher profits.

Advanced Real Estate Strategy No. 58: Structure Flexible Interest Rates to Match Seller Needs

Depending on the motivation and needs of the seller, an investor might be able to show the seller that she can benefit by giving the investor a lower interest rate at the beginning of a loan and increasing it as the loan ages.

Under this rising-interest-rate strategy, the buyer (investor) might propose, for example, that the seller hold a $20,000 second mortgage on a property. The current interest rate for second mortgages is 11 percent (for the purposes of our example). The buyer proposes interest that will be paid at a rate of 9 percent the first year and be increased 1 percent each year thereafter, up to a maximum rate of 15 percent. The buyer will benefit by paying a lower interest rate in the early years, when he is least likely to be able to make his mortgage payments. As the interest rate increases each year, the buyer will have to determine whether it is in his best interest to continue to pay the increasing rate or to refinance and pay off the loan.

As with many of the creative financing techniques already mentioned, the buyer or agent doing the negotiating must always be prepared to answer any objections put forward by the seller.

Many unsophisticated sellers will have difficulty understanding why they should accept an interest rate lower than the current market rate.

One solution is to combine this technique with another creative strategy. For example, should the seller balk at accepting a lower interest rate at the beginning, the difference between the interest rate quoted and the prevailing market rate can be made up by adding the difference to the purchase price. This would be advantageous to the seller, since the tax on the increased profit would be paid at capital gain rates rather than the ordinary income rates that would be paid on the interest alone.

The buyer benefits as well, since he gets a lower interest rate, which makes his monthly payments lower. The higher purchase price that he may be paying will be spread out over 30 years. The strategy is, as always, to keep an open mind and be prepared to combine several formulas for success.

Advanced Real Estate Strategy No. 59: Generate Cash with an Exchange/Sale/Buyback

Although similar to the discount/sale/buyback approach, the exchange/sale/buyback can be used to solve entirely different problems.

> **Example:** Johnson has 670 acres of developable land. Like many large landholders, Johnson needs cash to develop the property. The land has an MAI appraisal of $985,000, and there is a loan of only $97,500 on the property.
>
> Another investor, Andrews, owns an office building free and clear that is only one-quarter occupied because of poor management. Andrews recognizes his lack of man-

agement ability, and is willing to sell his building for $750,000 with terms.

Proposed Solution: Johnson offers to exchange a portion of his land worth $650,000 for Andrews's building, conditioned on being able to refinance the building. Johnson further agrees to buy back the land for $50,000 down, interest only, for 5 years at 8 percent. The balance would be amortized over 15 additional years at 8 percent.

This exchange/sale/buyback results in benefits for both parties.

To Johnson: Since the exchange/sale/buyback is subject to Johnson's being able to refinance the building, he is able to get his cash down payment for the buyback, plus the money he needs to develop his land. Although Johnson's basis in the land is now carried over to the building, the improved portion is now depreciable, giving him tax deductions that he didn't have before.

To Andrews: He is able to sell a piece of property that has been a poor producer for him, and he now has a management-free investment that will give him a yearly income of $52,000 for the next 30 years.

While this example may look almost too good to be true, the figures presented are the actual figures used in a real exchange. The building's vacancy problem was due to poor management, not to the fact that it was a bad building. We were convinced by comparables in the area that the building could be rented in a short period of time—and it was.

Since this entire chapter has been a checklist of sorts, we'll depart from our standard end-of-chapter practice of summarizing the key lessons. Instead, we'll list the 29 key lessons, all worth trying on for size! The *combined* lesson of these 29 lessons is that to succeed in real estate, you have to be creative and flexible. You have to build good relationships, which help both sides over the long run. And you have to figure out what you're good at and what you enjoy—and leave the rest to the other guys.

THE 28 STRATEGIES CHECKLIST

1. Use an imaginary down payment if you don't have a real one.
2. Discount the down payment.
3. Go for monthly down payments instead of the traditional lump sum.
4. Subordinate mortgages to create nothing-down buys.
5. Barter your services for a down payment.
6. Give equity for options on other property.
7. Use personal property to buy real estate.
8. Use the brokerage fee as a down payment.
9. Match investors with home buyers to create home partners.
10. Time-share small properties.
11. Create your own horizontal condominium complex for diversity.
12. Use a subdivided sale to break up properties into salable pieces.
13. Learn to make money from phantom ownership.
14. Make a profit on rejected offers.
15. Use subsidized interest payments to increase buyer interest.
16. Use a discount/sale/buyback to raise capital.
17. Refinance your life and reduce your stress.
18. Use a step mortgage to generate cash flow on a property.

19. Structure notes to match seasonal income.

20. Eliminate negative cash flow.

21. Use balloon mortgages to entice private lenders.

22. Amortize your balloon to defuse problems.

23. Use longer amortization to increase cash flow.

24. Use interest-only payments to increase cash flow.

25. Use multiple mortgages to increase flexibility.

26. Definance a property to increase salability and profits.

27. Structure flexible interest rates to match the needs of sellers.

28. Use an exchange/sale/buyback to generate cash.

CHAPTER 20

Protecting
Your Assets

F air warning: if you are new to real estate, this chapter can be
a little scary because it contains a great many words of caution. On the other hand, you might see this chapter as very positive. After all, it's entitled "protecting your assets," rather than
"how not to lose your assets."

The main lesson we want to convey in this chapter is that you
have to be realistic about being in business (including the real
estate business) because there are many things that can go wrong.
To protect yourself, you must be vigilant not only when you have
a problem, but *before* you have one. Planning for problems using
risk-management strategies is the best way to counter those problems when they do arise—and we always work on the assumption that they *will* arise.

Advanced Real Estate Strategy No. 60:
Set Up Your Investments in Legal Structures
That Offer Maximum Protection

The first place for us to start with a protection plan is with your legal structure. Most investors buy investment property in their own name, and they frequently buy it jointly with their spouse. This is a mistake for investment property because you immediately expose all of your assets and your spouse's assets to problems and lawsuits arising out of this one property.

Except for your home and property that you are trying to get financed as a second home, your real estate should be owned through an entity such as a corporation, trust, or limited partnership. The choice depends somewhat on your state law, but we prefer to use a particular type of corporation called a *limited liability company*, or LLC.

If someone gets hurt on one of your properties and sues you, then you and your personal assets are protected by the corporate shield that owns and "surrounds" the property. No, this does not mean that you won't get sued. Alas, attorneys sue everyone when they file an action for damages, and they try to get as many people as they can involved. It is part of the game, but from your point of view, it isn't a fun game.

Your attorney's job, if it ever comes to that, is to show that you have a properly set up corporation and that if there is any problem, it should be limited to the assets of the company and not involve you personally. If you have kept good corporate records and conducted yourself as we advise in this book, we think that you have little to fear because a corporation is a separate entity. The state government isn't too interested in seeing courts "pierce the corporate veil," because if the corporate veil gets pierced too often and too easily, people will stop using corporations, and then the big fees states earn from corporations will go away. This doesn't mean that a simple incorporation is a 100 percent surefire protector, but it is close.

We also take the corporate protection a step further, using a separate LLC for each property we own. If you put all of your assets into one LLC, then all of those assets are involved in any litigation involving any one of the properties.

The disadvantage of the multiple entity approach is cost. But believe us: this is *not* the area where you want to be saving money. Hire a good lawyer the first time to set up the right type of corporation or LLC to use in your state, and (if you like) tell him to show you how to do it yourself from then on, so that you can save the fee. Again, though, we don't usually cut corners when it comes to buying expert professional help.

We use LLCs instead of "regular" (or "C," or "straight C") corporations because you can elect to use individual tax treatments (for a single-owner LLC) or be treated as a partnership for multiple-owner LLCs.

LLCs are relatively new in the corporate world, and some professionals still use a Subchapter S corporation. We like the ease of using LLCs, and there are some benefits that we think make them preferable.

One powerful benefit of LLCs is that the stock isn't subject to attachment in civil lawsuits; instead, any plaintiff will be awarded a charging order against the assets. This allows you to continue to operate the corporation, and you can decide not to distribute income to the partners. Since you could continue this method of operation forever, it generally results in settlement discussions between you and the person who sued you, because he won't be getting distribution.

You can also structure different classes of stock for different roles and participation. For instance, class A stock could have all voting rights and class B stock just investment returns. You can also use classes of stock to structure preferred returns to one group of investors over another. In short, LLCs are very flexible, and are ideal for structuring investments.

If you decide to make real estate a business instead of just an investment, you will want to form a separate LLC for the business. The reason, as before, is to separate assets and insulate liability for each entity. Your real estate operation with multiple properties might look like this:

Each of the properties and businesses has a separate legal structure, and you and whoever you are in business with own the shares or interests in the LLCs. This structure also allows you to own some of the LLCs with different people.

Some advisers may suggest putting all of your interest in these separate LLCs in another LLC that forms a holding company. This is possible, but it does have some potential holding company tax issues. You should consult with your own attorney or tax adviser. It also creates the potential for the holding company to be sued, and that would put all of your assets in jeopardy. In general, our preference is to use separate structures rather than a holding company.

Advanced Real Estate Strategy No. 61: Use Insurance to Protect Assets

After the legal structure you operate under, insurance is your second line of defense. Like most things that are worthwhile, insurance is expensive. Someone (the insurance company) is stepping up and saying that for a small amount of money in the form of an annual premium, it will take some of your liability and potential worry off the table. Let the company do it!

You cannot afford to be without insurance. Your only decision is, how much of the risk are you willing to take on in the form of self-insurance. This means deciding how much of a deductible you are willing to accept. The higher the deductible, the higher the risk to you but the lower the cost of the premium. This risk quandary is the essence of the insurance predicament. You are always doing a risk/reward analysis, and the equation is a guess at best.

From a practical standpoint, the insurance company makes the risk analysis a little easier because any policy with a deductible of $500 or below will be too expensive for the difference in what you get for the price. Insurance companies do not want to deal with small claims ($500 or less), because they aren't worth the time for the companies to go through the process. So to keep you from making them, they make low deductibles very expensive. Deductibles between $500 and $1,000 are also high, but are more palatable. In this range, people start wanting insurance protection, and policies usually get written in this range as people balance price against reward and risk. The advice to you from this analysis is to check the insurance out at all prices and see where you think the balance comes into play for you.

What Type of Insurance Do You Get?

For most property, the big three are

1. Hazard
2. Wind
3. Flood

To those three, you can add

4. Specialty
5. Title
6. Umbrella

What Does Hazard Insurance Cover?

Hazard insurance is your basic protection against fire, theft, some wind, some rain, and liability. We added the "some wind" and "some rain" not as a joke, but because you don't really know how much you are getting until you read the policy. Not everything is covered, and we know that only because we have had a bad experience finding out that "rain" that is blown in by wind is different from rain that comes in because the roof over your head gets a hole in it. Sometimes one is covered and the other is not, and sometimes the deductibles are different. The problem is, you have to read your policy, or you have to ask, to know what type of protection you want. By the way, you want *both*, but you may have to buy two policies to get them.

An additional problem with insurance contracts is that even if you ask what the policy says, policies *change*. Remember all of those pesky little addendums to your contract that you get in the mail—the ones that most of us throw away? Next time, *read* one. You will be surprised, because they are the very things we need to understand.

Ask questions regarding coverage and deductibles as well and as often as you can. This is why a good insurance agent is worth the fee you pay.

Are All Wind Policies the Same?

The answer to this question, as you may already suspect, is a resounding *no*. Even if wind is included in a basic policy, it includes neither hurricane wind nor tornado. You have to have a special clause and coverage for those.

What happens if the wind knocks over the kerosene lantern you have burning in your house so that you can read, your neighbor gets hurt when the fire starts, and he knocks over the toilet bowl, flooding the property? Which of your insurance policies is going to pay off? The answer (before you even try to guess)—is, *who knows?* All we can tell you is that the great insurance contract drafters in the sky will have a formula to apply, and it will probably cost you more.

Flood Insurance

Premiums for flood insurance policies in areas that are hurricane prone or below flood plain elevations are very expensive. In Florida, we have such a difficult time with this that there is a special state insurance fund to cover certain policies. Many insurance companies have lost so much money writing policies that they have left the state. The remaining companies were charging premiums that were almost unaffordable, so the state had to step in.

There were good reasons for the state to intervene. Without the state fund, buying and selling beachfront property would have come to a standstill. Many people swore that they would start "going naked" (meaning having no insurance), but they forgot the clause in their mortgages *requiring* insurance. The lenders started writing nasty little letters saying, "Get insurance, or we will get it for you at an even higher price, and add it to your mortgage. If you don't pay, then we'll default you."

The bottom line is that you have to get flood, wind, and other insurance coverage if you're going to get a property that has a loan on it, so you'd better plan to shop around for the best deal. Often you have to shop each year at renewal time, because rates go up substantially once the "teaser" rate year expires.

What Is Specialty Insurance?

Specialty insurance can be many things. Earthquake insurance is one example. Special riders for certain personal property that you want protected under your homeowner's plan, such as your expensive watch or ring, can be another.

Sometimes you aren't told about what is available in the form of additional riders, so you need to ask. Sometimes the additional riders are so expensive that you decide to self-insure. As long as you self-insure with a true understanding of the trade-offs involve, that's fine. We rarely do add-ons for jewelry or other personal property, but we know people who do and who sleep better at night because of it. If that is you, go for it.

Title Insurance

As we have previously discussed, title insurance protects the policyholder against any title problems *for which the title insurance policy has not made an exception.* And that is the rub, because these policies make exceptions for most things. You as the buyer must always take it upon yourself to review the exceptions noted and get them stricken from the policy. In most cases, you can do this except for ones that are standard, such as the exception for "any recorded instruments." Recorded title instruments can be read by you or your attorney in advance, so you can decide when you see them whether or not they are important. Except for those, *you really don't want exceptions.*

Your lender will always get a title policy to cover property you buy. You will also pay for this policy, so read it as well. If the title insurance doesn't protect the lender, you will have to pay to correct any problem that arises, so see if you have any insurance backup. Don't forget to also ask the title company to give you a discount for writing the lender's policy. The seller will have to give you a policy when you go to closing for the full protection of the property, so you should get credit on the second policy, because it really covers only problems over and above what was covered under the owners. This discount is common practice, but only if you ask for it. So *ask.* (Note that in some states buyers pay for both title policies.)

Advanced Real Estate Strategy No. 62: Get an Umbrella Policy

The umbrella policy is a blanket policy that insures and protects you for anything you haven't been covered for, liability-wise, under any other policy you hold. If, for example, a problem develops on one of your properties and the liability claim is larger than your homeowner's or hazard insurance policy, your umbrella insurance would kick in to protect you for the balance. The umbrella policy is very inexpensive (a few hundred dollars per year) in light of its huge added protection, and we think everyone should have one.

The best place to buy your umbrella insurance policy is where you buy either your homeowner's insurance or your car insurance. You will find, if you haven't already, that insurance companies give substantial discounts to clients who place all of their insurance with the same company, so it pays to bundle things up and take advantage of the discounts. As long as you are asking for discounts, it also pays to ask your agent if there are any other discounts that you might qualify for, such as a senior citizen's discount.

Advanced Real Estate Strategy No. 63: Be Prepared with a Legal Defense Strategy

The more you have, the more someone is going to want to take it away from you. In addition to the fact that real things can go wrong and unfortunate accidents can occur on your properties, there will also be people who try to take advantage of you simply because they think you have more than they do, and somehow that is wrong. In both cases (the legit and the not-so-legit), you are going to be involved in a lawsuit. Lawsuits cost you in both time and money. The best defense is a good offense, and you will have to have an attorney to be your quarterback.

There are two ways to deal with the legal system. One is by hiring the best law firm for the type of problem you have, and the other is to use a form of insurance called *prepaid legal services*. Depending on the size of the case, you may have no choice but to get the best attorney you can find. On the other hand, prepaid legal services are a relatively easy way to handle initial problems that may go away if the other side concludes that you are going to be serious about defending your position.

With prepaid legal services, you are given the telephone number of a prequalified attorney to speak to about your type of problem. Telephone calls are for the most part completely covered under the plan, for about $25 per month. Additionally, you can have a legal letter written for no additional charge, and sometimes that is all that is necessary to let people know that you're serious.

Should the case escalate, you will get a discount on additional legal services, including going to court. If you like the attorney and are comfortable with her qualifications, sticking with her at discounted rates may be a good idea. On the other hand, at this point, you are also free to go out and hire someone else. The point is that the relatively modest sum of $25 a month covers you for some early legal forays, and it gives you a name and a firm to throw out to the other side when you say, "Hey, call my lawyer."

Advanced Real Estate Strategy No. 64: Operate Your Business Legally

A number of people in real estate (as in all businesses) don't always do things the right way. You will meet people who say, "It really isn't necessary to get a building permit to do that small a job." Or, when they talk abut disclosures to people you are dealing with, "Don't worry; what they don't know won't hurt them."

You can always choose to find an ethical dilemma in a complicated situation. We encourage you *not* to find the dilemma. Don't cut corners. Tell people the truth. In the long run, it will serve you well.

Sure, it may seem that people are getting away with things that you aren't, and your stance may even cost you money in the short term. But we're convinced that over the long term, sleazy behavior catches up to people. In addition to the fact that such behavior is just *wrong*, we believe that it also exposes you to risks that will, if nothing else, complicate your life unnecessarily.

In short, if you need a building permit to do some work, *get* a permit. If something needs to be disclosed, *disclose* it. Always dealing with people in an aboveboard way will gain you a reputation for being the kind of person people want to deal with. You will have more deals brought your way, and people will tend to treat you the way you are known to treat others. Sure, there will be some people who will try to take advantage of you, and we aren't suggesting that you let them do so.

Just do what you are supposed to do, and, again, don't cut corners: legal, ethical, or whatever. Don't expose yourself to risks just to do something that may be faster or more profitable in the short term. It's almost always too expensive in the long term—and you're in real estate for the long term.

THE ASSET-PROTECTION CHECKLIST

☑ **GET THE RIGHT LEGAL STRUCTURE IN PLACE.** There are lots of different ways to structure your business. Look into your options, and get good counsel. The general rule is to shield the assets in one corner of your life from trouble in other corners of your life.

☑ **GET ALL THE INSURANCE YOU NEED (AND THEN SOME).** All right, maybe not "and then some." But insurance, by and large, is cheap. It can buy you great peace of mind. Just read the fine print, and don't assume anything that you read there is nonnegotiable. Negotiate!

☑ **DO IT LEGALLY.** By this we mean two things. First, set up your legal defenses so that you look like a porcupine—not worth tangling with. And second, stay well within the spirit and letter of the law. Do things right. If it smells, looks, or sounds bad, stay out of it. You'll sleep better. You'll prosper.

Index

Success duplication, law of, 6–11
Successors and assigns, 268–269
Surveys, 80–81, 110, 125, 142, 157–158
"Survive closing" clause, 125–126
Sweat equity, 16–17, 76–77
Syndication, 27–28, 274–276

Take-away options, 145–146
Tax allocation clause, 117–118
Tax deeds, 316
Tax-deferred exchanges, 284–285
Tax lien certificates, 306–318
Tax lien sales, 244–245
Tax payments, 260–262
Tax returns, 155
Tax sales, 316–317
Tax shelters, 278–290
Teaser rates, 74
10-year retirement plan, 11–12
Tenants, 194–195, 198–201, 209, 211–212
1031 exchange, 284
Termites, 159
Thank-you notes, 58
Think and Grow Rich (Napoleon Hill), 48
Third mortgage, 42
30–year fixed-rate mortgages, 74
Time element, 300
Time extension clauses, 115–116
"Time is money," 163, 169
Time limit clauses, 110
Time management, law of, 300
Time on the market, 221
Time-shares, 337–338
Timing, 129, 162–163, 239

Title, 81, 142
Title insurance, 81, 97, 124, 157, 367–368
Title searches, 302, 317
Tornadoes, 366
Trainers, 28–29
Trans Union Corporation, 171
Transferring mortgages, 353–355
Transportation expenses, 286–287
Travel costs, 127–128
Trump, Donald, 93, 136, 137, 143
Trump National Golf Club, 93
Two-minute test, 222–228

Umbrella policies, 368–369
Underwriting, 182
Upgrading networks, 58
Upside growth potential, 309
Utilities, 262

Vacation-home deductions, 282–283
Voidable contracts, 98

Waiver of claims, 269
Waiver of right of partition, 270
Walk-through, 129–130, 161–162
Warranties, home, 70, 125, 130
Wasting assets, 285–286
"Weasel" clauses, 110
Web sites, 55–56, 221
Wind insurance, 366
Windstorms, 365
Written agreements/contracts, 98, 99, 249–250

Ziglar, Zig, 51